Sociology, Media and Journalism in China

This series provides an interdisciplinary and cutting edge approach to the key areas of media, journalism and communication in China. Offering titles cutting across these areas, *Sociology, Media and Journalism in China* addresses the rapid changes affecting how news is disseminated in China, how people communicate in daily life, and how mobile technologies are affecting contemporary human interaction in sociological and commercial settings. This series also examines major sociological trends in China and how these are developing, as well as rapid changes in how communication is affecting and being affected by China's growing population and internal migration. Providing a vital comparative approach, notably with western nations, this series considers the development of Chinese media, journalistic cultures and histories and sociological development on a global scale.

More information about this series at
http://www.palgrave.com/gp/series/16016

Wenbo Kuang

Social Media in China

palgrave
macmillan

Wenbo Kuang
Renmin University of China
Beijing, China

Translators
Hang Jiang
All Star (Beijing) Translation Co., Ltd
Beijing, China

Ying Zhang
All Star (Beijing) Translation Co., Ltd
Beijing, China

Quanli Wang
All Star (Beijing) Translation Co., Ltd
Beijing, China

Mifen Yang
All Star (Beijing) Translation Co., Ltd
Beijing, China

Based on a translation from the Chinese language edition: 新媒体舆论
by Kuang, **Wenbo**

Sociology, Media and Journalism in China
ISBN 978-981-13-0913-7 ISBN 978-981-13-0914-4 (eBook)
https://doi.org/10.1007/978-981-13-0914-4

The print edition is not for sale in China Mainland. Customers from China Mainland please order the print book from: China Renmin University Press. ISBN of the China Mainland edition: 978-7-300-18541-5

Library of Congress Control Number: 2018954354

Cover credit: PeopleImages

This Palgrave Macmillan imprint is published by the registered company Springer Nature Singapore Pte Ltd.
The registered company address is: 152 Beach Road, #21-01/04 Gateway East, Singapore 189721, Singapore

Contents

List of Figures

PART I

Theoretical Foundations of New Media's Public Opinions

CHAPTER 1

An Introduction to New Media

Looking back over human communication's history, we can easily see the historic role of the development of information technology as a lever for progress. A great transformation of information communication always follows an innovation in information technology. Each transformation exerts an immeasurable influence on people's political, economic, cultural and social lives and promotes the advancement of human civilization. Information technology has powerfully transformed people's production and daily lives, mainly as a result of changes in the modes of information communication. Within the history of human communication, which, up to now, can be divided into three stages—respectively, oral communication, typographic communication and electronic communication, every leap from the previous stage to the following one was achieved as a result of the revolutionary progress of information technology. The advance of computer-network technology, particularly the development of the Internet, laid the latest foundation for the development of information communication.

1.1 What Is the Definition of "New Media"?

Within industry and academia, as yet, no consensus has been reached on the exact definition of "New Media.".

W. Kuang, *Social Media in China*, Sociology, Media and Journalism in China, https://doi.org/10.1007/978-981-13-0914-4_1

1.1.1 The Concept of New Media

The term New Media first emerged in 1967 in a commodity development plan prepared by P. Goldmark, the Director of the CBS (Columbia Broadcasting System) American Institute of Technology. Later, E. Rostow, the Chairman of the US President's Special Committee on Communication, mentioned New Media several times in his 1969 report to President Richard Nixon. The term New Media spread rapidly over America and has since expanded to the whole world.

Experts throughout the world hold different opinions on the definition of new media. In the early stage, the United Nations Educational, Scientific and Cultural Organization (UNESCO) defined "new media" as the on-line media. Similarly, the term new media was also defined as "the media for information communication with digital technology as the basis and the network as the carrier."[1]

Jiang Hong and Xu Jian from Shanghai Jiao Tong University defined new media from the perspectives of connotation and denotation. According to them, in terms of connotation, "new media" refers to the new type of media established based on the digital technology that emerged in the social information communication sector thanks to the great progress of science and technology in the late twentieth century and enables the wider range, faster speed and more diversified methods of information communication, which is vastly different from the traditional media. Regarding denotation, the new media consist of the fiber-optic cable communication network, the cable TV network, teletext, the computer communication network, the large-scale computer database communication system, the direct broadcast satellite system, the Internet, the short message service (SMS), the multimedia information interactive platform, the multimedia technology broadcasting network, and so on.[2]

Professor Huang Shengmin from the Communication University of China considers Internet protocol television (IPTV), terrestrial mobile TV and mobile TV as the three major parts of the new media.[3]

[1] Tao Dan, Zhang Haoda, *New Media and On-line Advertising*, Page 3, Beijing, Science Publishing, 2001.

[2] Jiang Hong, Xu Jian, *Introduction to New Media*, Page 14, Shanghai, Shanghai Jiao Tong University Press, 2006.

[3] Guo Yabing, Huang Shengmin, Wang Lanzhu, *Report on Development of Digital New Media in China*, Page 1, Beijing, Communication University of China Press, 2006.

Gong Chengbo holds that portal sites, search engines, virtual communities, e-mails, Internet literature and on-line games all belong to new media.[4]

Therefore, we believe that the biggest issue in the definition of new media lies in the too extensive range and the logical confusion.

Some people believe that the new media also include a few new communication approaches that arose in the recent decade due to technology improvements or a few channels and carriers that have existed for a long time without their value in communication being discovered.[5] They include the mobile TV, IPTV, webcast, blog, podcast, office-building TV, vehicle mobile TV, the fiber-optic cable communication network, the urban two-way transmission cable TV network, high-definition TV (HDTV), the Internet, SMS, the digital magazine, the digital newspaper, digital broadcasting, digital TV, digital movie and touch media in the list of new media. In addition to the too-wide range, this definition is also exposed to logical confusion by putting all these media on a par with each other, since the sum of the subclasses should be equal to the parent class and subclasses should be mutually exclusive as per the logic of classification. Currently, many people make logical mistakes when defining the connotation and denotation of new media.

1.1.1.1 Interaction Is the Essential Characteristic of New Media

Though commonly known as "new media," the complete expression should be "digital interactive new media." That is to say, the "new media" are technically digital and are highly interactive from the perspective of communication characteristics. "Digitalization" and "interaction" constitute fundamental characteristics of the new media. Being a non-linear form of communication, the new media may have information sending synchronous or asynchronous with information receiving. For example, office-building media and vehicle mobile TV do not fall into the category of "new media."

As a relative concept, the connotation of "new media" will always develop along with the progress of communication technology. However, from the perspective of the history of human communication, it should be

[4] Gong Chengbo, *Introduction to New Media*, Page 1, Beijing, China Radio & television Publishing House, 2007.

[5] Chen Xiaoning, *Research on Policies and Regulations on New Media of Radio and TV*, Page 16–35, Beijing, China Legal Publishing House, 2001.

confined to a certain era and indicate "the new for today" but not "the new for yesterday" or "the new for tomorrow." The new media should not be defined by the standard of "the new for yesterday," as radio and TV, which emerged in the early twentieth century, are traditional media now though they were new at that time. It also shall not be defined by "the new for tomorrow," otherwise there is no new media now.

Moreover, the international standard should be applied as the criterion for the "new" in "new media." Some media forms that appear to be "new" to Chinese people have actually been in existence for many years in developed countries and, therefore, are not considered as new media—an example would be vehicle mobile TV.

The concept of "digital media" is not recommended, since here "digital" could refer to the digital production process. If so, many more media would be listed as digital media.

Compared to traditional media, new media are characterized by immediacy, openness, individuation, audience-segmentation, massive information, low-cost global communication, quick search, integrativeness and so on. However, the essential features of new media lie in its digital technology and interactive communication.

In traditional media, the communicator and audience were clearly positioned—the communicator distributed information and the audience accepted information passively without a way to express their views, whether positive or negative. By contrast, the new media create a fuzzy boundary between the communicator and the audience, where the audience no longer consumes information passively, but engages in information exchange with the communicator and may even play a part as a communicator.

The magazine *Online* once defined "new media" as "communications for all, by all." The traditional media divided the world into two camps, communicators and audiences, when people were writers or readers, broadcasters or viewers, performers or appreciators. New media, on the contrary, offer everyone the opportunity to listen and talk and realize unprecedented interaction. Therefore, the concept of "audience" is not now used in new-media research—it is recommended to replace the word "audience" with "user."

Judging the current various forms of new media by the interaction criterion, we can see that some so-called "new media" are actually "traditional media that are new," typically represented by vehicle mobile TV, outdoor media, and office-building TV.

Vehicle mobile TV and outdoor media are simply traditional media that have recently appeared in China, as they show no interaction, the essential characteristic of new media. Vehicle mobile TV has no interaction with users at all. Instead, it exists in an enclosed space, where users have no choice but to accept the information without the option to change the channel or shield the advertisement; and users have to watch it as they move, independent of their will.

Office-building TV transmits through cable. As with traditional radio and TV, it is characterized by a wide audience, great timeliness, rich and visual content, voluntary acceptance, sequential acceptance and fleetingness. Office-building TV can and should be considered as cable radio or closed-circuit radio based on its transmission mode, and mainly displays advertisements. Someone 0spending time in a very boring space (such as waiting for an elevator) would rather watch advertisements, which leads to the psychological coercion utilized by office-building TV. Thus, the information transmission by office-building TV exhibits strong audience passivity and goes against two essential characteristics of new media—users' initiative and interaction.

1.1.1.2 Which Media Should Not Fall into the Category of New Media?

Academia has reached a consensus that the print media and the traditional analog radio and TV are traditional media. However, does this mean that all other media forms can be considered as "new media?"

In the author's opinion, not all media forms that newly appear are new media. For example, bicycles and even people's foreheads are used as advertisement media; and these cannot be considered as new media but can only be called the traditional media that are new.

Then, how about digital TV? Digital TV is a kind of TV where the digital TV signal is applied to every link from the studio to transmission and reception, or where all signals of the system are transmitted through a binary data stream composed of numeric strings of 0 and 1. Compared to analog TV, it features smaller signal loss and better reception.

However, the digital TV popular in China now only increases the number of TV channels and improves definition, but still lacks interaction. For example, the video-on-demand service has not yet been popularized.

Hence, currently, in my view, digital TV is not a kind of new media. However, as with the mobile phone, TV constantly evolves following technical developments and may become a type of computer in the future. By then, digital TV provided with interaction will become a member of new media.

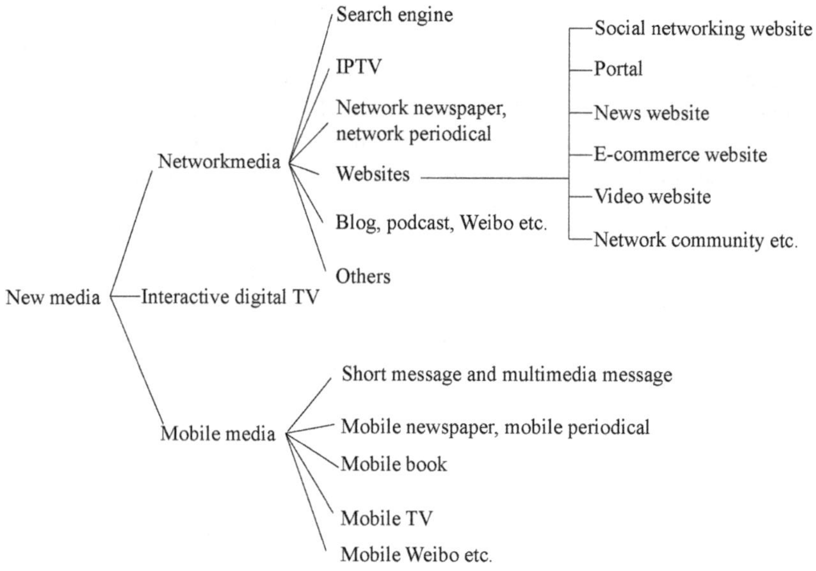

Fig. 1.1 The extension of new media

The extension of new media is listed in Fig. 1.1. It should be noted that the extension will expand along with the technical development.

The new media, the focus of media development in the future, points out this inexorable trend and direction for development of media communication.

1.1.1.3 Scientific Definition of New Media: The Carrier that Communicates Information by Means of Computers

The current new media consist of the Internet and mobile media, since only these feature real interaction. While the Internet is the product of computer technology development, mobile phones nowadays are no longer just hand-held phones, but are mini-computers provided with communication functions.

In the early stage of the mobile phone—the age of the first-generation (1G) mobile phone—it was only used as a hand-held phone and had no function to communicate news.

Looking back on the development of the mobile phone, it can be seen that the mobile phone has followed a trend towards a lighter design, more functions and a lower cost. Currently, the 3G, 4G, 5G... NG mobile phones are no longer just hand-held phones, but are mini-computers provided with communication functions. The central processing units (CPUs) of mobile phones have started to apply "multi-core" functionality.

The smart phone constitutes the mainstream of mobile phone development nowadays, and shows two essential characteristics, the CPU as the hardware and the operating system as the software.

Like the CPU of a computer, the CPU of a mobile phone functions as the central control system of the whole mobile phone as well as the control center of the logic. The microprocessor monitors the whole mobile phone by operating software in the memory and using the database in the memory.

The development of the mobile phone processor shows great similarities with processor progress in the PC industry, both from the single-core to the multi-core, but multi-core smart phones arrived more quickly than expected. The smart phone with its computer functions has become the mainstream of mobile communication.

In conclusion, the new media can be defined as the carrier that communicates information by means of computers (or digital equipment featuring essential characteristics of computers).

1.1.2 Relevant Concepts

Concepts closely associated with the new media include network communication, network media and mobile media.

What is meant by network communication? The network communication refers to the human information (including news, knowledge etc.) communication through computer networks. Information exposed to network communication is stored in the optical or magnetic or other storage media in digital form, communicated at a high speed through computer networks and read and used by computers or similar devices. Network communication realizes information dissemination, exchange and utilization based on computer networks, thus achieving the goal of social and cultural communication.

The computer networks included here have a broad range, including not only the popular Internet, but also the mobile communication network based on computer network technologies and modern communication technologies as well as the next-generation high-speed Internet. The network communication shall not be confined to the current Internet communication.

Similarly, the network media, in addition to the Internet, also comprise the mobile media, IPTV (interactive personality TV) and many other forms. A medium is a carrier that carries information. According to *The Contemporary Chinese Dictionary*, the medium means "the tool to communicate and disseminate information, such as newspapers, radios and advertisements etc."[6] Thus, the network media can be defined as the tools to communicate information by means of computer networks.

Some people called the network media the "fourth media," as they believed that the print media was the first media, radio the second, TV the third and the Internet the fourth. The annual meeting of the United States Information Committee in May 1998 officially mentioned the network media as the "fourth media." Nevertheless, it is only an informal statement and is not precise.

The mobile media communicates information through mobile phones. Along with the development and popularization of communication technologies and computer technologies, the mobile phone has become a mini-computer provided with communication functions; and now it is also an extension of the network media. However, the mobile media must integrate into the network media, which contain massive information, otherwise it will suffer from information deficiency.

It must be noted that the short message service (SMS) is only an important form of the mobile media at the current stage and does not represent the totality, or the future, of mobile media. Many people in China have mistakenly seen SMS as the only element of mobile media and thus list the SMS as the "fifth media." As a matter of fact, the huge quantity and highly developed culture of short messages in China result from China's specific telecommunication management system and charging mode.

The network media, the mobile media and the interactive digital TV all play as important members of the new media.

1.2 Strengths of the New Media

Communication is commonly divided into five categories: intrapersonal communication, interpersonal communication, group communication, organization communication and mass communication. The new media is

[6] The Dictionary Editorial Office, Institute of Linguistics of Chinese Academy of Social Sciences, *The Contemporary Chinese Dictionary*, 5th edition, Page 928, Beijing, The Commercial Press, 2005.

a brand new and special communication that integrates interpersonal communication and mass communication.

Essentially characterized by digital technologies and interactive communication, the new media also feature massive information, easy use, quick and convenient retrieval, a combination of pictures, texts and sounds, great interaction, high-speed information communication through computer networks and quick information acquisition, quick transmission and quick update, as well as the function of computer retrieval and hypertext. As a kind of communication media revealing a strong vitality, it has exerted profound influences on human society. The new media realizes network communication between readers and writers and thus provides timely feedback, which alters the traditional way of academic exchanges. Specifically, the new media reveal the characteristics discussed in the following subsections.

1.2.1 Quick Communication and Update and Low Cost

The new media is a kind of digital communication with a quicker update and a lower cost. The new media is updated every several minutes or seconds, compared to days or hours for updates of TV and radio, days and even weeks for print newspapers and even a longer time for print journals and books.

Combining synchronous communication and asynchronous communication, the new media improve news timeliness by real-time refresh and enable the audience to receive news anytime anywhere based on "asynchronous reception." As a result of asynchronous reception, the audience may receive information whenever they want, free from the restraint of the time of media communication.

1.2.2 Massive Information and Rich Content

All users share global information resources through the Internet and no other media can compare with this network media with its massive quantity of information. New media digital information is stored on a hard disk. The strength of the large capacity is also reflected by the feature stories and databases of the new media. The new media are capable of storing and communicating information of any size at any time and of running various information databases where readers can search for any historical document at any time.

1.2.3 Cost-Free Global Communication

The new media break the restraint of the national boundary and cost little for transnational communication. Information communication, internationally or locally, shares the same cost and speed, from the perspective of either the communicator or the audience. In other words, the distance and range of the new media communication have no effect on cost, which is entirely different from the traditional media. Though the print media, radio and TV are also theoretically able to launch global communication, their costs are directly proportional to the distance of communication.

1.2.4 Convenient Retrieval

Retrieval is hard for traditional communication. By comparison, providing the data are stored on the Internet, merely by using their fingers netizens can quickly acquire the information they need by using various search engines and databases.

1.2.5 Multimedia Communication

Multimedia makes the computer a variety of medium that acts on people's different perceptions and conveys information by combining multiple media forms (such as texts, sounds, pictures, animations, videos etc.). As a kind of multimedia communication, the new media communicate information by means of either, or a combination of, texts, pictures, images or sounds. In this way, the new media not only play the part of TV, but also make practical use of their multimedia characteristic based on large capacity and convenient retrieval. With the popularization of the broadband network, it has become fashionable to report news in a multimedia format.

1.2.6 Interaction

From the perspective of communication studies, interaction constitutes the fundamental characteristic of the new media,. The network news communication is an open and interactive form of communication, while the traditional media only provide one-way communication and do not allow two-way communication between the writers and the readers.

1.3 Impact of the New Media on the Media Industry

1.3.1 Change the Current Pattern of Communication

The development of the new media has changed the current modes of communication; broken the boundaries among the media industry, the communication industry and the information technology industry; broken the fragmentation of the wired network, the wireless network, the communication network and the TV network; integrated various media forms; and shaped the new pattern of communication.

1.3.1.1 Form a New Communication Environment

In the era of the new media, theoretically, everyone is playing the role of the communicator, and the gap between the communication organizations and individual audiences has been narrowed. Global communication sees a smoother channel, and global interconnection will probably be realized based on real-time network communication, network blogs and the wireless Internet, which further reduces geographic segmentation and brings the "global village" into reality. The previous static way of information reception has been replaced by dynamic and real-time information reception, achieving both timely interaction of information and temporary delay of information reception. Discourse spaces of interpersonal communication have been perfectly integrated, where the point-to-point private space and the minority-to-majority public space (generated by connection with the wireless Internet), while independent from each other, and also can be connected with each other in real time.

1.3.1.2 Make the Media Ecology More Complicated

Being a brand new communication media, the network makes the media ecology more complicated, the communication subjects more diversified and audiences more differentiated. As a result of the high-speed development of media undertakings and profound changes of communication technologies, the world witnesses a huge quantity of media, new and emerging media forms, various communication channels and an increasingly complicated media ecology. The competition among different media is becoming fiercer. Some traditional media may see a narrower coverage as a result of the rapid development of the new media and may even be marginalized by the Internet.

1.3.1.3 Make the Communication Subjects More Diversified

As a result of the development of the new media, more diversified subjects are engaged in news information communication. In particular, individuals are controlling more and more communication tools. Therefore, their status in information communication has been promoted to an unprecedented level, while their ability to publish information, form public opinion, "mobilize society" and "penetrate" management is constantly improving, Unfortunately, at the same time, unhealthy information and uncontrollable factors are more likely to increase. All these will inevitably impact mainstream public opinion.

1.3.1.4 Make Audiences More Differentiated

Human's news communication has gone through a long course of development from minority communication to mass communication, and from mass communication to focus communication. Primarily reflecting individuals' interests and demands, the new media is a completely personalized communication platform. The network information communication will maximally present individual differences and demands and realize individual values in information demand. The application and popularization of the new media will further change the ways for people to acquire and receive information and boost the development of focus communication and minority communication. Hence, to some extent, the traditional mainstream media often fail to reach certain audience groups, which has an influence on the publicity effect of news.

1.3.2 Impact on the Public-Opinion Regulation Mechanism

The new media, showing a public-opinion trend, offer a free publishing platform for users and allows them to express themselves as they want. However, as a result of the interaction, openness and anonymity of the new media as well as the unpredictable communication content and the uncontrollable mass messaging and forwarding, "monitoring" becomes more difficult, and the "monitoring" mechanism loses effectiveness or is missing. Moreover, as no universal standard is applied to the development of the whole industry and the new media, the public-opinion trend of the new media also brings many practical and potential problems.

1.3.2.1 Impact on the Traditional Public-Opinion Regulation Mechanism

The new media enable more timely information communication and a wider range of communication and form a "5a" network environment, which means, theoretically, "anyone" can communicate "any message" through "any media" at "any time" and "anywhere" by using the new media. New media exert profound influences on the traditional public-opinion regulation mechanism. (1) In terms of the guidance of hot topics, a local incident reported by a few media may rapidly draw the attention of nationwide media through the new media, and will rapidly develop from a "local hot topic" to a "global hot topic"; and a "xx Incident" or "xx phenomenon" may be made within a few days or even a few hours. No sign can be seen before and no responsible party can be found after, but it often exerts a huge adverse influence. (2) In terms of the positive publicity, diversified forms of the new media and massive and disorderly information may easily cover the content of the positive publicity, when the expected social effect can hardly be achieved and the wrong ideas and irrational public opinions will find their communication channels and living spaces. In this way, new media exert an impact on the traditional public-opinion regulation mechanism and propose a new challenge of how to assure the correct orientation for public opinion.

1.3.2.2 Impact the Order of Information Communication

On one hand, along with the development of the public-opinion trend of the new media, some hearsays and rumors spread quickly, spam messages and vulgar information are seen widely, and viewing or downloading pornographic novels, pictures or videos is "popular." The information communication order of the Internet has been disturbed. On the other hand, instead of bringing equality of information, the public-opinion trend of new media aggravates the information asymmetry already caused by the traditional media and the new media. As early as in the 1970s, the American communication scholar P. J. Tichenor et al. had put forward the hypothesis of "Knowledge Gap Theory," which explains "as the infusion of mass media information into a social system increases, segments of the population with higher socioeconomic status tend to acquire this information at a faster rate than the lower status segments, so that the gap in knowledge between these segments tends to increase rather than decrease." This theory has been further demonstrated along with the birth and development of new media. The public-opinion trend of the network information communication, as the latest progress of media development, further aggravates the information asymmetry.

1.3.2.3 Impact the Environment for Media Development

The public-opinion trend of network information communication constantly impacts the environment for the new media development and influences the construction of new media credibility. On one hand, the new media technologies lead to the lack of the "monitor" and failure of the "monitoring mechanism," which intensifies the public-opinion trend of new media. Integrating the characteristics of point-to-point linear communication and group-to-group reticular communication, the new media theoretically have boundless communication paths. Meanwhile, the "monitoring" mechanisms, built by the government at a macro level or established by operators and providers at a micro level, are all exposed to vulnerabilities and lags. Therefore, it is increasingly difficult or even impossible to conduct "monitoring," and the public opinions of the new media enjoy a larger free space. On the other hand, the public-opinion trend of the new media constantly shock the "monitor" and the "monitoring mechanism" conversely. More and more people express their opinions freely through the platforms provided by the new media, and more and more people may expect to become "opinion leaders." The increasingly diversified public opinions in the new media are exerting greater impacts on the "monitoring mechanism" and creating a more complicated environment for the new media development.

1.3.3 The Print Media Is Withering Away

"Whether the print media will wither away" is not only a theoretical controversial hot topic, but also a practical issue that involves the career development or even livelihood of millions of people. Some people are quite emotional in the argument, and some emotionally point out many "strengths" of the print media compared to the new media. Nevertheless, as a matter of fact, these so-called "strengths" of the print media are not true if we analyze them rationally without emotions.

1.3.3.1 Is the Print Media Portable?

Some people believe that the traditional print media has its own advantages, such as being portable, intuitive and convenient to read. Is that true? Actually, they have ignored an important fact that the density of information storage in a piece of paper is much lower than that of the new media, since the new media features a small volume, a large capacity and an extremely high storage density. For the same amount of information, the new media is much more portable than the print media.

For an instance, a DVD disc, only several grams heavy, can save information of 4.7G, equal to 4.7 × 1024 × 1024 × 1024 = 5046,586,572.8 B ytes (i.e., 2,523,293,286 Chinese characters). Considering that a book has about 200,000 Chinese characters on average, a DVD disc provides room for 12,616 books. It is obvious which, between a several-gram disc and more than 10,000 books, is more portable.

In fact, it is exactly the portability, convenience and low cost that are the strength of the mobile media and E-books.

1.3.3.2 Is the Print Media More Authoritative and Authentic than the New Media?

According to some people, the print media is more authoritative for following reasons: (1) The print media have established the perfect system of editing, production and release based on over a thousand years' experience; (2) Most of the print media strictly observe a standard process of news gathering, editing and release of news reports; (3) Publishing houses and periodical presses have established and improved the academic review committee or similar organization to assure the academic standards of the works to be published.

However, the authoritativeness and authenticity of different kinds of media should be analyzed on a case-by-case basis. While there is no denying that the information published on the bulletin board system (BBS) and personal blogs is less authoritative and authentic than the traditional media, the authoritativeness and authenticity of information published on famous websites is also undeniable. Regarding the print media, is the information in tabloid newspapers authoritative and authentic? Some other people think that new-media reports do not have sufficient depth, but this should also be analyzed case by case. Positive and negative cases of in-depth reports are widely found both in the new media and the traditional media. There is no necessary contradiction between the promptness and depth of news release in the new media. Actually, the new media show greater immediacy, objectivity and authenticity than the traditional media for reports of some emergent and sensitive incidents. For example, the images taken by mobile phones are more authentic and accurate.

Some people state that, within China, the new media lack original news since the new media only have the right to reprint and edit news but no right to interview. Nevertheless, it is only a special policy in a special period in China not to provide the new media with the right to interview, and currently major domestic portals are allowed to publish original content in entertainment, sport and some other news sectors.

In the academic sector, many foreign universities and research institutes have started to recognize academic literature published on the academic new media. These academic new media have transcended national borders and gathered top experts within an industry, who can discuss academic issues conveniently through the Internet.

As demonstrated by research, the news credibility of the new media is no less than the traditional media.

We have conducted telephone surveys of mobile phone users. Based on random sampling, the investigation covered the four most representative cities in China: Beijing, Wuhan, Guangzhou and Chengdu. Surveys were done between June 1 and July 31, 2010. Respondents were categorized by gender, age and occupation. The sample size was designed to be 4000 people, 1000 from each of the four cities. By the end, 3421 valid samples had been obtained.

Quantitative analysis of the use of the new media provided the following interesting result: the credibility of the new media represented by the Internet and mobile phone is no less than the traditional media.

Though some people believe that the new media has a lower credibility than the serious traditional media, particularly the print media such as newspapers, according to our investigation the credibility of the mobile phone, the network, newspapers, radio and TV is respectively 22.4%, 19.6%, 20.7%, 12.6% and 34.2% (see Fig. 1.2).

Many people's prejudice about the low credibility of the new media's news coverage has been overturned by our investigation on news credibility. As a matter of fact, false news is not necessarily associated with media forms, but is determined by the interest driver behind the scenes—whether anyone is making false news to boost circulation and audience rate for improved profit.

The *Journalist Monthly* appraises and selects the "Top 10" false news stories of the previous year in its first issue every year. With the Top 10 false news stories of 2010 as an example, other than a few false news from websites of some traditional media, none of the ten is truly derived from the new media.

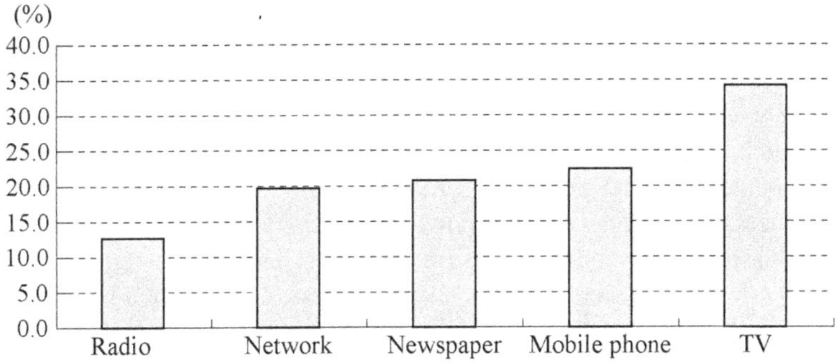

Fig. 1.2 Credibility of different forms of media

1.3.3.3 Is the Print Media More Economical?

Some people think the print media needs no special reading tool and thus the reading cost is lower. However, considering the total social cost, the print media is far less economical than the new media.

Cutting out the process of platemaking, printing, binding and delivery, the new media saves the expenses of printing and release as well as the paper costs, and thus significantly reduces the overall cost.

The print media consume a large quantity of forest resources and causes severe pollution during paper production. The price of digital technology products such as computers and mobile phones is reducing together with technical developments, while the print media will become increasingly expensive as the forest resources become scarcer and more precious.

1.3.3.4 Is the Print Media More in Line with People's Reading Habit?

Some people believe that human's dependence on, and attachment to, the print media and the habit of linear reading formed through thousands of years cannot be fundamentally changed in one day. As the print media has accompanied people for millennia, people have got used to it and have a feeling for it.

We consider that emotions and habits can be changed. For the elderly who, from their childhood, have only read paper books, the print media meet their reading habit more than the new media do but for the new generation of readers, who have used the new media since they were very young, they may well get used to reading new media more than traditional books.

1.3.3.5 Does the Print Media Have Less Influence on Readers' Health?

According to some people, when reading paper books or magazines people not only acquire the information delivered by books and magazines but also intuitively enjoy their beauty. The print media, characterized by its beautiful appearance, a great contrast between ink and paper, the high resolution, stable characters and a good color effect, is suitable for reading and exerts less influence on readers' health, particularly the health of their eyes.

This is only an theoretical judgment, since no authoritative data of medical comparison demonstrate that the print media have a less negative influence on readers' health than the new media. In fact, long-term desk-bound reading, regardless of whether print media or new media, will definitely impair readers' health. It is the unscientific lifestyle and incorrect reading habit, rather than the screen, that affects people's health. Many readers are near-sighted now just because they read print media when they were young. With the upcoming technical developments and increasing humanization, such as the wider application of ergonomics and improvement of the display screen, further doubt will be cast on the idea that reading new media impairs health more than print media.

1.3.3.6 Is It Easier to Preserve the Print Media?

Some people think that the print media is easy to preserve and has a high collection value. A large quantity of print media has been preserved until now thanks to many collectors' relentless pursuit for collections. While absorbing information and knowledge from the print media, readers also intuitively appreciate the sublime and unsophisticated beauty. For example, the press plates of the Song Dynasty widely use the Song typeface with its forceful structure and pleasing appearance, so that these prints are considered as ancient treasures among readers. By comparison, optical disks, magnetic tapes and magnetic disks may be easily damaged by dirt, scratches, wear, or even the sunlight or organic solvent. Moreover, a computer system may easily be destroyed by computer viruses.

Nevertheless, the extremely high density of information storage and the extremely low cost of information storage per unit constitutes one of the greatest strengths of the new media, so it is practical to reproduce many copies of digital information as a backup at an extremely low cost. Meanwhile, it is impossible for the print media to do so. For example, all the newspapers in the whole history of the *People's Daily* can be stored on a few DVDs at a cost lower than 100 Yuan. In comparison, the print media can hardly be reproduced in a large size and may be more easily damaged.

The collectable value placed on print media exactly proves that it will wither away.

When someone says the print media is very beautiful, we can't help asking don't the new computers and mobile phones present the beauty of high technology and humanization.

1.3.3.7 *A Lesson from Kodak: The Most Dangerous Opponent Is Outside the Industry*

Two decades ago, nobody would have believed anyone who said Kodak would go bankrupt; and a decade ago, fierce controversy would arise if anyone said the film camera would be replaced by the digital camera. According to statistics, Kodak's income and profit respectively hit their peak in 1996 and 1999 at USD 16 billion and 2.5 billion.

Kodak's businesses were exposed to great impacts with the popularization of the digital camera. The progress of science and technology is unstoppable. After the time of George Eastman, though Kodak possessed approximately 1100 patents in the digital area, it lost its courage to explore and research, hence, fell behind in the new era. At present, the digital camera and camera phone have dominated the market, while the film camera has become a collectable item. As a result, Kodak applied for bankruptcy protection to the court in New York on January 19, 2012, marking the end of an era.

Two reasons contributed to the failure of Kodak. First, the working principles vary between the traditional camera and the digital camera, so Kodak's strengths in the supply chain and the patents of the traditional camera reduced in value. Second, even though a Kodak employee invented the digital camera, Kodak's success essentially depended on its traditional businesses, so its traditional business division played a greater part in the company's decision making and resources went to traditional businesses first, leading to its slow exploitation of the digital camera.

In turn, the card digital camera is being replaced by the smart phone camera. According to statistics, people are increasingly using mobile smart phones to shoot videos and pictures, while fewer and fewer people are using a traditional camera or video camera.

1.3.3.8 *Smart Phones Accelerate the Extinction of the Print Media*

Integrating interpersonal communication and mass communication, the new media are essentially characterized by digital technologies and interactive communication. Moreover, the new media have the advantages of quick communication and update, massive information, rich content, globalization and interculturality, convenient retrieval, multimedia, hypertext, interaction and low cost.[7]

The new media are rapidly overcoming their deficiencies through constant progress and improvement. On the contrary, a technological leap is now impossible for the print media, which has over a thousand-year history. For example, people can draw lines, write notes, mark some words or phrases, fold a page and even tear a page when reading the print media, but, in the past, they could not do it in the new media; but now many e-books provide the function of writing notes or marking on the book.

Many functions of the new media are not achievable for the print media, especially the quick and convenient retrieval and knowledge clustering. Regarding knowledge clustering, the new media are capable of automatically clustering knowledge for a knowledge item on a certain basis as required, and then performing new clustering from another perspective based on another basis. At the same time, shortages of the print media are becoming increasingly evident, such as the inconvenient retrieval, the small density of information storage, the incapability in transnational multimedia communication and the high cost of printing and release.

Along with the trend of the hand-held computer and the popularization of the 3rd generation of mobile phone technologies, the mobile phone is becoming the important new media, compared to which, the print media have lost thier advantage in portability. As the new generation of readers who have started to use the new media from childhood give up the traditional reading habits, they will easily accept e-books that can fill people's pockets with an entire library. The new media are ready to change the reading format of the whole world—from paper reading to screen reading.

Some people think that earlier predictions about the extinction of print media are wrong, but we believe the general trend for the print media to wither away has only been postponed a little. Being a prophet is a hard job. It is impossible to make accurate predictions for everything, and anyone who could point out the general trend correctly should be regarded as a great prophet.

As readers of the print media in major countries including China, Japan and the United States are over forty years old on average and their average life expectancy is less than ninety years, we predict that the print media will

[7] Kuang Wenbo, *Introduction to Network Communication*, 2nd Edition, Page 24, Beijing, Higher Education Press, 2004.

step down from the stage of history in major countries within fifty years. In view of the imbalance of global social, economic, scientific and technological development, print media will only exist in a museum a hundred years from now.

Philip Meyer, a professor from North Carolina State University, stated in *The Vanishing Newspaper: Saving Journalism in the Information Age* by, "In 2044, or more precisely in October 2044, the last newspaper reader will pay the last bill."[8]

However, it shall be noted that people's act of reading will not disappear, the newspaper offices, publishing houses, periodical presses and libraries will not vanish, and workers of the industry will not lose their jobs, but the form of information communication will be fundamentally changed. The new media today will be replaced by a newer media form later. Let's bid farewell to our attachment for paper, one of the Great Four Inventions in ancient China, and embrace a brand new era of the digital new media.

[8] [US] Philip Meyer, *The Vanishing Newspaper: Saving Journalism in the Information Age*, Page 12, Beijing, Xinhua Publishing House, 2007.

CHAPTER 2

New-Media Public Opinion Becomes Mainstream Social Opinion

New-media public opinion refers to the influential opinions or comments on specific issues that are expressed by the public through new media like the Internet and mobile phones. It is also the expression of actual public opinion through new media. Network public opinion, including opinion on the wired and wireless Internet, is the main body of new media currently. In rigorous theoretical studies, network public opinion is a subset of new-media public opinion, but in reality, it is difficult to show precisely the differences between network public opinion and new-media public opinion. As wireless Internet has increasingly become the mainstream, both are often seen as having similar meanings, even synonyms.

In recent years, a few big events in China caused great sensations in the "virtual society" after being brought under the spotlamp by new media, attracting extensive attention from the real society showing people the influence of new-media public opinion. New media have become an important platform for the Chinese people to express their opinions, discuss public affairs, participate in economic, social and political life, and play the role as supervisors. Currently, new-media public opinion has become a significant part of social opinion in China and is playing a role that is more and more influential on government behavior.

New media, as an emerging media form, has a growing influence on social development and people's lives, and has gradually penetrated each and every field of social life like politics, economy and culture, and begun to play an increasingly important role in social development and public

W. Kuang, *Social Media in China*, Sociology, Media and Journalism in China, https://doi.org/10.1007/978-981-13-0914-4_2

life. New media becomes a new discourse platform for the public and new-media public opinion, which emerged along with new media, is playing a more and more important part in social opinions on the whole as a new form of opinions. "Sun Zhigang event," "event of BMW hitting pedestrians," "Zhou Jiugeng event," "'hide-and-seek' event," "70 yards event," "Deng Yujiao event" and "Shishou event" all indicate that new-media public opinion has developed from the less-influential margins into a mainstream position and become an important factor that affects the development of social events and a component of mainstream opinion.

This explains why new-media public opinion is not only a focus of attention for government departments at all levels, but also one of the hotspots of academic studies.

New-media public opinion is a new field of research involving extensive aspects. Worldwide, the studies of the dissemination of network crises are the most similar to domestic studies. In China, the studies of new-media public opinion are made up of the following parts:

- *Comprehensive studies*: like "A study of the use of new media and its impacts," a project to tackle major problems in philosophy and social scientific studies under the Ministry of Education that was presided over by Prof. Xie Xinzhou from Peking University.
- *Empirical studies*: mainly refer to quantitative studies of network public opinion, and analyses of content of online information like *Annual Report on Public Opinion in China (2012)* written by Prof. Yu Guoming from Renmin University of China, and research reports issued by yuqing.people.com.cn, xinhuanet.com/yuqing, and Public Relations & Public Opinion Institute of Communication University of China (CUC).
- *Case studies*: are mainly demonstrated in various kinds of case libraries. In terms of monographs, there are, for example, *Internet Realtime-Public-Opinions Index [IRI]* (2010) by professors Ding Junjie and Zhang Shuting from Communication University of China and *Research on the Opinion Leaders of Political BBS: A Case Study on Sino-Japan BBS of Strong Nation Forum* (2010) by Prof. Yu Hong from Huazhong University of Science and Technology.
- *Studies of countermeasures*: The treatises are many, but the so-called countermeasures they suggest are neither original nor operational.

However, theoretical studies both at home and abroad on new-media public opinion, especially theoretical framework studies, are a weak point, which is exactly the priority of this study. As regards the theoretical framework studies on new-media public opinion, the chaos-theory-based model is often referred to abroad; and early treatises in China included *On the Butterfly Effect of New Media Communication* (2009) by Kuang Wenbo and *A Study on the Butterfly Effect of Network Public Opinions* (2011), the doctorial dissertation of Dang Shengcun, one of Kuang Wenbo's PhD candidates.

2.1 Characteristics of New-Media Public Opinion

2.1.1 Definition of the Concept of New-Media Public Opinion

New-media public opinion refers to the influential opinions or comments that are expressed by the public on specific issues through new media like the Internet and mobile phones, which is also the expression of actual public opinions through new media.

2.1.1.1 Definitions of Public Opinion

Public opinion is an extremely rich and complicated human spiritual phenomenon, and has various definitions. Chinese and foreign scholars have different opinions about how to define it, and there have been as many as seventy or eighty definitions so far, yet none has ever been publicly recognized.

Public opinion, also known as "舆诵," "舆颂" and "清义" in ancient China, refers to public views. Now many experts and scholars see public opinion as public views and think that public opinion includes effective public views, of the majority of the people, on some event.

In *Many Voices One World*, a UNESCO thematic report, public opinion is defined as a phenomenon of collectivity which usually can't be accurately analyzed with science, and that it is intimately associated with people's social nature. But public opinion is not changeless nor could it form an entirety from a geographical perspective.

Lippmann made a rough description of public opinion in his book *Public Opinion*—"images in people's mind of themselves and others, their needs, purposes and relations etc."[1]

Liu Jianming pointed out in *Principle of Public Opinion*, "Public opinion is the collective consciousness and common perception of the majority in a certain scope."[2]

[1] [US] Walter Lippmann, *Public Opinion*, p22, Beijing: Huaxia Publishing House, 1989.
[2] Liu Jianming, *Principle of Public opinion*, p70, Beijing: Huaxia Publishing House, 2002.

Li Guangzhi pointed out in *The General Theory of Public Opinion*, "Public opinion is the common trend that is formed by the free expression and spread of their opinions by the public on events involving personal interests."[3]

Gan Xifen believed, "Public opinion refers to roughly similar views, of people or social groups that have basically the same economic and political strata in social life, on the development of some state of affairs."[4]

In *Public Opinion and Information*, Xiang Desheng pointed out, "Public opinion is the open comment by the public or social groups on situations of general concerns to people."[5]

Yu Guoming believed, "Public opinion is the common perception of the society or social groups on the same controversial social issue of general public concern that happened recently."[6]

Sha Lianxiang pointed out in *Social Psychology*, "Public opinion refers to the sum of most people's views on controversial issues of common concerns. It is the unanimous public reaction to and judgment of some events in society, and representative and comprehensive view as well."[7]

Chen Lidan held, "Public opinion is the sum of beliefs, attitudes, views and emotions expressed by the public on the real society and social phenomena and problems. It is unanimous, intense and sustained, and affects social development and the evolution of the state of affairs, both rationally and irrationally."[8]

In *News and Public Opinion*, Hu Yu pointed out, "Public opinion is the sum of specific views of specific social groups on specific events."[9]

In line with these definitions, it is easy to see that public opinion has the following characteristics: it is the opinion of the public; there must be a central issue; public opinion is always developing and changing; public opinion is an enormous social spiritual force (see Fig. 2.1).

[3] Li Guangzhi, *The General Theory of Public Opinion*, p4, Harbin: Heilongjiang Educational Press, 1989.

[4] Gan Xifen, *Journalism Theory*, p42, Beijing: China Renmin University Press, 1982.

[5] Xiang Desheng, *Public Opinion and Information*, p9, Zhengzhou: Henan People's Publishing House, 1992.

[6] Yu Guoming, *Public Opinion Analysis: A Quantitative research into the Public in Modern China*, p26, Beijing: Huaxia Publishing House, 2001.

[7] Sha Lianxiang, *Social Psychology*, p44, Beijing: China Renmin University Press, 2002.

[8] Chen Lidan, *Public Opinion*, p14, Beijing: China Radio Film & TV Press, 1999.

[9] *News and Public Opinion*, p112, Beijing: China Radio Film & TV Press, 2001.

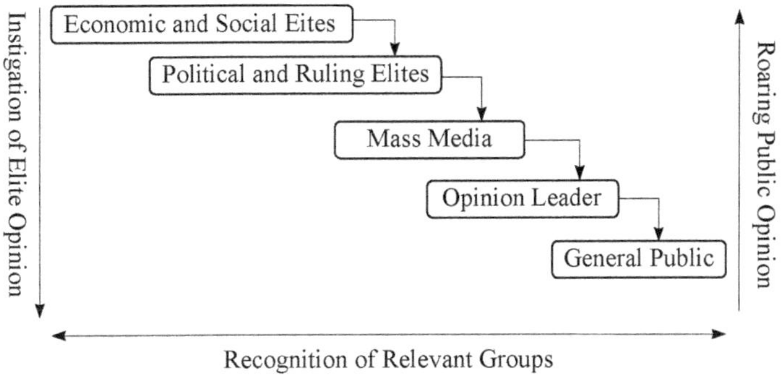

Fig. 2.1 Deustcher④ "waterfall model" of public opinion formation

In reality, people usually equate the opinions expressed by mass media or media to social opinion; and public opinion to social opinion; and opinion of the masses or public perception to social opinion.[10]

2.1.1.2 Network Public Opinion and New-Media Opinion

As a collectivity of the opinions expressed by the public, public opinion was passed on through mouths and ears in ancient society, and the carriers of public opinion were people themselves. Modern public opinion emerged in close association with mass media. Before the 1990s, carriers of modern public opinion were mainly mass media like newspapers, broadcasters and TV. As the Internet emerged as "the fourth medium," a new type of public opinion—network public opinion—appeared.

Related to public opinion in the traditional sense, "network public opinion" is different because it has different dissemination entities, carriers, ways of dissemination and audience characteristics. However, as an extension of public opinion, network public opinion is by nature public opinion, therefore we define "network public opinion" as a special form of public opinion that emerges as network dissemination becomes popular. It

[10] Isaac Deustcher (1906–1967) was a Judaic Marxist writer, journalist and social activist who was born in Poland and moved to Britain after the Second World War broke out. His best-known identity would be as the author of biographies of Leon Trotsky and Joseph Stalin and commentator of current events in the Soviet Union. His three-volume biography of Trotsky, "Leon Trotsky" made up of *The Prophet Armed: Trotsky, 1879–1921*, *The Prophet Unarmed: Trotsky, 1921–1929* and *The Prophet Outcast: Trotsky, 1929–1940*, deeply influenced the new left wings in Britain. As the universally acknowledged most authoritative work to study Trotsky, it has been translated into several languages.

is the sum of common views, attitudes, beliefs and emotions expressed by cybercitizens on the phenomena and problems online or in reality (both more than often superimposed), is consistent, influential and sustainable, and affects social development and the progress of relevant states of affairs. That is, network public opinion is the product of public opinion together with online dissemination media. As long as these two conditions are met, that is, being dissemination of the collectivity of public opinions through the carrier of network media, it is network public opinion.

The emergence of network public opinion is inevitable in the process of social development. China is now at a transitional period and sees a sharply growing number of social conflicts, with different groups pursuing different interests and possessing different cultural demands. It is, therefore, necessary to provide an active public discourse platform for them to fully and legally express their views to reach the ultimate goal—communicating and eliminating prejudice and conflicts. The Internet meets this requirement exactly, and an active public discourse platform is thus built. In the era of network media, with the help of emails, BBS, blogs, and microblogging, among other information interactive tools, cybercitizens, in combination with content discussion, show even greater enthusiasm in media construction, greatly enhancing the influence of public opinion. Also, network public opinion enjoys a fair degree of freedom of speech, and many network users express, online, their opinions which they would rather not say or dare not say in real life. Therefore, network public opinion is also a distribution center for social opinions on contentious issues, and its status has attracted increasing attention from the people.

As mobile phones become increasingly popular, mobile-phone media also becomes an important platform for expressing public opinions. Since remarks that are spread with mobile phones are more open and democratic, more profound and extensive, and are spread in various forms even faster, the expression of social situations and public opinion is even more free and efficient, making mobile-phone media a new platform for citizens to participate in politics. China is no exception to this phenomenon and mobile-phone media has become an important channel for the Chinese to participate in politics. Therefore, "new-media public opinion" including network public opinion and mobile-phone media came into vogue.

As a form of media, new-media public opinion of course has all the characteristics of public opinion. However, relative to traditional public opinion, it has different dissemination space, plus the influence of the new media dissemination mechanism—especially the traditional "gatekeeping" role, which has partially lost its effectiveness—means new-media public opinion becomes a form of public opinion that is quite different from traditional mass-media public opinion.

2.1.2 *Characteristics of New-Media Public Opinion*

2.1.2.1 Rich and Diversified

New-media public opinion is rich in that it is all-embracing and universal. The characteristics of new media being virtual, anonymous, limitless and interactive in real time make online public opinion diversified and off the mainstream in value transmission and the pursuit of interests. Also, the traditional "gatekeeping" role is partially ineffective. Positive and healthy, or vulgar and gray content can all found here, explaining why the content of new-media public opinion is extraordinarily rich.

2.1.2.2 Open, Free and Interactive

Hundreds of thousands of cybercitizens in different regions, who usually express their views and opinions online anonymously and are highly virtual make the body of new-media public opinion. This determines the characteristic of new-media public opinion being open and free.

Because new media is interactive in real time, the dissemination process can be continued and completed. The audiences of new-media public opinion are no longer completely inactive "targets" and the disseminators no longer hold absolute discourse domination or the control right. What's more, in new-media dissemination, the roles of the disseminators and the audience are ambiguous and may be shifted in a flash. Relative to mighty traditional media, individual cybercitizens have gradually become the body of online information release, and their strength is being enhanced.

2.1.2.3 Fast

The rapid development of new-media public opinion benefits from the advantages of new-media dissemination. The Internet breaks the limits of time and space, and the fast nature of new-media public opinion is mainly demonstrated by the shortened time and narrowed space of its development.

Thanks to the advantages of new-media dissemination, information can be released quickly and, with the help of new media, disseminated fast. Replies or remarks, once attracting cybercitizens' attention, will be forwarded repeatedly and spread at an astonishing speed.

The nature of new media being interactive in real time makes communication a dynamic system that enables cybercitizens to respond rapidly to online opinions. Information dissemination on the Internet is extensive. Although cybercitizens, as the body of public opinion, spread in each and every corner of the world, they can have rapid opinion interaction beyond the limits of region and space, and thus develop public opinion very fast.

New-media public opinion always “leans to one side.” In many cases, the majority of the cybercitizens had simple and direct understanding and views, which were neither profound nor comprehensive, and always “leaned to one side.” On issues of popular concern for the cybercitizens, for example, sensitive issue of international relations, the dark sides of the society, corruption cases and negative outbursts, extreme statements spread even faster than positive mainstream remarks, and in even extensive scopes to the level of “one-sided” or “avalanche at crucial moment,” leading to “a high concentration” of cybercitizens’ opinions, even when irrational and emotional.

The Internet is an open and highly participatory world. Anybody, rich or poor, well-educated or poorly educated, regardless of their social strata or race, are equal on the Internet. The most prominent thing is that in network forums, any visitor can release their own information or express their views.

2.1.2.4 Co-existence of Rational and Irrational Factors

New media, as an important platform for expressing public opinions, is playing an important role and has great influence that cannot be ignored by society. New-media public opinion has gradually become the government’s “barometer” in its administration. Since new media is anonymous and open, it is viewed as a place for people to give vent to their emotions, which gives birth to a kind of emotional public opinion, which may be a political emotion-type, asocial emotion-type, a cultural emotion-type or a lifestyle emotion-type.

The emergence of emotion-based new-media public opinion on the Internet helps the Party and the government understand real public opinions. New media is becoming a “driver” of public democratic life.

However, emotional public opinion may be irrational, passive, infectious and diffusible. The anonymous and interactive characteristics of new media make new-media public opinion more perceptual and less rational, and somewhat blind, impulsive and radical, and lack reasoning.

The irrational characteristic of new-media public opinion may possibly cause conflicts. New-media public opinion is conflictual in that its enhancement of ethical relativism is in conflict with its basic ethical guidelines.

In many cases, new-media public opinion tends to "be grouped." For one thing, the irrational characteristic of groups is very prominent in cybercitizens; for another, groups, which cluster under new media, very easily raise questions of group concern. Through the convincing mechanism, cybercitizens approach biased results after discussion. Because of that, cybercitizens usually express their opinions radically, and the struggle for prominence leads to extreme utterances designed to shock.

2.1.2.5 Hard to Control

New-media public opinion is hard to control. To control public opinion in traditional mass media, governments may—by setting a mass communication system and developing relevant laws, regulations and policies—distribute communication resources, examine and register newly built media, and prohibit, censor or limit the dissemination of some information. For traditional media, thanks to this "gatekeeping" role, controlling public opinion is not difficult. However, the Internet is a highly open space where every person has a "microphone." New-media information disseminators can be counted by hundreds of millions, making it impossible for the news publishing department to examine and approve the dissemination of information online.

The openness of new media makes each user a "news publisher" in theory. Given the big population of new media users, it is impossible to examine all remarks "on the information highway," let alone make comprehensive and objective comments on them. The control of new-media public opinion therefore becomes complicated and difficult. Being hard to control is the most important characteristic of new-media public opinion, as a result of which new-media public opinion is rich, complex, plural and conflicting.

It is hard to control new-media public opinion in that:

1. The domination of new-media public opinion does not reside on websites but is up to the intensity and concentration of the population of cybercitizens participating in the discussion.
2. The openness of new media enables information disseminators to circumvent barriers in order to release information, and it is impossible for web managers to examine online remarks individually.

3. New-media public opinion is complicated. New-media public opinion, whether considered or spontaneous, is chaotic and disorderly. Since cybercitizens can say what they want to say online, new-media public opinion is mainly spontaneous.
4. New-media public opinion is plural. The ideology of new-media public opinion is plural. There are opposite social and political systems and ideologies in the world. As new media develops, it is unrealistic to expect complete control of online remarks. Information may be disseminated online infinitely from any place in the world to another, so the ideology of new-media public opinion presents pluralism.

2.1.2.6 Easily Manipulated

The existence of the "Internet water army" (e.g., paid posters) makes new-media public opinion easily manipulated. The "Internet water army," hired by network PR companies, opens new topics and reply to topics for the formation of public opinion. Paid posters may be full-time or part-time. As regards how the "Internet water army" manipulates new-media public opinion, will be examined in detail later in the discussion of network forums.

2.2 Management of New-Media Public Opinion

2.2.1 Functions of New-Media Public Opinion

Supervision. Government decision making and the development of laws and regulations can be affected by public opinion on the Internet or mobile phones.

Disseminating information. The existence of new media makes information dissemination faster and faster. The network surpasses traditional media thanks to its function of instant information dissemination. Because new-media public opinion has the collection and distribution, dissemination, and even magnification effect, the network becomes an important channel for people to get information. The phenomenon of opaque and asymmetric information in the past has been greatly ameliorated.

Exchanging ideas. New-media public opinion usually has many voices, making the network a place where different ideas meet.

New-media public opinion somewhat affects government behavior, too, which is embodied in the following aspects.

First, it produces instant influence with quick response. The dissemination of new-media public opinion is more agile and faster, setting a higher requirement on government's administration efficiency. The public has the right to question the government, so the government is obliged to reply to the public. When questioned, the government needs to respond quickly and show enough concern, announce relevant information in a timely way, and give feedback on social issues of public concern so as to eliminate public doubt. In many cases, the public has doubts and speculation mostly because information dissemination is not smooth, and in a few cases, because of the misconduct and nonfeasance of a few departments.

Second, it produces demonstrative influence with plural responses. The emergence of new media makes possible infinite and instant information transmission from one place to another in the world. Any organization or individual can find the space to release information online. The openness of dissemination and disseminators' pluralism break the monopoly of public-opinion dissemination via traditional media.

Third, it produces complicated impacts with tremendous responses. Relative to traditional media, new media breaks through many restrictions like newspaper layout, fixed time periods in radio and TV programs and program capacity. Because the dissemination entities are plural, each cybercitizen may become a potential information provider, and network information becomes endless. Meanwhile, the existence of databases enables storage of historical news. It is the accumulation of information collection in depth and breadth that contributes to tremendous information for new-media public opinion.

Fourth, it produces exploring influence with interactive responses. That new media enable rapid responses makes interaction a necessary and regular way of communication. In the era of traditional media, there was interaction in the traditional sense, but because of limited scope and influence of such interaction and the need to examine carefully the content of such interaction, it was actually "time-sharing" interaction. The Internet turns that into "instant" interaction. Online investigation, timely comments and multi-channel participation make the development of new-media public opinion far faster than traditional public opinion. A hotspot issue together with an emotional opinion can become the fuse to ignite public opinion to spread rapidly and widely.

2.2.2 *Problems of New-Media Public Opinion*

Its enormous influence makes new-media public opinion highly "lethal," even leading to online violence. The absence of the "gatekeeping" role in network dissemination can lead to public opinion becoming out of control. Over recent years, new-media public opinion has presented the following unhealthy phenomena.

First, slandering and attacks. The characteristic of the network being anonymous makes it common that cybercitizens attack or slander others. In particular, the phenomenon of abusing and blaming characters in news reports, specific people or work units in news comments, post bars and forums of web portals is common and mostly abreaction of emotions.

Second, releasing false information. Given the convenience of online information release, and the great differences between network information examination and the information examination practiced by traditional media, it becomes very easy to release false information online.

Third, a great deal of civil infringement. New-media public opinion infringement may infringe upon *jus personarum* or property rights like the right of reputation, the right of privacy, the right of image, copyright, and the right to network dissemination of information. Making public, without permission, other people's names, phone numbers, addresses and other personal information online, for example, phone numbers and addresses of some famous stars, will disturb the tranquility of their life and infringe their right of privacy. Randomly posting other people's photos online, even spoofing them, infringes upon their right of image. The phenomenon of reprinting articles without the authors' permission, which infringes other people's copyright, can be seen everywhere.

It is not that the network does not have laws. The acts of tort in new-media public opinion bring to the users corresponding legal responsibilities.

2.2.3 *Management of New-Media Public Opinion*

New-media public opinion is liberating ordinary people's scope for commenting. It meets, even stimulates ordinary people's desire to speak. The Internet, full of different rational and irrational perceptions, is a huge market for public opinion. New-media public opinion has concentrated hotspots, and mainly focuses on people's livelihood, medical treatment, housing, education and remuneration, as well as government official-related or craft-related political topics. New-media public opinion is sometimes true and sometimes false, and frequently highly emotional. It covers both well-founded, accurate, reports and groundless hype.

New-media public opinion may be about expostulation or complaint. Expostulation deserves award, and complaints are not necessarily that formidable. Effective social participation is an important link in crisis governance, and allowing people to express their discontent usually helps alleviate conflict and eliminate some potential hidden troubles. Ignoring, even suppressing people's discontent is unwise, because accumulated mass discontent, if not pacified, could well lead to serious crises. Control of new-media public opinion has become an extremely important aspect of social management. How to guide online public opinion, balance cybercitizens' moods, and rationalize cybercitizens' feelings are concerns for the general situation of development and stability.

Currently in China, the main platforms for new-media public opinion are network forums and microblogging. Network forums are places where users exchange information, and new-media public opinion forms, develops and is disseminated. The Internet's characteristics make the development of new-media public opinion faster than traditional dissemination of public opinion and make opinion disputes fiercer. Therefore, the network plays a role that is not to be ignored in the dissemination of public opinion in today's society.

Cybercitizens discuss hotspot issues fiercely and their opinions on such issues may become very influential, even affect relevant departments' decision-making process and administration. However, the public-opinion function of network forums has its confines—it can only supervise, but not substitute independent judicial procedures and legal administrative procedures to make final decisions. Online public opinion, regardless of its influence, cannot replace independent judicial investigation or direct participation in the decision-making process, and its most fundamental function is to reflect public feelings and popular wishes, supervise the decision-making process while exerting whatever large or small influence it possesses on these decisions.

It must be remembered that cybercitizens can express their opinions freely online, both good and bad opinions and these may have a negative influence.

The characteristics of new media enable all to promulgate their views with a virtual identity as long as they are online. Everyone has a "microphone"; the audience's position is promoted unprecedentedly, and the disseminator's dominating position is weakened. The audience in traditional sense, after getting rid of their passive position, begin to become positive participators in information dissemination. Topics are therefore diversified, the conformability of public opinion is dissolved, and public opinion presents extreme diversity and dispersity.

In eye-catching competitions, some websites, in order to attract an audience, fabricate hearsay information before posting it online, forwarding or citing false news to mislead and confuse the public, which then has great negative influence.

New-media public opinion is the product of an era of development and social progress, and we must face it actively instead of avoiding it passively. New-media public opinion needed be controlled in the way Da Yu controlled the flood, that is, the priority is dredging, not blocking, and the positive role of new-media public opinion needs to be given full play.

The characteristic of new-media public opinion being diversified and dispersed sets a new requirement on public opinion management—be integrated and targeted. Integration is a word with extensive meanings, mainly inclusiveness, tolerance, seeking common ground, and organization into an organic whole.

Being targeted is an important requirement on managing new-media public opinion. The network is a world of pluralism, where different ideological trends actively seek their own space online.

It must be emphasized that we cannot demonize new media, or blame new media for the chaos of new-media public opinion. New media is simply a tool for communication, and a channel for information circulation. Some information spread through new media may be detrimental, but more is harmless. The positive social benefits created by new media are far greater than new media's negative effect.

Compared to mighty governmental discourse, folk public opinion remains in a disadvantaged position, and is a rare discourse resource in China. New-media public opinion expresses the voices and words in a nongovernmental position in civil society and is extensively radioactive and influential. It plays an irreplaceable role in the development of a pluralism pattern of public opinion. A benign view of public opinion is exactly the purpose of the concept of freedom of speech and is a major step in building a harmonious society.

CHAPTER 3

Theoretical Models for Studying New-Media Public Opinion

The rapid rise and vigorous development of new media has not only led to a fundamental reform of the information dissemination technology, but also changed people's productive activities, way of life, interpersonal communication and way of thinking. It has extensively and profoundly influenced each and every field of social life and human survival and development. In the 1950s, the famous communication scholar Marshall McLuhan asserted that as a consequence of the media revolution all individuals and social life would need to be adjusted to fit the new perception model that was being built in order to adapt to new technologies. However, frequently, fundamental theoretical studies lag behind the development of the corresponding new technologies.

3.1 Theoretical Models of New Media Studies

Currently, the new media industry with its rapid development has gained enormous social influence and has penetrated all social aspects like politics, economy, science and technology, education and culture. However, around the globe, the basic new media theories are weak.

The following theoretical models are recognized and have been adopted extensively by the international academic community.

W. Kuang, *Social Media in China*, Sociology, Media and Journalism in China, https://doi.org/10.1007/978-981-13-0914-4_3

3.1.1 Diffusion of Innovations Theory

Advanced by the American scholar Everett Rogers in the 1960s, the diffusion of innovations theory convinces people to accept new concepts, new things and new products through media with particular emphasis on the social and cultural influence of mass communication. The diffusion of innovations theory is extensively applied to new media studies in Western academic circles.

Rogers believed that innovation was a concept, practice or thing that was deemed original by individuals or other adopter units; that diffusion of innovations referred to a basic social progress, during which individuals subjectively felt that information about some new voice was disseminated. In a social construction process, the significance of some innovation becomes clearer and clearer.

In 1962, Rogers studied a number of cases on the diffusion of innovations before publishing his book *Diffusion of Innovations.* He observed the process of diffusion of innovations and the influential factors, summarized basic rules of diffusion of innovative things in a social system, and put forward the famous S-curve theory of diffusion of innovations.

Rogers summarized the studies on the diffusion of innovations. The book divided the diffusion process of innovations into awareness, persuasion, decision-making and determination, and put forward the basic hypothesis of "diffusion of innovations" (see Fig. 3.1).

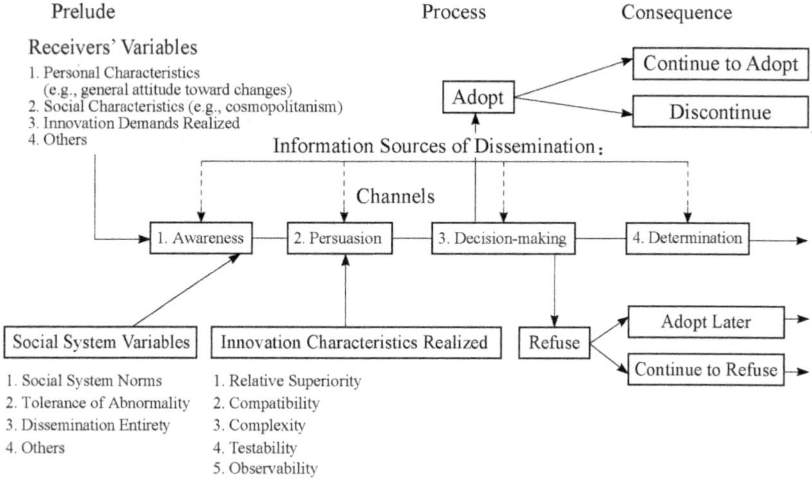

Fig. 3.1 Diffusion of innovations theory model①

In the 1970s and 1980s, studies of the diffusion of innovations shifted to communication media and the audience in social and cultural scenarios, and studies that highlighted two-way and macro levels like coding and decoding, media and social development became hotspots.

3.1.1.1 Levels of Individual Innovativeness[1]

Rogers divided "individual innovativeness" into five levels, namely five different types of adopters—innovator, early adopters, early majority, late majority and laggards.

The *innovator* was the pioneer adopting "innovations" but, unfortunately, was a thrill-seeker and reckless and might accept "innovations" too fast.

Early adopters usually have the charisma of opinion leaders, and their prudent characteristics and leadership decisively influence later adopters, so they had profound influence on the promotion of "innovations." Early adopters' work enthusiasm, interpersonal relations and influence made them the best candidates for "innovation media" in an organization.

The *early majority* accepted "innovations" after careful consideration.

The *late majority* was a suspicious group, and gradually became adopters after eliminating misgivings about "innovations."

Laggards were traditional and conservative, and adopted "innovations" as the last resort.

3.1.1.2 Stages of the Process of Diffusion of Innovations

Awareness: Contacting innovations and roughly knowing how they operate;

Persuasion: Developing an innovation-related attitude;

Decision making: Deciding whether to adopt or refuse an innovative activity;

Implementation: Putting innovation to practice; and

Determination: Enhancing or revoking innovation-related decisions.

3.1.1.3 Innovation Features Affecting the Adoption Rate

Relative superiority: the degree by which an innovation is superior to the old idea that it substitutes;

Compatibility: the degree of co-existence of the innovation with existing values, past experience and expected adopters' demands;

[1] Refer to [US] Everett M. Rogers, *Diffusion of Innovations*, p10, Beijing: Central Compilation & Translation Press, 2002.

Complexity: the degree of difficulty in understanding and using the innovation;
Testability: the degree that an innovation can be tested on a limited foundation; and
Observability: the degree that an innovative result can be seen by others.

The communication process of diffusion of innovations can be described by an "S" curve (see Fig. 3.2). At the early stage of diffusion, the number of adopters was small, and diffusion progressed slowly; when the number of adopters expanded to 10~25%, diffusion sped up suddenly, and the curve rose rapidly and maintained the trend, that is, the so-called "take-off period;" when diffusion was close to its saturation point, its progress began to slow down, leading to the "S"-shaped curve.

In the process of diffusion of innovations, early adopters made necessary preparations for subsequent takeoff. This seemingly weak group was capable of playing a great role in interpersonal communication and persuading other people to accept innovations. To Rogers, early adopters were people who were willing to take the lead in accepting and using innovative things and take risks for them. They were highly tolerant of the deficiencies at the early stage of innovation, and were capable of persuading the opinion leaders of groups where they were members to accept and adopt innovative products. Then innovations diffused rapidly by opinion leaders. In this way, innovations were already close to the "take-off period."

Rogers pointed out that an innovative thing, in order to continue diffusing in a social system, must first be adopted by a certain number of people. Normally, it was 10~20% of the total market. Once the proportion

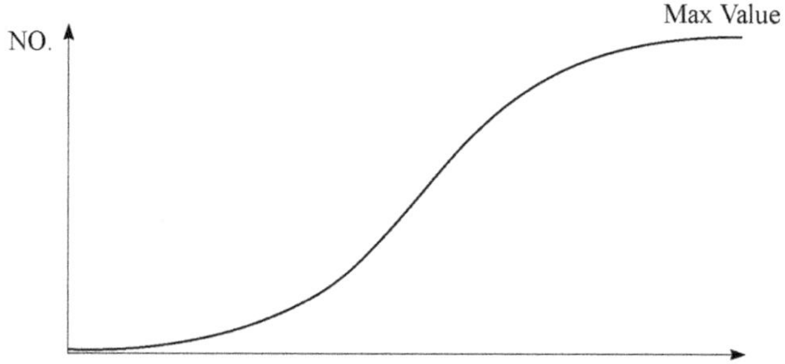

Fig. 3.2 S curve of the diffusion of innovations model

of diffusion of innovations reached the critical level, the diffusion process took off into the stage of rapid diffusion. The concept of saturation point means that innovation normally cannot diffuse 100% in the social system. As a matter of fact, many innovations can, eventually, only diffuse to a certain percentage of the social system. When the innovation adopters in the system stop growing, the scalar (expressed in absolute scalar) of innovation adopters in the system or the percentage (expressed in relative scalar) of innovation adopters is the diffusion saturation point of the innovation.

Rogers believed that the diffusion of innovations could always proceed with the help of certain social networks, and that in the process when innovations were promoted and diffused to society, information technology could effectively provide relevant knowledge and information but, in terms of persuading people to accept and use innovations, interpersonal communication seemed more direct and effective. Therefore, the best way to popularize innovations was to apply information technology in combination with interpersonal communication.[2]

3.1.2 Technology Acceptance Model

The Technology Acceptance Model, TAM for short, was developed by Fred Davis in 1989 on the basis of Fishbein and Ajzen's theory of reasoned action (TRA) in order to study users' acceptance of new media. According to TRA, consumer behavior was determined by consumers' behavioral intention, while consumers' behavioral intention was affected by their behavioral attitude. TAM is applied extensively to studying new media, especially users' behavioral intention. The so-called behavioral intention refers to the subjective probability that individuals attempt to execute a specific behavior, and is individuals' willingness to engage in some behavior. According to TAM, the users' behavioral intention to use new media is affected by both their attitude and perceived usefulness. Attitude refers to the degree that individuals like or dislike specific behavior, and is affected by perceived usefulness and perceived ease of use. Perceived usefulness refers to the degree that a specific system can improve individuals' work performance, and may directly affect their participation intention. Perceived ease of use refers to the degree that the use of a spe-

[2] See page 12 of *Diffusion of Innovations* by [US] Everett M. Rogers for Figs 3.1 and 3.2 and views.

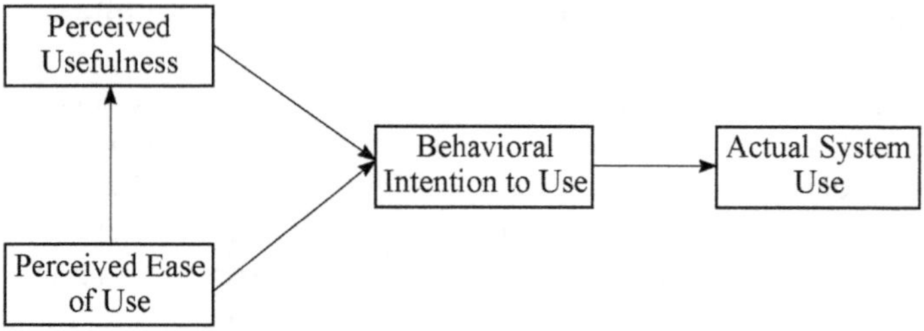

Fig. 3.3 English expression of TAM

cific system can save individuals' energy. It affects the behavioral intention through perceived usefulness. TAM is more frequently cited in the international communication circle.

TAM has two commonly seen expressions (see Figs. 3.3 and 3.4)[3]:

3.1.3 Theory of Planned Behavior

The Theory of Planned Behavior, TPB for short, can help us understand how people change their behavioral models. TPB believes that people's behaviors are the results of cogitative plans.

TPB, put forward by Ajzen (1988, 1991), was the successor of the Theory of Reasoned Action (TRA) that was developed by Ajzen and Fishbein together. Ajzen discovered in studies that people's behaviors were not always voluntary, but were under control. He therefore expanded TRA and added a new concept—self-"behavior control cognition" to it before developing it into a new model for studying behavior theories (see Fig. 3.5).

3.1.3.1 Five Elements of the Theory of Planned Behavior

Attitude refers to the positive or passive feeling that is held by individuals on some behavior. It also refers to the attitude after individuals' comments on a specific behavior are conceptualized. Therefore, the components of attitude are often deemed as functions of individuals' significant faith in such a behavioral result.

[3] Martin Fishbein and Icek Ajzen, *Predicting and Changing Behavior: The Reasoned Action Approach*, Psychology Press, 2010, p.43. (Figs. 3.3 and 3.4 are from the book; the Chinese in Figs 3.3 and 3.4 is translated by this book's author.)

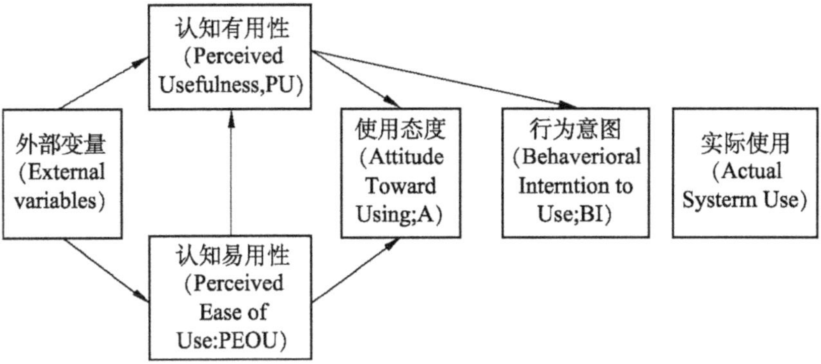

Fig. 3.4 Chinese expression of TAM

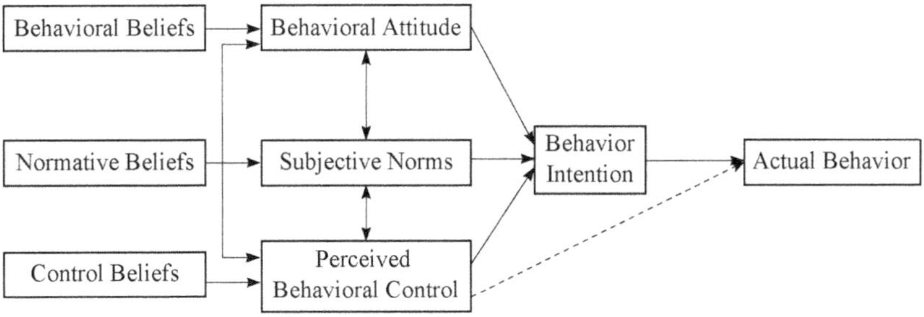

Fig. 3.5 Illustration of Theory of Planned Behavior model[①]

Subjective norm refers to the social pressure that individuals feel about whether to conduct a specific behavior or not, or the role of individuals or groups—which have influence on individuals' behavioral decision-making—in whether individuals conduct a specific behavior or not when they predict other people's behavior.

Perceived behavioral control reflects individuals' past experience and expected obstacles. The more the resources and opportunities individuals think they have, the fewer their expected obstacles, the stronger their perceived behavioral control. It exerts influence in two ways—first, it has a motive meaning to behavior intention; second, it can predict behavior directly.

Behavior intention refers to individuals' judgment of subjective probability of conducting a specific behavior. It reflects individuals' willingness to take actions over a specific behavior.

Behavior refers to acts that are actually taken by individuals.[4]

Ajzen believed that all the factors that may affect behavior would indirectly affect behavior performance via behavior intention. Behavior intention was influenced by three relevant factors: first, it stemmed from individuals' "attitude," that is, the attitude toward some specific behavior; second, it stemmed from "subjective norms," that is, the subjective norms that would affect individuals' specific behavior; third, it stemmed from "perceived behavioral control."

Generally speaking, the more positive an individual's attitude toward a behavior was, the stronger the individual's behavior intention would be. Similarly, the more positive an individual's subjective norms over a behavior were, the stronger the individual's behavior intention would be. The more positive the attitude and subjective norms and the stronger the perceived behavioral control were, the stronger an individual's behavior intention would be. In the basic hypothesis of the TRA, Ajzen advocated seeing individuals' will control over their behaviors as a continuum, one end of which was behavior completely under will control and the other end of which was behavior completely out of will control. Most human behaviors were somewhere between the two extremes. Therefore, to predict behaviors that were not completely under will control, it is necessary to enhance the variable of perceived behavioral control. However, when individual control of behavior was close to the most intensified, or when the issue of control was not a factor to be taken into consideration by individuals, the prediction effect of the Theory of Planned Behavior was similar to TRA.

3.1.3.2 Main Views of the Theory of Planned Behavior

Behavior that was not completely under individuals' will control was not only affected by behavior intention, but restricted by actual controlling conditions like the individuals' capabilities of executing the behavior, opportunities and resources. Under the circumstance where the actual controlling conditions were sufficient, behavior intention directly determined behavior.

[4] Martin Fishbein and Icek Ajzen, *Belief, Attitude, Intention, and Behavior: An Introduction to Theory and Research*, Addison-Wesley Publishing Company, 1975, p53.

Accurate perceived behavior control reflected the situation of actual controlling conditions. It therefore can be seen as an alternative measurement indicator to directly predict the possibility of the occurrence of a behavior (as shown in Fig. 3.5 by dotted line) and the accuracy of prediction relied on the degree of truthfulness of perceived behavior control.

Attitude to behavior, subjective norms and perceived behavior control were three major variables that determined behavior intention. The more active the attitude, the greater the supports from other important people, the more intensified the perceived behavior control were, the greater the behavior intention would be, otherwise the smaller the behavior intention would be.

Individuals had a lot of behavior beliefs, but only a small number of behavior beliefs could be accessed at specific times and in specific environments, and these accessible beliefs were known as salient beliefs and were the cognitive and emotional foundation of attitude toward behavior, subjective norms and perceived behavior control.

Individual and social and cultural factors (e.g., personality, intelligence, experience, age, sex and cultural background) indirectly affected the attitude toward behavior, subjective norms and perceived behavior control by affecting behavior beliefs, and eventually affected behavior intention and behavior.

The attitude toward behavior, subjective norms and perceived behavior control could be completely differentiated in concept, but sometimes they may have a common belief foundation. They, therefore, were mutually independent and interconnected.

3.2 Butterfly–Effect Model in Studies of New–Media Public Opinion

3.2.1 *Butterfly Effect of the Evolution of New-Media Public Opinion*

3.2.1.1 Definition of the Butterfly Effect of Network Public Opinion

Since the concept of "public opinion" was first put forward by Walter Lippmann in *Public Opinion*, public opinion has presented multiple characteristics. A definition that is universally recognized is the common opinion of the majority in a specific scope in society that eliminates the differences of individual views and reflects social perception and collective consciousness. The main part is "opinion" and the dissemination of public opinion is also the process that views flow.

If the network is only seen as a communication tool, "network public opinion" may have the following definition: "Network public opinion refers to influential and biased views or remarks that are expressed by the public over some focal issue and spread on the Internet." As a matter of fact, the basic definition of "network public opinion" goes beyond basic technical-level interpretation. Seeing it as an expression channel in society conforms more to the current national conditions of China.

The concept of the butterfly effect was put forward by Edward Norton Lorenz in 1963. The butterfly effect of network public opinion is a metaphor of the enormous social influence of network public opinion. The butterfly effect explains that complicated and chaotic systems cannot be accurately predicted and completely controlled; and that despite the lack of controller power in traditional sense, individuals all have butterfly power which has subtle influence, that is, "power of the powerless."[5] Some scholar held that the butterfly effect in network public opinion was a phenomenon of non-linear irregular chaos that was formed at the expression of opinions under the circumstance when the initial conditions for network public opinion were not yet certain.[6] The definition highlighted "non-linear irregular" and "chaotic" characteristics of online expression of opinions in the butterfly effect, but regarded the subtlety of initial conditions of network public opinion and uncertainty of results thus caused as "uncertainty of initial conditions for network public opinion" and ignored the original meaning of a butterfly flapping its wings and the possibility of windstorms; there were also researchers who held that the butterfly effect should refer to the enormous chain reactions of "normal" trivial things in day-to-day life in the field of the Internet, which caused wide repercussion in the cultural, ideological, even political world.[7] Using this analogy from nature highlighted that "trivial things" can evolve into public opinion "tornados" or have "shock effects," and emphasized the neutrality of the butterfly effect. But as a definition, it is extensive, and fails to analyze the evolution process, so it is not specific.

[5] Czech writer Havel put forward "the power of the powerless," cited from *Seven Life Lessons of Chaos* by [US] Briggs and [UK] Peat, Shanghai: Shanghai Scientific & Technical Publishers, 2008.

[6] Refer to *A study of the characteristics and management of online public opinion supervision from perspective of chaos theory* by Li Ruobing, available at www.people.com.cn/20091221.

[7] Refer to *Psychological phenomena and analysis of different roles in network society* by Wang Yifu and Shen Kejun, *Journal of Huaiyin Teachers College (Social Sciences Edition)*, 2009(3).

We hold that the butterfly effect of network public opinion refers to the multiplication effect of public opinion which is formed after relevant parties in the real society give feedback on the synergy effect of network media and traditional media, while this synergy effect is triggered by micro contents after micro contents are refined and superimposed by cybercitizens—the group exerting public opinion pressure.

Such a concept first highlighted that the initial conditions for the forming of network public opinion were sensitive; then it stressed that the effects of the butterfly effect were not sudden windstorms, but were similar in nature; later it pointed out that the results of the initial conditions after evolution were uncertain, but not necessarily destructive; and eventually, the process of the butterfly effect was chaotic, orderly amidst disorderly, and fractals and iteration were its order.

3.2.1.2 Elements and Characteristics of the Butterfly Effect of Network Public Opinion

In the evolution of the butterfly effect of network public opinion, cybercitizens, by refining and superimposing details of online events, build an information tree. For some hotspot issues, the audience will use their emotions and inclination within their knowledge and cognition as synergistic agents to mix and multiply such hotspots into new information and form new public opinion in many ways like ordinary web pages, news, forums, blogs and replies to topics. Meanwhile, they turn from pure information recipients into information discoverers and conveyers and, while sending information, give information feedback in different directions to different groups online, thus inducing ideological and behavioral "resonance" of multiple strata in large areas. With the unique two-way and multiple-way interaction function of the network, the "resonance" cycles and repeats before producing the superimposed effect.[8] As areas of "resonance" get expanded, so does the "resonance" margin, the exponentially growing diffusion speed lets out explosive influence, and leads to the "avalanche" effect. A public opinion storm is thus formed and continues to be advanced, with an increasingly stronger social mobilization function.

As can be seen, the butterfly effect of network public opinion needs three elements to occur: the release of micro content, synergistic response of network media and traditional media and feedback from interest stakeholders.

[8] Refer to Ren Xianliang, *The Guiding Art of the Public Opinion*, Beijing: Xinhua Publishing House, 2010.

The butterfly effect of network public opinion can multiply and exponentially magnify public opinion, and that is mainly embodied in the following aspects: first, the contrast of social resources held by the micro contents publisher and those held by the party (parties) involved in the event, which demonstrates the power of the powerless; second, the contrast of the "micro" initial contents and the huge changes of material, information and energy that are caused by the public opinion tornado; third, the enormous population of the public opinion pressure group, and the profoundness of their opinions.

The butterfly effect of network public opinion includes both social events and cultural events. The former are featured by news characters as the main part and media, especially network media, as the main channel to implement relief; and the latter are featured by some character as the representative of some culture and public pursuit of a heterogeneous culture, which then forms social public opinion. This book gives priority to discussing social events involved in the butterfly effect of network public opinion.

3.2.2 *Model and Variables of the Evolution of New-Media Public Opinion*

3.2.2.1 *Model Overview*

In order to explain the evolution route of network dissemination producing social influence, it is necessary to build an evolution model of the butterfly effect of network dissemination and stereotype the seemingly complicated network dissemination process with elements such as information sources, communication entities, feedback entities and feedback indexes. However, "a model that meets all purposes and all analytical levels does not exist at all," and any model has its applicability and limitations. In addition, given limited data and restrictions of studies at the present stage, the model built in this book can only be called a helpful try.

The butterfly effect of network public opinion is a non-linear system. In non-linear equations, even a subtle change of a variable may have disproportionate, even overturning influence on the other variables. The reciprocity among the elements can be maintained relatively unchanged in a fairly big scope, but split at some critical points, leading the system to a new state. Similarly, at different stages of public opinion evolution, the subtle changes of some variable will influence other variables, and then exponentially magnify the communication effect of public opinion, making it substantially difficult to establish a model.

Meanwhile, a model has to not only reflect the complex association between the Internet and the outside world but also represent the roles and interrelationships of the elements at each and every stage of dissemination, thus it organically combines the whole with the local, elements with factors, and internal structure with external relations. What is the most important is that the Internet communicates with the external environment in a combined way, namely it is a point-to-point, many-to-many, two-way and horizontally spread webbed model. In such a webbed model, a great deal of data and experiments are needed in order to explicitly understand which factors are central.

The model built in this book has characteristics of a structural model in that it focuses on describing the structural system for the occurrence of the butterfly effect of network public opinion. It also has the characteristics of a functional model in that it describes the relationship and interaction between the dissemination system and the dissemination elements from such perspectives as dissemination functions, energy and directions of information flow.

It has to be pointed out that the occurrence probability of the butterfly effect of network public opinion is not necessarily connected to the degree of importance of the information itself. Some significant and sensitive events may not go into the orbit of the butterfly effect, because traditional media have paid enough attention. Events of equal importance may have quite opposite effects due to different publication platforms and interpretation mechanism. Therefore, an important question to ask about the evolution model of the butterfly effect of network public opinion is—for events that are equally important and sensitive, what factors contribute to the multiplication effect of network public opinion? This book puts forward a simple formula, that is, the butterfly effect of network public opinion = network participation × participation of traditional media/positive feedback from stakeholders.

As can be seen, the model includes the following several elements (see Fig. 3.6).

First, *the disseminators*. In the butterfly effect of network public opinion, disseminators present multiple characteristics, and include cybercitizens, network media, traditional media, public agencies and web hypers. A feature of the disseminators of network public opinion is that each type of disseminator—including cybercitizens—has the self-agenda setting function and has already got rid of the authoritative status of former paper media and the aphasia state as well. In the butterfly effect of network

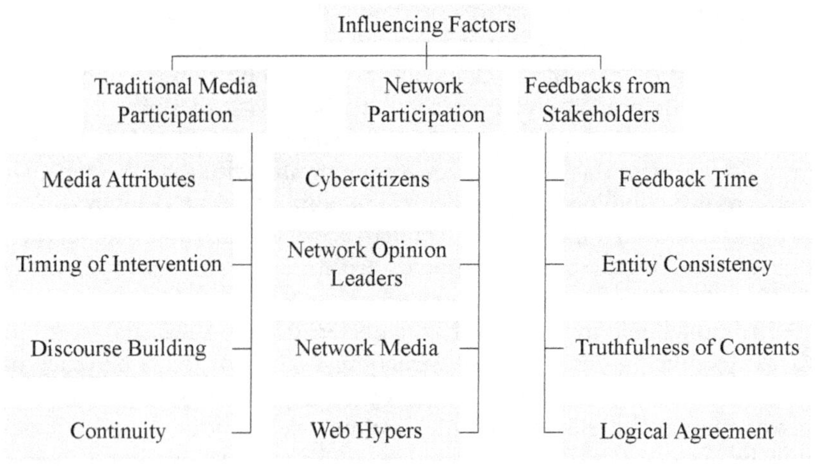

Fig. 3.6 Influencing factors of network public opinion

public opinion, the disseminators can similarly determine the time, content and form of dissemination, but do not check or filter information.

Second, *the audience*, namely information recipients. The audience is information recipients in the dissemination process, the dissemination objects or "destination," as well as disseminators' active and positive recipients and feedback providers. Audiences in the traditional sense are characterized as numerous, extensive, complicated, scattered, unorganized, irregular, uncertain and anonymous. In network dissemination, the audiences (network users) go from anonymous to open and turn from recipients into publishers.

Third, *the media*. With technical progresses and increasingly extensive application, the media get integrated on a large scale. Dissemination media not only incorporate traditional media and network media, but also have new forms inside network media like microblogging, blogs and streaming media. It is noteworthy that sudden news events may evolve from the incubation stage, media intervention stage directly to the outbreak stage. There are also hotspot events that form waves of public opinion because they keep developing and there are constant updates. With the development of portable terminals, network public opinion is no longer confined to the Internet, and Mobile Internet will also become a field that deserves attention.

Fourth, *the dissemination content.* Generally speaking, the occurrence of the butterfly effect not only involves original micro content, but content of paper media. Both emerge alternatively, presenting a multiplier effect. Seen from their quantity, original micro content are small in volume, but big in capacity, appear in a centralized way in a short time, generate new views in the exchange of information and views, and grow surprisingly fast. Paper media content overlap the former, and its rate of appearance is in direct proportion to the former. Seen from their quality, original micro contents are not always good because of the absence of the traditional "gatekeeping" role that filters and screens information. Paper media content may be a little bit behind time but, because of rigorous work procedures and many restrictions in real society, need to meet higher requirements on balance and objectiveness. Both may explode and be incubated.

Fifth, *the dissemination direction.* The dissemination direction of the butterfly effect of network public opinion is most prominently characterized as multiple-way interactive. Between network media and traditional media, cybercitizens, ordinary cybercitizens and opinion leaders, online virtual world and offline real society are always in a state of active interaction. Given that network media is interactive and immediate and involves multiple forms, information dissemination direction is clear-cut in a small scope of the network community, but is webbed in a large scope.

Sixth, *the dissemination effect.* In terms of the dissemination effect, the biggest characteristic of the butterfly effect of network public opinion is exponential magnification, prominently embodied in the huge contrast between the initial conditions and the final results in terms of level, quantity and influencing scope, as well as the large number of people affected, and great impacts of views. Since information dissemination in the butterfly effect proceeds in a centralized way in a short time, information noises are a protruding problem. The process of information noises is also the process of interaction between disseminators and audience, online and offline, network media and traditional media. The intervention of traditional media and feedbacks from real society both magnify the dissemination effect.

3.2.2.2 Network Participation

China Internet Network Information Center publishes an "interactive participation index" to reflect cybercitizens' social participation. According to its report, the interactive participation index of Chinese cybercitizens was 49.0% in 2009, higher than 47.0% in 2008, and 45.8% in the United States.[9] A prominent demonstration of such characteristic in sudden public events is increased public participation in the public sector.

3.2.2.2.1 Internal Synergy of Cybercitizens

Cybercitizens, as a form of We Media, play an important role in the evolution of hotspot network events that originate from micro contents, and have a series of synergy advantages.

First, a huge user group plus instant communication create a "pressure group." Network dissemination has involved from the linear type into the non-linear type; the audience from "listeners" and "the educated" into information publishers who have almost the same say as the media; and dissemination from a "church-like dissemination" of traditional media, where only one preaches, to "bazaar-like dissemination," which allows different voices. The huge base of users pushes network media to the position of mainstream media. Besides, the supervision within the system, which is rendered by supervision outside the system, is, in the special management system of China today, enormously influential.

Second, strong self-empowerment awareness. Empowerment is generally defined as "to give authority or power; to give ability; to enable; to give opportunities." Quinn Miller, the famous management scientist of Harvard University, pointed out that empowerment referred to developing positive self-ability awareness, having critical and analytical understanding and knowledge of the surrounding social political environment, and that empowerment could increase resources held by individuals and groups. Network communities form temporary alliances based on opinions, and conduct self-empowerment over the release of opinions and social mobilization. Such empowerment is not a simple handover of the power of government and established authoritative departments, but a long-term gaming process during which different forces interweave with one another, and wane and wax.

Third, high degree of trust and a strong sense of restriction. The complicated self-adaptation system of network public opinion is binding. It is firstly binding upon opinions. New media technologies endow people with a growing ability to "filter" information and "self-selection," while casting into high relief the problem of segmentation of public network

[9] Refer to *The 25th China Statistical Report on Internet Development in China*, China Internet Network Information Center, available at the website of China Internet Network Information Center.

space. As public opinion is constantly pushed forward, network public opinion will automatically take two sharply opposing sides, and other sparsely supported opinions will gradually be squeezed out of public view. This restriction presents a differentiation tendency of the entities of network public opinion, and makes the public opinion entities even more prominently homogenous. Then it is binding upon future moves. The public opinion entities not only express opinions on an event itself, but develop plans and steps to display the social mobilization function of the network. How effective these two kinds of restraining mechanism will be depends on network opinion leaders' organizational ability and cohesion.

Fourth, a high preference for sharing. When the butterfly effect of network public opinion occurs, cybercitizens have a high preference for sharing, and are ready to share their own goals, technologies and information with others. Kollock believed that information could be shared extensively, even if without direct benefits, because of the characteristics of online interaction and the culture of Internet participators. Unlike the exchange culture of physical communities, the strict, two-way and real-time mutual advantages are not necessary in network. For the contributors, providing information costs far less than the potential returns they may get, makes them well-informed characters in the network world, and enhances their sense of self-fulfillment. Besides, the enormous number of the recipients contributes to a scale economy and a positive external effect.

Fifth, the function of the network as a database. The database function and memory characteristic brought about by information digitalization make possible the application of search engines and technologies in an even broader scope, providing cybercitizens with the ability to satisfy their information demands. Personal remarks and deeds recorded online, despite the fact that their authoritativeness cannot be assured, have a constantly updated and expanded capacity and, after being mutually demonstrated, become sort of authoritative. Meanwhile, the network is open to the public, that is, anyone, after completing simple registration formalities, can access information in time and space. In network events, the deeper some information goes through data digging, the more attractive it will be. The more objectively recorded by others, the more authoritative some content will be deemed. Reflective interpretation of these details functions as "the knocking brick" in many events.

Sixth, digging of hidden topics. At the initiation of a network event, information always presents an explosive trend. Many cybercitizens cluster around micro content, and their way of thinking is like a tree. Information demand is three-dimensional, having not only details relating to the height of the event itself, but also institutional reflection on its background and causes and effects. It makes the "information tree" of a network event extraordinarily huge.

3.2.2.2.2 An Analysis of the Influencing Factors of the Synergy Effect Inside Cybercitizens

First, self-agenda setting effect. After the butterfly effect of network public opinion, cybercitizens give feedback to, discuss and disseminate some important issues in network forums, blogs and by clicking news or leaving messages to realize self-agenda setting, to make traditional media and power departments pay attention to hotspot events, and guide the resolution of such hotspot events. After the entity of agenda setting changes, agenda setting is equally intensified, and in an interactive setting with traditional media, the agenda topics are even more extensive with even greater influence. In traditional media, agenda setting goes one way, from agenda setter to the media and then to the audience, while in network media, it goes in loops in a three-dimensional way among cybercitizens, network media, traditional media agenda setter, and traditional media.[10] Another aspect not to be ignored is that the change of agenda setting entities may breed rumors when it is difficult for the opinion-dependent free market to get sufficient information, thus it will cause rampant online violence, and add fuel to the fire in the interaction between network media and traditional media.

Second, times of topic change. The Internet has unapproachable advantages in information diffusion and mobilization with its technical features. Whether it can construct effective public opinion or not depends on the segmentation degree of network public opinion. On the one hand, the polarization of cybercitizens' attitudes reduces this segmentation degree. In the early days after the forming of public opinion, the higher the degree of polarization of cybercitizen's opinions is, the more easily the forming of influential public opinion and the entry of traditional media into the selection system will be. On the other, in the late stage after the forming of public opinion, whether network public opinion is consistent or enduring depends on the digging of hidden topics. Network public opinion has a common goal. When network technologies are adopted to accomplish this

[10] Refer to Jiao Dewu, Online agent setting and cybercitizens' self-empowerment, *Journal of Huainan Normal University*, 2009(6).

virtual goal together, even offline moves are taken, such degree of segmentation will be bridged by common action objectives and pace. To some extent, it makes up for the shocks brought about by risky online public actions.

Third, the three-dimensional degree of public opinion information tree. At the initiation of a network event, information demand will present an expansive trend. Many cybercitizens, by gathering micro contents, have a tree-shaped way of thinking. Network public opinion always starts with a central point. Each keyword becomes a sub-center or stimulates association. Together, they radiate all around through infinite branched chains, or attribute to the same center.

Fourth, the level of relevance of historical events online. A network event, after being incubated for some time, will form a hotspot, and then remain in a frozen stage for lack of new information, that is, it is not completely forgotten by the cybercitizens, but it will not "soar up" again because there are no new stimulants. For such events, if similar events happen, the association mechanism will play a role and form hotspot news once again.

Another aspect of the association mechanism playing its role is the ascending threshold of network events. In other words, the threshold of occurrence of the butterfly effect keeps rising. As extreme social events happen one after another, the news media—which has an inborn interest in "bad news," and even takes it as its credo that "bad news is good news"—become insensitive to once-sensitive news. Similarly, cybercitizens' sensitivity to news and social sympathy and sense of responsibility become blunt in the face of a growing number of network events.

3.2.2.2.3 Network Opinion Leaders

Network opinion leaders refer to characters who often provide information, views or suggestions for cybercitizens, and exert influence on cybercitizens on the Internet platform. The Burson-Marsteller research group (2005) discovered in its investigation that there was a group of "e-influentials" online, that is, network public opinion leaders. They disseminate information or change public opinion, develop trends and lead the fashion in chat rooms, forums, company websites and blogs.

Public opinion leaders in the butterfly effect of network public opinion refer to groups of people who can keenly sense and judge the importance of publishing micro contents of network public opinion, develop distinct personal opinions on events, influence other cybercitizens, realize information implementation, and go from the virtual world to the real society. After power is dispersed to individuals, the most important capital is no longer money or position alone as it was in the past, but also includes imagination, personal traits and decision-making power.

First, the three elements of network opinion leaders. "Opinion leaders" refers to the "active people" who always provide information for others while exerting impacts on them in the network of interpersonal dissemination. They play a significant intermediate or filtering role in the forming of the mass-media effect, and diffuse information to the audience before forming two-step information delivery. Relative to traditional opinion leaders, network opinion leaders are faced with an even more complex environment, receive even more information, and find an even higher threshold of opinion forming and dissemination. It's like an information contest that never ends. Opinion leaders in traditional media have three traits: first, they demonstrate some values that attract their followers; second, their ability to access tremendous information; third, social connections, that is, the people they know. Prof. Xiao Qiang from the University of California Berkeley held that "representative characters" or "spokesmen" in online activities should possess the following elements: have a platform for them to speak; remarks that can form a sense of identity; earnestly practicing what they advocate; experts in a specific aspect; and with reliable morality. In other words, "values that are based on the attention to public fields," "advantages in cognition, judgment and action force" and "extensive social connections" are the three major elements of network public-opinion leaders.

To start with, their values speak for the grassroots. Relative to traditional opinion leaders in the past who had rich social capital, higher social statuses and elite values, network public opinion leaders come from an even wider scope and are more grassroots. They emerge through non-political system channels, but not formal institutional arrangement, appointment or election, and their emergence is a result of natural selection in accordance with cultural and psychological factors like online replies to topics, click-through rate and influence. Network opinion leaders' values distinctively speak for the grassroots. The selection result of network public opinion leaders also proves that having grassroots values is an important condition for becoming network opinion leaders. Of course, we are not saying that officials can't represent public interests, but that, under the current social conditions, on the basis of public reason, grassroots opinion leaders who pay close attention to public fields are more than often responded to.

Then, they have cognition of network information, and judgment and action force over network events, and are authoritative and reliable at three levels: cognition, attitude and action. In terms of cognition, they are highly familiar with and can accurately use information; in terms of action, it is important that they practice what they advocate and are brave enough to take responsibilities and pressure.

Lastly, "extensive social connections." Network opinion leaders' status in the butterfly effect of some network public opinion may match their professions, interests and hobbies in real society, which facilitates them to better use their knowledge, skills, experience and connections.

Given the above three elements, opinion leaders of network public opinion at the present stage can be roughly divided into three categories: first, traditional opinion leaders who migrate to the world of network public opinion, including writers, scholars, artists and traditional media journalists; second, amateur observers and free-lancers in other industries who are experts in some industry in the real society, but do not belong to the traditional cultural circle, and have got rid of the limits of industries in network public opinion and exert influence with their own knowledge resources; third, self-employed, even unemployed people, who are the most grassroots of all.

Second, network opinion leaders' behavioral motives. To analyze network opinion leaders' behavioral motives, an important perspective is the new characteristics of knowledge power. The power in network society shows three characteristics—knowledge-based, flat and decentralized. The knowledge-based power is primarily demonstrated by its knowledge-based source of power. It is a kind of non-compulsory power, some sort of "soft power." Alvin Toffler once said, of the pillars of power—violence, wealth and knowledge, knowledge produced high-quality power, not only for punishment, award and persuasion, but even for power shift, thus it was more flexible. The prominence of knowledge power not only changed the form of power, but also the way of manipulating power, so it was persuasive and sharing. Manipulating knowledge power could control information production and flow, sell self-values, and struggle for the domination of the "gaming" rules. Therefore, network opinion leaders have the following two main behavioral motives in network events.

The first is their network prestige as virtual social capital. Network opinion leaders' prestige plays its role in the occurrence and promotion of the butterfly effect of network events, and network prestige is the biggest benefit that network opinion leaders get from the events by devoting time and energy. The obtainment of network prestige can meet network opinion leaders' subconscious need to become the authority and hero, although it may not actually change their real life, and even bring negative influence sometimes. A typical example of collective social capital is that people believe supporting meaningful causes will promote their dignity and helping people will make them happier.

The second motive is their business interests as physical capital in society. Network opinion leaders will be lured by business interests. For example, the editors of many forums have established a relatively stable cooperative relationship with web hypers. When web hypers seek private interests or seek interests for some enterprise or organization, the editors of well-known forums will—for the need to create network hotspot issues and for the business interests to be paid by web hypers—serve as incubators and pushers of the chain reaction of major network public opinion while fomenting the overflow and spread of vulgar culture.

Third, network opinion leaders' influencing factors. In the incubation of public opinion, cybercitizens are easily affected by the authoritative effect, and become followers of non-governmental opinion leaders. In the chain reaction of network public opinion, the decisive factors for network opinion leaders to produce an effect are as follows.

To start with, the ambiguity of facts is positively correlated to the network opinion leaders' role in the butterfly effect of public opinion. After a network event occurs, it is actually a gaming process where cybercitizens attempt to break information asymmetry under network opinion leaders' leadership and realize the balance of supply and demand of the network information chain. One side sees the network as an organic component of social capital, struggles for complete manipulation of network power, requests the right to know and to participate in event-related information, and has many information demands; the other side is the information supplier, which has control of traditional information resources and sees information as a part of power. The more uneven the strength of both sides is, the greater the space for network opinion leaders to display their abilities will be. When the facts of controversial news are unclear, "network opinion leaders" will make independent judgment and express opinions with rational imagination, prejudice and bias, and such opinions will attract cybercitizens to follow so that network public opinion goes out of the virtual world to the real society, scaling up the interactions.

Then the development and progress of network technology are positively correlated to the display of network opinion leaders' role. The ever-changing communications technology has become a sharp weapon for network opinion leaders who are always ahead of the other people in sensing and understanding network technology and using them to promote their authoritativeness. The emergence of search engines and similar technologies makes information more transparent. Despite the inevitability of negative behavior like infringing personal privacy, search engine, Internet manhunt and other technologies keep any behavior of any individual under the control of the Internet and increase opinion leaders' ability to act.

Network opinion leaders' stability is positively correlated to the butterfly effect of network public opinion. Network opinion leaders' performance is stable in the butterfly effect of network public opinion. Some groups of people pay close attention to topics of a specific type. In particular, when social topics of public concern appear, they will get as many news details as they can in the shortest time with network search engines and like technologies, integrate cybercitizens' opinions, and make the most influential and propelling comments on such events before developing plans and suggestions for the next move. In terms of social mobilization of network public opinion, network opinion leaders weigh heavily.

Network opinion leader's innovativeness is positively correlated to the butterfly effect of network public opinion. Network opinion leaders lead and practice network innovations. The more their innovations in hot network topics are, the greater the probability of the butterfly effect will be.

Network opinion leaders' well-known-ness and distinctiveness are positively correlated to the butterfly effect of network public opinion. Network popularity comes from two sources: first, well-known-ness in the real world is directly turned into influence on the Internet; second, network popularity. Although many opinion leaders exist anonymously, their cyber names have already had celebrity effect and brand effect, so opinion leaders' concerns and remarks are of information value.

Finally, the range of network opinion leaders' social connections is positively correlated to the butterfly effect of network public opinion. There is an interesting pull between the virtual world and the real world. Some virtual relations will develop into participation in actions in real life. As a matter of fact, when involved in the butterfly effect of network public opinion, network opinion leaders can always find important others to enhance understanding and stimulate their sense of identity. The butterfly effect of network public opinion occurs along with the appearance and rise of network opinion leaders. Such rise usually appears along with the series connection of opinion leaders and traditional media. After the butterfly effect of network public opinion is triggered, the cooperative mechanism between network opinion leaders and traditional media takes shape—they negotiate about the selection of topics, testify the truthfulness of such topics together, question the organs of public power, and carry out reliefs. This way of complementing resources and cooperating with advantages greatly enhances the social influence of network public opinion, and also forms the synergy effect of network media and traditional media.

3.2.2.2.4 Network Media

"Published online (in forums)—recommended by webmasters—focused on by cybercitizens—intervened in by traditional media journalists" has become the basic route of occurrence of the butterfly effect of network public opinion.

Network media's influencing factors on the butterfly effect of network public opinion include network media's well-known-ness, the degree of alliance between network media and traditional media and network "gatekeeper's" sensitivity to news.

First, network media's well-known-ness is highly correlated to the butterfly effect of network online public opinion.

Second, the degree of alliance between network media and traditional media is correlated to the butterfly effect of network public opinion. The unique media management system in China determines that both can get maximum benefits only by sharing resources. Traditional media has the right to interview, but also a number of restrictions, while network media has a lot of news clues to develop further. The intervention of network media turns reports in local newspapers into focuses of nationwide concern, greatly stimulating the enthusiasm of "alliance" between traditional media and network editors. Such alliance, namely resource sharing, allows both to win some advantages in market competition, and "alliance" has gradually become one of the motives for the occurrence of the butterfly effect of network public opinion.

Third, the butterfly effect of network public opinion is related to network editors' ability to produce and dig hotspot events. The role of influential forums like Tianya.cn, mop.com, kdnet.net and xici.net in the butterfly effect of network public opinion depends largely on network editors' performance.

A problem deserving attention is that, as the butterfly effect of network public opinion is becoming more and more well-known and gaining a reputation, the network is becoming increasingly monopolized. Although being brand-oriented and featured is a correct direction of network development, it is increasingly significant that a few websites have the right to say and serve as the network "gatekeeper." The tendency of the right to network discourse is much too centralized, and network monopoly emerges gradually. Possible hazards of network monopoly include: abusing the discourse right, representing bogus public will, conspiring with other stakeholders, selling public discourse right, and having a serious commercial inclination.

3.2.2.2.5 Web Hypers: An Auxiliary Variable

Public opinion, as a public object, is always faced with the risk of being consumed or excessively exploited by individuals. At the explosion of network information and during dissemination of network voices, websites or network companies having multiple network relations are able to manipulate public will and gain a "public opinion monopoly" with their advantages in users, information service technology and resource centralization, forming the vicious cycle of "disclosing information—charging—eliminating negative impacts." Such an effect of "public opinion monopoly"—if gradually extending from unfair competition among enterprises to the field of administrative power and public interests, and making network public opinion manually manipulated—may reduce the significance as a public discourse platform. Whether there is a web hypers' operation behind the scenes or not is also an auxiliary variable that determines whether the butterfly effect of network public opinion will occur and what will it be like.

As the network becomes popular and increasingly influential, web hypers extend their operations from entertainment and commercial planning to the planning of social problems and public events in an ever-broadening scope.

Web hypers, network backstage manipulators and paid posters reflect a kind of bogus public will. As products at the development stage of new media when the network is highly developed and the network dissemination effect is eye-catching, they are built on the basis of the demand to develop a multi-culture. The three are different in that they resort to different means. Web hypers adopt legitimate planning to attract cybercitizens' attention to finally realize control of the development direction of public events; network backstage manipulators realize business benefits by spreading rumors and resorting to other illegal means; while paid posters sell their own discourse right and benefit from replying to topics.

Driven by interests, media cooperation is realized tacitly, which also explains why web hypers only initiate network events, but operational network marketing events develop with ups and downs. Given that, scholars express the opinion that, in hotspot issues on the Internet, traditional media has fallen from its traditional "gatekeeping" role into the danger of being channelized.

3.2.3 Participation of Traditional Media

A popular view holds that network media, with its technological advantages, can produce a huge public opinion resultant, even exert pressure on traditional media and agenda set for the latter through network onlooking alone. We think it much too optimistic about network public opinion's agenda setting function in that the cybercitizens are mostly grassroots, which means that the agendas set by them depend on the height of their own interests. By setting agendas, the disadvantaged groups try to seek expression of their interests. Although network media normally becomes the first point of call for news, to be truly verified and display the social mobilization function, news must enter the view of traditional media. It is de facto a second check. If not relayed by traditional media, network media talk does not become mainstream.

3.2.3.1 Synergy Motives of Traditional Media

Traditional media's participation is positively correlated to the occurrence of the butterfly effect of network public opinion. After a network hotspot is formed, traditional media begin to follow it up, and consider it with traditional media's gatekeeping requirements before publishing it through newspaper or TV. Once into the development period after latency, network public opinion begins to change the network competition ecology—traditional media and network media struggle for the right to report and interpret the news and regard it as latent earnings of public trust in media and an opportunity to get explicit earnings like commercial benefits. Specifically speaking, traditional media have the following four synergy motives.

3.2.3.1.1 "Symbiotic Public Opinion Eco-System" that is "Full of Opportunities"

After a hot event on the Internet passes the network opinion leaders' "pre-gatekeeping" check and realizes platform shift, the public opinion system becomes a social environment "full of opportunities." Such "opportunities" mean the realization of the media's public functions as social observer and functional monitor, and the attention benefits in an economy. Such public opinion ecology "full of opportunities" is the most beneficial and attractive to traditional media which pursues social benefits and is unwilling to give up economic returns. It is the active intervention of network public opinion that makes it possible for traditional media to comment and report and promote positive development of the state of affairs.

For network media, although the network world sows the "seed," to further expand the diffusion effect of public opinion and be truly capable of changing the real world, an authoritative and mature media operational mechanism like traditional media is needed in order to make up for the defects of network media having miscellaneous information and poor accountability. In this sense, in complicated self-adaptation system of network public opinion, network media and traditional media both find the best timing and way of cooperation, and form a "symbiotic public opinion eco-system."

3.2.3.1.2 "Spiral of Silence" in Media Competition

Pursuing news hotspots is what the media live for. Performance in major events is a decisive factor for media positions. Noelle Neumann put forward the view that the public had a panic inside over opinion isolation. Once they discover that their opinions are different from the mainstream opinions, they will deliberately conceal their opinions, making the opinions of the majority louder and clearer and those of the minority more and more silent. In media competition, mass media has a similar mentality. If discovering that the other media are following up some hot news, urban newspapers especially will be afraid of lagging behind in the pursuit of such news. Absence from a hot event will cost the media public trust in them, and the opportunity to guide public opinion as well. Therefore, a media assembly effect will appear, that is, a large number of media are attracted by the same news topic, and a great deal of attention and reporting concentrates on some news figure or public opinion of news, making news reporting, including network public opinion, homogenous. Of course, it cannot be denied that, without such concentrated firepower and wisdom pool, neither the synergistic effect nor the social mobilization function will form. But how to cooperatively distribute media resources and try to avoid the negativity of the assembly effect is a major topic that is deserving of scholarly study.

3.2.3.1.3 Temptation of Business Benefits

Network life goes from virtual to real and from online to offline, gradually releasing enormous business potential and marketing opportunities. Cybercitizens are enthusiastic in discussing public affairs. The richer the "attention resource" that a website gets, the more the benefits it gives in return. Network media—by integrating resources and enriching the public discussion agendas—will also process the content of replies to hot news topics to establish a value system for public discussion, and the influence of business driving force is not to be sneezed at.[11] How to face serious challenges from new media and get a slice of the market pie is a question on which the vast traditional media practitioners have to ponder, and is also the reason why they work so hard in major network events.

3.2.3.1.4 Media's Sense of Responsibilities Under "the Broken Windows Effect"

Social sciences put forward "the broken windows theory," namely if the windows are broken and left unrepaired, they have a demonstrative effect. Given the rising momentum of the network and the expanding influence of network news, traditional media takes into consideration the source of news and reporting perspective when reporting news. Also, the media's social responsibility theory also provides an explanation of traditional media's paying attention to the butterfly effect of network public opinion. The traditional media in China have been confined by institutional restrictions and have not been able to report sensitive issues that are highly relevant to people's interests, and the emergence of network public opinion serves as a platform for such topics. Once a momentum has formed, network public opinion will be an incentive to traditional media.

3.2.3.2 Synergistic Advantages of Traditional Media

The first advantage is the accountability resource accumulated in the development of journalism. In 1999, Huang Xiaofang defined it as "charms of the media themselves which are accumulated in media development and widely authoritative and reputed, and have profound influence in the audience" in *Credibility and Media Authoritativeness*. Media accountability has two dimensions: relative accountability and absolute

[11] Refer to Hu Hanhan, Media building and generation of public fields—a study of "replies to news" business at 163.com, *The Journalist Monthly*, 2010(4).

accountability. Relative accountability refers to the most trusted media of several; and absolute accountability refers to the degree of public trust that is won by each investigated media. Zhang Guoliang of Fudan Journalism School presided over a topic-setting investigation in 2001. According to the investigation, from the perspective of absolute accountability, both China and the United States had the problem of reduced media truthfulness and accountability.

Second, the regular news process ensures information authoritativeness. Process management is important to news productivity. News dissemination by traditional media is controlled by media editors in chief, executive editors and journalists. In recent years, some media practitioners have proposed to realize "the mode of lean production" of news process management. Although the production of online information is simple and online information spreads quickly, there is the problem of fake or redundant information. Traditional media can test and verify the falsehood of information on the Internet through network news agencies and by applying a strict news process. Of course, it is undeniable that the network has penetrated and optimized each link of news interview and the editing of traditional media. Traditional media is affected by network media, from getting news judgments with information, to investigating and ascertaining facts, and then to arranging space of pages. But on the whole, with rigorous and constantly optimized news processing, traditional media, as a professional news production and release organizations, ensures greater accountability than network dissemination, which, mainly, is information dissemination by individuals.

Third, its in-depth reporting enables it to track the depth and breadth of news events. Traditional media produce in-depth reporting: in terms of genre, the language of traditional media is more formal and regular, and traditional media present news following the principle of "objective more than subjective," "more facts than comments" to show the author's stance and views with news facts themselves. Only when the news has a greater value can it easily attract attention and be reprinted.[12]

Finally, the increasing integration of traditional media and network media and the bold reform of traditional media are also among the sufficient and necessary conditions for the occurrence of the butterfly effect of

[12] Refer to Yi Shenghua, Dissemination resonance of the new and the old media, *PR Magazine*, 2010(2).

network public opinion. The "intimate contact" of traditional media and the network has developed from the stage of simple reproduction of contents to the stage of integration and participation featuring full digitalization. The best-quality network information resources are still from traditional media which, against the background of technology confluence and media integration, actively involves itself in the "omnimedia" role competition as communication operator, content provider and service supplier, and does not exist only in newspapers or TV in the simple sense.

3.2.3.3 Factors Influencing the Synergetic Effect of Traditional Media

3.2.3.3.1 Media Attribute

"Media is content." Media in itself is information. Participation in reporting is one of the most crucial factors, followed by the length and form of the reporting. In the media ecology in China at the present stage, media nature is related to media type, source of capital and stance, as is the propelling role played by the media in the butterfly effect of network public opinion. The network breaks the pattern of information competition, but the different media are still struggling for the high-ground of public sentiments. Take, for example, the dissemination function, central network media have changed traditional media's state of lagging behind in information release in the past, and Xinhuanet.com and people.com.cn have become important sources of news. The central traditional media, including *People's Daily*, Xinhua News Agency and China Central Television (CCTV), although relatively lagging behind in terms of timely attention to topics with high public concern, having narrow focuses when selecting major hot events that are influential nationwide and have been fully incubated—are highly authoritative and profound in reporting, and have an extremely large influence on cybercitizens.

3.2.3.3.2 Timing of Intervention

In the era of network media, traditional media—in order to deal with increasingly fierce news competitions—joined the process of media integration, formed a multi-layered and three-dimensional media map, and has gradually developed a pattern of gradient dissemination and remarks: the Internet system that takes seconds as its dissemination scale; flat paper media that takes a day as the dissemination frequency, and a broadcasting and television system that takes images and voices as three-dimensional language; and a magazine and weekly newspaper system that take a week as the dissemination cycle. this pattern gives them the superiority in substituting one another at different points of a story's development. When the butterfly effect of network public opinion is incubated and escalates, traditional media, with its resource advantage, selects the right timing to participate in event reporting and mobilization.

3.2.3.3.3 Discourse Construction

Traditional media's method of discourse construction affects the occurrence of the butterfly effect of network public opinion. The more traditional media's discourse system tallies with non-governmental public opinion circumstances, the more significant the multiplication effect of network public opinion will be. Studies show that traditional media's selection of topics for discussion is closely linked to network public opinion. At the micro level, the closer traditional media's discourse system is to non-governmental discourse, the more helpful it will be to the continuance of the chain reaction of network public opinion. In particular, for mainstream values which are widely recognized in society or "main frames" of protests, once they are diffused by the media, the cost of mobilization of them will be reduced.[13] In this sense, media strategy is a tool of "topic construction" and "consensus mobilization."

3.2.3.3.4 Continuity

China has a unique media system in the world, that is, a unitary system, but binary operation. The decision made by traditional media—with a sense of social responsibility and under marketization pressure—to participate in the follow-up reporting of an event, may be changed by systems within the institution, that is, event stakeholders may impede traditional media's participation in the reporting of an event through non-information communication channels, breaking the reaction chain. Under such circumstance, different types of media may collaborate with one another to wage an anti-blocking war. One method is to provide information for these media, and have the event reported by other media resources. Such cooperation among individual media is also an "open secret" in the industry to avoid news censorship. Another resolution is—after the event is sup-

[13] Gao Enxin: Topic construction and consensus mobilization of public events on the Internet—Exampled with several network public events, *Journal of Publish Management*, 2009(4).

pressed for some time—resuming the interrupted reporting of the event and continuing it in a faster and fiercer way through another news outlet like the outbreak or disclosure of another similar news event. Under such circumstance, there might be retaliating mobilization, that is, mobilization on a scale that the event could not reach before. After it is resumed, energy will be even greater, and the public opinion multiplication effect will be even more significant.

3.2.3.3.5 Hierarchy: The Building of a "New Map" of Network Public Opinion Pattern

To build a "new map" of the network public opinion pattern, the first thing is to accept the important characteristic of network public opinion hierarchy, that is, the "new map" of network public opinion does not take administrative jurisdiction or geographical boundaries as the watershed, even its original planar characteristic has already been broken; and the hierarchical and three-dimensional characteristics of network public opinion are becoming increasingly significant. A specific example is: topics led by network public opinion are no longer given by administrative orders, and positive reporting is the main way to guide network public opinion; and increasing the weight of typical reporting will no longer work. The hierarchy of network public opinion is also demonstrated by the fact that the pluralism of network public opinion has a logic to follow, and gets segmented gradually as news facts develop and become more detailed before forming three interaction models with traditional media, that is, resonance of network public will and media reporting, revision of media reporting by network public will, and social mobilization by network public will after traditional media reporting. Although the "resonance" between network public opinion and the reports of traditional media appears only when it involves national interests or in the early stage of natural disasters, the enormous patriotism and national morality and justice in such "resonance" enable public opinion to have a more profound influence on national characteristics and traditional culture, and play an important role in external dissemination as a non-governmental force. Acts that are against journalistic professionalism—which are done by traditional media either under role restriction due to administrative subjection or under the temptation of commercial interests—will be supplemented or corrected under the assembly effect of the micro content of network public opinion, and the correction effect helps generate a more rational society and a group of cybercitizens with higher media attainments. The role of network public opinion in differentiating and mobilizing traditional media, which is the sharpest challenge against the government and traditional media, is a comprehensive test for the entire society.

3.2.3.4 Final Way to Make Good Use of Network Public Will: Full Social Mobilization

Network public opinion has to be guided effectively. Facing an increasingly complicated map of public opinion, relying simply on positive propaganda and guidance of mainstream media is of little help to realize the established dissemination effect. Truly effective guidance of network public opinion should be full social mobilization, including improvement of government transparency, accountability and efficiency, improvement of traditional media's authoritativeness, accountability and influence, and gradual improvement of the social legal system. For the government, it means deepening its understanding of the rules of network information flows, strengthening its media accomplishments, and comprehensively improving its governance. For the media, it means a higher pursuit of comprehensive and truthful news facts, more profound questioning of the significance behind news, and more real presentation of news details. Only in so doing can the dissemination effect be ameliorated under the reality that traditional media is the "gatekeeper" of the expression of network public opinion. For cybercitizens, it means improving their media accomplishments, and the gradual formation of rational network rules. For academia, it needs to strengthen the studies of network topics and the rules of changes of network information flows, and enhance scientific and targeted public-opinion guidance.

3.2.4 Feedbacks from Stakeholders

Feedback, one of the most central concepts of system science, refers to the process whereby after inputs act on a controlled system, the outputs are routed back through proper devices and have influence on the system's re-inputs and re-outputs. Negative feedback is the changing trend of suppressing or weakening the element that first sees changes. It is a purpose-oriented behavior that increases the influence of the system's inputs on its outputs in order to enable the system to realize or maintain a state of equilibrium or stability. Positive feedback is the opposite.

As can be seen, on the Internet, a place where opinions are collected and diffused, due to the lack of a "gatekeeping" role and capacity multiplication, voices are repeated and refined rapidly in a fragmented state. Network public opinion, traditional media public opinion and organs of public power all play the role of a feedback loop. Their feedback may be positive or negative. Negative feedback function to adjust, while positive feedbacks function to multiply. The more the positive feedback, the greater the possibility of a public opinion tornado, and the greater the possibility of triggering the butterfly effect of network public opinion. The more the negative feedback, the smaller the possibility of the butterfly effect of network public opinion, the more frequent the occurrence, the smaller the negative influence. All these feedback loops fully collide to change one another, wane and wax, and their energy is superimposed. When the energy of positive feedbacks increases sharply, the scale and intensity of public opinion will grow exponentially, triggering the butterfly effect. It is a new structure when the system reaches an orderly state after chaos, and has adopted the new environmental conditions. The dissolution of the butterfly effect depends on the progressive increase of the energy of negative feedback.

3.2.4.1 Factors Influencing Stakeholders' Responses

3.2.4.1.1 Response Time

The response time is in direct proportion to the butterfly effect of network public opinion. Timeliness is the primary principle to follow to handle a crisis. Information needs to be released along with the development of the situation, not after all facts are ascertained, or it will only make the government passive in crisis management. Therefore, in traditional crisis-diffusion theories, experts put forward "prime twenty-four hours," meaning that the first twenty-four hours after the formation of a hotspot issue is the most crucial period for the success of crisis management. In the era of network dissemination, the characteristics of prompt dissemination on the Internet, rapid diffusion, three-dimensional thinking and interaction determine that twenty-four hours are not enough to stop the diffusion of a crisis. The experts, of people.com.cn, in public opinion studies then put forward "prime four hours" to highlight the importance of timely news release. A long response time and aphasia at crucial moments together cost the prime time of information release, and rumors and hearsay appear at the information ambiguity stage and rapidly occupy "the free market of opinion."

3.2.4.1.2 Logical Coincidence

During the occurrence of the butterfly effect of network public opinion that aims at correcting wrongs, one of the stakeholders' positive responses is the agreement of the response logic with the logic of the media and cybercitizens. A crisis event involves multiple entities, but there must be a core entity that plays a crucial role in the emergence, development or shift of the trend of the event. Stakeholders' responses should take into consideration the other parties' thinking logic and claims. Otherwise there will be more polarized public wills, which will trigger a greater distrust crisis and the request for more correction once stuck in the behavioral model of "shrinking responsibilities—warning—explaining." To achieve an agreement in the thinking and behavior logic between the two parties in the butterfly effect of network public opinion, requires fundamental institutional planning, which must include the capacity to include the public's opinions and interests within the institution's planning orbit.

3.2.4.1.3 Consistency of Principals

The number of information feedback principals is in direct proportion to the butterfly effect of network public opinion. The greater the number of information release principals, the higher the probability of the butterfly effect of network public opinion. Once information is released, it carries weight. If information comes from multiple sources, it may be contradictory and less authoritative. Meanwhile, it will aggravate the state of affairs and attract more onlookers.

3.2.4.1.4 Truthfulness of Content

The truthfulness of the content in information release is in direct proportion to the butterfly effect of network public opinion. Releasing conclusions in a rush or shifting the focus of public opinion will also stimulate the diffusion of network events, and produce the magnification effect. Such a practice helps little in guiding public sentiment, and will cause more doubt and greater dissatisfaction in the cybercitizens and will be attacked online by public opinion under the network assembly effect.

As can be seen, introducing the factor of responses to the government to studies of the butterfly effect of network public opinion realizes the equilibrium of forces in the gaming of public opinion. In particular, at the present stage, to weaken the butterfly effect of network public opinion, deeper observation of such variable needs to be done.

3.3 Life-Cycle Model of the Butterfly Effect of New-Media Public Opinion

The Product Life Cycle (PLC) theory put forward by Harvard University Prof. Raymond Vernon suggests that products had a four-stage life cycle, namely introduction, growth, maturity and decline. Corporate Lifecycle Theory and Crisis Lifecycle Theory were later additions. The life-cycle theory of the butterfly effect of network public opinion is of great significance to understanding the components, internal structures, and so on of network public opinion.

To observe the evolution model of the butterfly effect of network public opinion, it is necessary to divide different evolution stages of network public opinion. The network public opinion initiated by any hot topic will go through the process from something to nothing, and its evolution and development conforms to the periodic law from the incubation period, to the outbreak period, and then to the digestion period (see Fig. 3.7).

3.3.1 Specialness of the Life Cycle of the Butterfly Effect of Network Public Opinion

The life cycle of network public opinion is both universal and special. It is universal in that the occurrence of the butterfly effect of network public opinion also has a life cycle. What makes it special is considered in the following paragraphs.

First, the life stages are uneven—public opinion's forming period is relatively short, its growth and maturity periods relatively long, and its recession period temporary. During the diffusion of an event, new information needs to be added in order to keep the chain reaction going. Each time new information comes in, information becomes more stimulating. After the dissemination of the event reaches the peak point temporarily, it slides down slowly. Without new information, it will tend toward recession. The diffusion of a network event goes through the process of initiation, climax and recession, and it is a changing and developing process that usually lasts one to three months. Each hotspot topic of network public opinion lives 16.8 days on average, and mostly within two weeks. Most network hotspot events live from one to fifteen days, that is, what are more online are clamors, indicating cybercitizens' low concentration on a topic for discussion that's less changed. A topic for discussion does not have a long "preservation time" for cybercitizens unless new variables and elements enter its information system.

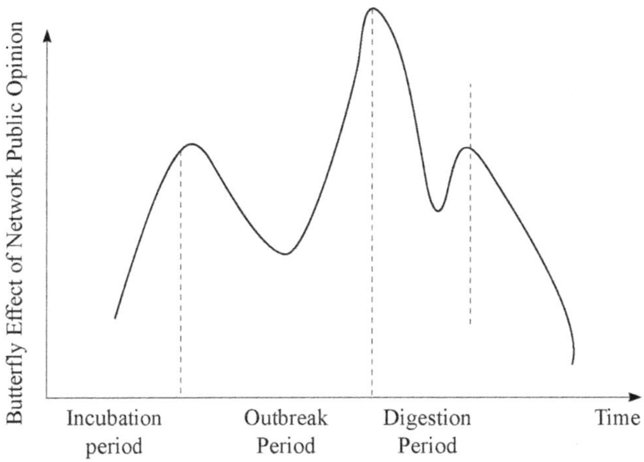

Fig. 3.7 Life cycle of the butterfly effect of network public opinion

Second, the life cycle of network public opinion is linked, that is, new hotspots of public opinion will emerge one after another and compete with the old ones, and the emergence of new topics for discussion will cause the old ones to decline. The huge amount of network information leads to new hotspots one after another, which will definitely distract people, and public attention to old topics will, therefore, be weakened. Without new information being added, the hotspots of public opinion are balanced. The total number of hotspots of public opinion is always maintained at a certain amount, because cybercitizens' attention and the attention of network media and traditional media are always limited.

Third, the life cycle of rumors, an element in the butterfly effect of online public opinion, is also somewhat special. The issue of the life cycle of rumors in the butterfly effect of network public opinion is an antinomy. On the one hand, the increase in the information sources of the network public opinion platform, the weakened "gatekeeping" role, and webbed topological structure all get the channels ready for the spread of rumors; on the other, the cost of producing and diffusing false information is reduced, and the diffusion efficiency promoted, and various assumed and speculated information appears in public opinion without censorship. It directly leads to the formation of a circular chain of the butterfly effect of network public opinion of rumors.

All in all, introducing the life-cycle theory to interpret the butterfly effect of network public opinion is of special guiding significance, and the concept of chain reaction of the butterfly-effect theory also provides a feasible perspective for explaining its evolution.

3.3.2 *Incubation Period of the Butterfly Effect of Network Public Opinion—"A Butterfly Flaps Its Wings"*

The topics of network events arise from two major sources: the Internet and traditional media. Specifically, there are two situations: first, public opinion is formed online, and relayed and responded by traditional media; second, news is first reported by traditional media before causing great concussions online. Two different sources of information and public opinion evolve through different routes, but reach the same goal.

The incubation period of the butterfly effect of network public opinion follows the operating rules of media politics (information simplification, expression with images, personification of politics, narration) and cyber-citizens' media consumption habits (being more easily attracted by images than by words, and preferring illustration to abstract). Specifically speaking, after the three-dimension vibration of "politics—technology—social psychology," information is sublimed into public opinion and begins incubation; sensitive factors are touched, and the nature of topics for discussion begins to play the sieve role. Meanwhile, the selection and the decoding mechanism of the information release platform have also constituted the screening mechanism of the multiplication effect of network public opinion. After screening is accomplished, selected individual topics enter public purview, and network media and traditional media start the synergy process, and topics enter the stage for public discussion.

In the process, there are opinion flows and information flows. When a network public opinion tornado comes into being, the most prominent thing would be changes of the information flow—the information flow increases sharply in a period, information agents grow, information flow slows down, and information content becomes even more decentralized.

Information flow is always a webbed penetrating structure on the Internet. It penetrates along the physical structure of the network, in which process information gets replicated and reproduced and forms bypasses before eventually growing exponentially. Duplication ensues while entering the new round of information release, that is, information is released again in a linear, aligned and hierarchical way to start its next life cycle. Therefore, the information release structure will continue playing a role in information flow.

Since the network is anonymous, timely and interactive, cybercitizens can have discussions more freely and openly, and therefore will have a higher demand for information. After a news event occurs, whether it is first exposed by traditional media or network media, it will trigger cybercitizens' demand for information disclosure, namely information sharing. Once the demand is not responded to in a timely way, information will be magnified and distorted by the intermediaries, leading to even intenser, deeper and even frequent information sharing. When information flows from the original supplier to the client terminal, information will be distorted and gradually magnified without effective information sharing, leading to growing fluctuations of the information demands.

3.3.3 Outbreak Period of the Butterfly Effect of Network Public Opinion—Formation of a Public-Opinion Tornado

After topic and platform selection and decoding in the incubation period, network public opinion goes into the self-loop state of self-evaluation—self-assumption—self-verification and, as information is rapidly refined and superimposed, forms a network hot spot. At this time, "butterfly flapping its wings" has changed the network ecology and the micro-ecology of news competition as well, and a chain reaction with tremendous energy is triggered, causing a turbulence state. A typical characteristic is the operation of an integrated dissemination model and a burst of plural, multiform and multi-layer dissemination content together; the questioning process of network public opinion goes from the surface to the essence, from being biased to being comprehensive, and from false appearance to truth. The scope of information sharing keeps expanding, and the event may possibly evolve into a nationwide one. With the support of public opinion, the media, as spokesman of public interests, games with the organs of public power. In the gaming, the scale of public opinion gets further expanded and the media, while exercising its discourse right, carries out right relief, and improves its own social capital. From "seed posts," that is, "butterfly flapping its wings," to a public opinion tornado, takes only a few days. It is hard to explicitly separate the incubation period from the outbreak period of network public opinion.

In China today, those who can touch off the expansion of public opinion and gather more audience in the butterfly effect of network public opinion—for right relief—are still representatives in public power organs in most cases. Their responses to public opinion, especially their improper responses, hinder the speed of information flow, make information not that crystal clear, and would more easily cause sudden changes in public opinion, attracting a larger audience, escalating the state of affairs to a wider scope, and causing more information demands and real requests. Introducing the major agent of stakeholders' feedback helps realize the evolution law of the butterfly effect of network public opinion in its development and outbreak periods in an even objective way.

After assembly and distribution, synergy and feedback, network public opinion develops from micro contents to a public opinion tornado before exerting super influence and transformative power (see Fig. 3.8).

3.3.4 *Dissipation Period of the Butterfly Effect of Network Public Opinion*

The butterfly effect of network public opinion dissipates partially because it realizes the participators' wishes and needs. When consumers and the media, that is, agents of public opinion, have consumed all social resources and emotions, or the event has been placed under effective control, the attention to the event will fade away.

The dissipation of the butterfly effect of network public opinion is in direct proportion to the degree and speed of information disclosure. If the information agents can meet cybercitizens' information demands, even initiatively guide the development direction of topics for discussion, the occurrence of the butterfly effect of network public opinion will be instant in character. Some network events may become very popular in a short time, and cause many questions, but if the information agents make timely responses, it would cause the event to dissipate rapidly.

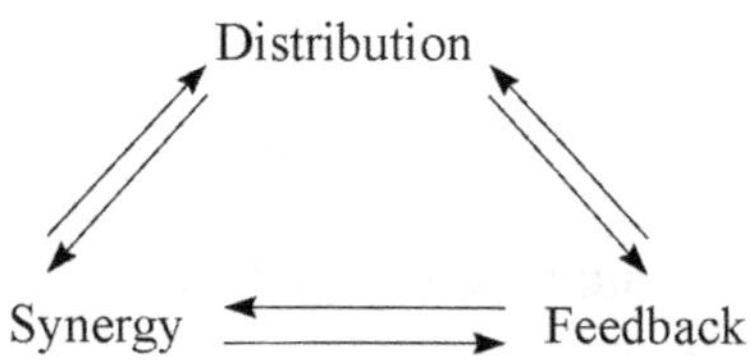

Fig. 3.8 Dynamics mechanism of the evolution from micro content to public opinion tornado

Otherwise, if the information agents are unable to adapt to the butterfly effect of network public opinion and can partially meet cybercitizens' information demands only after going through media interaction-based agenda setting, synergistic operation of plural dissemination ways and in-depth digging of topic switch, cybercitizens will not trust the information releaser(s) at all. Even if an event ends, the negative public opinion will last for some time instead of dissipating immediately. Under such circumstance, the information agents need to provide additional effective information for information compensation in order to win cybercitizens' trust back, and turn failure into victory.

Another characteristic is that, if a similar event occurs, public opinion, as a result of the memory function and being always sensitive to such kind of events, will gather quickly. That is to say, the dissipation period of the butterfly effect of network public opinion, besides having the long tail effect, may be rekindled. If social mobilization failed in the last public-opinion tornado, it will leave behind serious public opinion traumas. Under these specific conditions, the kindling point of an event is low after its inception.

3.3.5 Model of Network Topic Emergence, Existence, Public Opinion Integration and Dissipation

Taking a close look at the network public opinion events in recent years, the emergence, gathering and final dissipation of network public opinion match well with the theory of the public opinion formation stages described by Davidson and Bower, that is, a topic appears → the topic triggers discussions → individuals' expression of opinions is effected by multiple parties → expression of individuals' opinion begin to gather → it triggers social discussion and has social influence → problem involved in the topic disappears → a new topic appears. Then the process repeats in loops. Events and problems of public interest, which are closely related to mainstream social morals and values and have expected influence, usually attract people's attention. All public opinions originate from personal opinion, so personal views or opinions on some event are where public opinion starts. If such views or opinions are agreed with or echoed by the majority, there will be social discussions. When public opinion induced by personal opinions is constantly replied to, re-posted and commented on by cybercitizens, followed up and reported by traditional media, and disseminated by opinion leader, it will possibly escalate. After being argued about by cybercitizens, opposite opinions will be screened and personal opinions that are recognized by the majority will get an upper hand and form final conclusions in public opinion. Traditional media continues following up the event and reporting it and cybercitizens continue re-posting and discussing the event. When public opinion escalates along the original route, its influence keeps growing, and opinions of different parties get further integrated before forming a big public opinion campaign. Then as the government or relevant parties take actions and resolve the problem, network public opinion dissipates. When network public opinion appears on a large scale, its direction will shift if the government intervenes in it immediately or the media resets the agenda and government intervention will help resolve the event. By now, network public opinion disappears.

Therefore, in combination with relevant theories on the formation of public opinion and actual development of network public opinion events, we adopt the longitudinal analysis method to divide the formation and evolution process of network public opinion into four stages: (1) topic appearance period; (2) network public opinion existence period; (3) network public opinion integration period; (4) network public opinion dissipation period. On this basis, we establish a four-stage theory model that mainly involves topic appearance, network public opinion existence, network public opinion integration and network public opinion dissipation periods, and call it "Topic Appearance, Existence, Integration and Dissipation Model of Network Public Opinion" (see Fig. 3.9).

In terms of time, the four stages, namely topic appearance, topic existence, public opinion integration and public opinion dissipation periods of network public opinion, generalize the whole formation process of network public opinion. There follows a detailed analysis of the characteristics and influencing factors at each stage.

3.3.5.1 Period of Topic Appearance

Once a topic for discussion appears on the Internet, it must involve a topic or event of public concern. What kind of topics or events attracts cybercitizens' attention? Take the network public opinion events in 2011 for example, the "July 23" rear-end collision of bullet trains, Xiao Yueyue event, Guo Meimei event, salt-scrambling disturbance, the Palace Museum theft, the case of Yao Jiaxin … analyzing such events once much discussed by cybercitizens, we will see that the nature of topics themselves and the source of topics are two important reasons affecting people's attention to them.

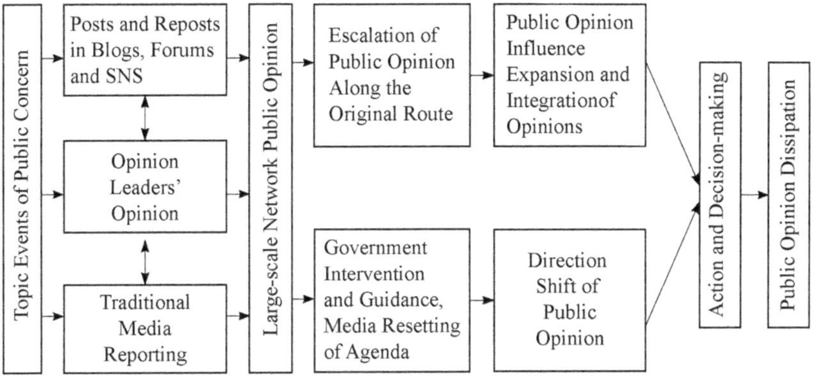

Fig. 3.9 Topic Appearance, Topic Existence, Public Opinion Integration and Dissipation Model of Network Public Opinion

In the era of network media, information is unprecedentedly open and clear; the roles of information disseminators and recipients are completely changed—cybercitizens are not only information recipients but publishers; the "gatekeeping" role is weakened, and the scope of network supervision is even wider than traditional media. Therefore, to a large degree, the emergence of network public opinion is spontaneous, that is to say, cybercitizens' spontaneous discussion of topics and the concentration of their opinions lead to the emergence model of public opinion. Under such circumstance, the nature and characteristics of topics themselves become important influencing factors in the topic-appearance period of network public opinion. We illustrate the hot events that easily generate public opinion in combination with the network hot spots in recent years.

First, topics that involve social contradictions. China is now in a transitional period of reforms of social politics and economic system, with deep economic system reforms and big changes in social structure and profound changes of people's ideology thus caused. Bringing vitality to the reforms, bring a series of social contradictions and problems into public view: the psychology of hating the rich and the officials, educational reform, corruption and housing prices.

Second, topics that involve social "fairness and justice." As people's consciousness of citizenship keeps growing, their consciousness of protecting their democratic rights and interests is being strengthened, and their requirement for fairness and justice is more intense. The space for free information and opinion communication that is provided by the network serves as a real expression platform for these demands.

Third, topics that involve morality and ethics. Traditional Chinese culture is not sufficiently and properly carried forward today, and the phenomena of "ceremony disintegration" and "prevailing materialism" cause much concern to cybercitizens, so they detest and scourge events that are against basic social morals and ethics.

Fourth, topics on major sudden events that involve public security, major accidents, natural disasters or environmental pollution. Recent years have seen many major sudden events which, besides attracting wide attention in the real society, became focuses of cybercitizens' discussion on the Internet. Such events included the "May 12" Wenchuan earthquake, the water pollution of Songhuajiang River, and the mine disaster in Nandan.

In the topic-appearance period, the second factor that attracts more attention from cybercitizens and triggers discussion in cybercitizens in the beginning is the sources of topics.

3.3.5.2 Topic Existence Period

Whether a topic can survive on the Internet or not depends on whether the relevant event can attract forum members' attention continuously, a demonstration of which is continuous new posts of opinions or replies to topics on the event on the Internet. Any topic for discussion, to attract continuous attention, must accumulate sufficient page views and replies. The more the page views and replies are, the higher the topic will be on the web page, and the more concerned it will show. Therefore, to attract cybercitizens' attention and develop network public opinion on that basis, it is necessary and important to keep the topic from "sinking" down in the forum. The network public opinion events in recent years were hot topics in each and every major forum, each with millions, even tens of millions of page views. Once a topic survives in a forum, it will be visited and replied to continuously by cybercitizens, or cybercitizens may re-post similar topics, which will build a platform for expressing opinions, and large-scale network public opinion will gradually come into being.

In the topic-existence period, opinion leaders also play a very important role. "Opinion leaders," originated from the "two-step dissemination" theory put forward by Paul Lazarsfeld, refers to people who are active in the interpersonal network and capable of influencing others' opinions and views. It is because of the emergence of opinion leaders that the process of mass media turned into the "mass media → opinion leaders → the audience" model, and two-step dissemination came into being. In the era of traditional media, opinion leaders played the "gatekeeping" role in the dissemination process and had direct influence on the audience's information recognition and acceptance, attitudes, and even behavioral changes.

In the network-media era, the dissemination characteristics of information bring about fundamental changes in the relationship between the media and the audience; cybercitizens' ability to accept information gets enhanced and cybercitizens have the ability to release information. Take network forums for example. Network forums have developed to a fairly large scale in China. Except special network forums, almost all web portals in China have set a BBS forum. In mainstream media and web portals, almost all news reports have the function that allows the audience to reply to the news. Cybercitizens may express their views on the news that interests them. Under such circumstance, network opinion leaders present new characteristics.

Three indicators are used to measure network opinion leaders' influence: first, whether a topic initiated by network opinion leaders is viewed and replied to by a big population of cybercitizens, which is an essential condition for the topic to survive; second, whether the topic is sticky, and placed on the homepage of a website or a forum, which directly determines if a topic can exist and emerge continuously in a forum; third, whether the topic is re-posted by other forums or websites, even reported by traditional media, which ensures the topic's continuous vitality and extensive communication effect.

3.3.5.3 Public Opinion Integration Period

Once a topic survives, it is like a tornado that has initially "taken shape." Its subsequent development will be the result of a series of factors—cybercitizens' attitudes and behavior, changes in the network media environment—checking and gaming. On the one hand, network public opinion is born turbulent because of cybercitizens' publicity and emancipation of their personality, values and moral orientation; on the other, after a topic survives and becomes a public opinion "climate" of a certain scale, and therefore attracts attention from numerous cybercitizens, even social public and mass media, social ethics, even laws and regulations will intervene in the operation of public opinion and become an important factor that restrains or guides the development direction of network public opinion.

Under the circumstance where an event is continuously reported and reprinted by the media, and discussed, replied to and forwarded by a big population of cybercitizens, network public opinion develops in two directions—it may escalate along the original route, during which official opinions, cybercitizens' views and media reports interweave to further expand the influence of public opinion; or it may derive from the event itself because it is intentionally guided by the government, or influenced by the latest information supplements or media setting of new topics. Integrated opinions and commentary remarks, and parties that hold different attitudes toward the event itself begin to split apart into the pro side and the con side after a period of online discussion and communication. During the process, the discussion of both sides on network public opinion also becomes highly intensified. At this stage, opinions are concentrated, highlighted and enhanced in network public opinion, making it an important link for cybercitizens to speak and express their opinions in a centralized way.

3.3.5.4 Public Opinion Dissipation Period

After expressing their opinions in the network public opinion integration period, as time goes by and the event is further processed, cybercitizens' participation in discussion becomes less, and the intensity of their expression of opinions reduces. Network public opinion goes into the dissipation period.

From the time perspective, the dissipation of the momentum of network public opinion always goes with the final settlement or phased settlement of the event. After cybercitizens express their opinions in a centralized way, the network public opinion has exerted pressure on the development of the event, and affected the development of the event to different degrees. The dissipation of the momentum of network public opinion is also embodied in the following—no substantial growth of the page views of event-related replies, apparent reduction in replies and followers, significant decline in new posts that continue event development, an always sinking trend of the posts in the forum, and less and less attention from cybercitizens. As the page view rate and the reply rate decline, the posts that are on a specific topic will finally be replaced by new topics, and centralized opinion expression by cybercitizens on the topic weakens accordingly till it finally disappears.

PART II

Study of the Main Body of New-Media Public Opinion—Users

CHAPTER 4

Study of the Characteristics of New-Media Users

Given the interactive characteristic of new media, the disseminators and the audience have a vague boundary in the dissemination process. Normally, new-media users are both disseminators and the audience. Therefore, in new-media studies, the study of new-media users, especially the quantitative analysis of the cybercitizens, has always been a hotspot of academic studies and a focus of concern in the industry.

4.1 Audience Theories in the New-Media Era

4.1.1 Audience, Network Audience and Cybercitizens, Users

Audience, to put it simple, refers to people who receive information. Audience in the traditional sense is a collective name of spectators, listeners and readers. Audience, the destination of information (sink) in the dissemination process, can be simplified as information → news communicators → mass media → few information feedback from the audience. Here, audience is a relative fixed group of people who are different from news communicators and passively receive fully identical information content that news communicators disseminate to them. In new media where the audience has many choices, qualified members of the audience get rid of the passive position and become active information communication participators like the former news communicators.

W. Kuang, *Social Media in China*, Sociology, Media and Journalism in China, https://doi.org/10.1007/978-981-13-0914-4_4

Audience includes not only groups in large-scale information dissemination like newspaper readers, broadcasting listeners and TV audience, but also individuals in small-scale information communication. With the emergence of new media, there is a new member of the audience: network audience. Audience has a new meaning on the Internet. In new media, either information releasers or the audience first are common users of network media, and qualified audience can both receive and release information online. The so-called network audience can be defined as information recipients of new media. Network audience may be individuals, or groups, or societies or the country.

Since new media is initiative and interactive, network audience has many new characteristics that the audience of traditional media does not have. Communicators and recipients can change roles in a flash in new media, which is especially obvious in BBS, emails, online chatting and WeChat. Under many circumstances in new media, it is difficult to clearly distinguish information disseminators from information recipients, and there is an ambiguous boundary between both. Of course, communicators and recipients in new media can be differentiated in a static state.

The term "cybercitizens" generally refers to people who surf the Internet. Besides receiving information by browsing web pages, people who surf the Internet also release and disseminate information in BBS, emails or through online chatting, that is, they play the role of both information disseminators and that of information recipients. Only when people who surf the Internet are in the state of purely receiving information can they be called "network audience." "Cybercitizens" and "network audience" are two intimately related concepts. Sometimes, cybercitizens both receive and release information. Seen from its denotation, "network audience" is a subset of "cybercitizens," or a component of the latter. In terms of logics, studies of cybercitizens inevitably include the studies of network audience.

"Users" generally refers to Internet users and mobile phone users. Chinese mobile phone users have exceeded 1.3 billion, and cybercitizens who use mobile phones to surf the Internet have gradually become the mainstay of cybercitizens. The word "users" is more frequently used.

Limited by objective conditions (economy, technology, time, knowledge skills, etc.), users are primarily information recipients at least in most cases now, that is, they appear in new media as network audience. On the whole, users can't compete against news websites or business websites, which are financially and technically capable, in terms of the influence, truthfulness and reliability of the news released and disseminated. Most users, when surfing the Internet, browse, retrieve, download and receive information far more frequently than they upload or release information. However, as new media develops rapidly, especially the increased popularity of microblogging, more and more users will release high-quality information as their self-awareness and sense of democracy get further enhanced.

Obviously, in theoretical studies or in practice, it is hard to completely differentiate "users," "cybercitizens" and "network audience." Since new media is interactive, the boundary between disseminators and recipients are vague, and both can switch roles in a blink, "users" may be used to replace "audience."

Using the current audience theory, developed on the basis of traditional media, it is hard to explain the phenomenon of cybercitizens rationally. From the audience perspective, new media is highly selective, initiative and interactive. All these characteristics—which traditional mass media lacks—necessitate the updating of the former audience theory.

4.1.2 *Interactivity of New Media*

The biggest difference between the Internet and traditional media is that the Internet realizes a two-way information dissemination model that is similar to interpersonal communication, that is, the Internet is interactive, which is a revolutionary reform of the old way of dissemination. The Internet is capable of two-way and multiple-way communication. Interactivity is a big advantage of new media over traditional media. In new media, the audience enjoys unprecedented participation and becomes a part of the media. It becomes active from passive, and can "drag" out the information it wants at will from the media, or participate in media dissemination activities. The media and the audience realize sufficient two-way communication.

The interactivity of new media catalyzes changes in the relationship between the disseminators and the audience. Thanks to the initiative that is brought about by the interactivity of new media, the audience becomes even more active in participation in new-media activities.

4.1.3 *Information Access Initiative Brought to the Audience by New Media*

New media breaks through the one-way dissemination model of traditional mass media, and makes information delivery two-way, interactive and point-to-point. This dissemination characteristic determines the way that the audience accesses information: being initiative—the audience gets information by themselves from the network, and being individualized—the audience makes selections according to personal needs. This shift from groups to individuals undoubtedly enhances the audience's autonomy.

In new media, the audience no longer receives information passively, but discovers and processes information actively. The relationship between the disseminators and the audience sees fundamental changes—"the audience center" substitutes "the disseminator center" and the status of the audience is fully respected.

The audience now is no longer satisfied with the old mode of dissemination featuring "passive listening" and "passive watching." The shocks within the market economy and the openness of people's minds have split the audience structure apart into "niche" groups with different wishes and demands. Enhancement of the subject consciousness greatly strengthens the audience's sense of participation. The development of new media has promoted the trend of personalized communication. Alongside the reform of the way of dissemination, China's politics will become even more democratic, and its economy, culture, society as well as personal life, study and work will become even more diversified. All these changes have accelerated the trend of personalized dissemination that features multiple information sources, a large space for selection, and an enhanced ability to think and judge independently, as well as strengthened personal independence. The audience—being well-educated, with broadened horizons, and enhanced ability and habit to think and judge independently—will become less blind. This together with a plural life and rich and diversified opportunities to select make the audience highly independent. The audience's demands will become even more personalized.

4.1.4 New Media's Breakthrough of Users' (Audience's) Right of Access to the Media

The right of access to the media refers to "the freedom that the public, namely each member of the society, should have to express opinions by accessing and using the media." Jerome A. Barron, the American scholar who initiated the theory, believed it a must to confirm the masses' right to "access" the media in the Constitution in order to protect the freedom of speech for the masses.[1] Seen from the theoretical background, it was reconfirmation of the basic nature of the media as a public instrument. With the development of the practice, the views of classical liberalism proved to be too idealistic, and people were much too concerned about the power of the media. The theory attempted to weaken the power that was too densely demonstrated by the media.

From the perspective of communication, highlighting users' right of access to the media is of prominent significance. First, it helps promote the communication efficiency; second, it helps build a healthy and positive media environment; third, it properly settles the relationship between information source and information disseminators.

Despite the positive significance of users' right of access to the media in theory, there are many difficulties in order to truly realize it in reality. The real difficulties are discussed in the following paragraphs.

First, traditional mass media is limited by time and space. Users' opinions and facts therefore can't be fully reflected, and only a very small number of them may be disseminated by mass media.

Second, traditional media is highly selective. It is generally considered that the media is selective because of the limitation of time and space. The media, out of the consideration of its own stance and interest relationship, will inevitably have preferences and make avoidances, so it does not see the users' opinions and facts equal.

The emergence of new media shows us light in the plight. First it was BBS and microblogging that enabled the users to release information, exchange ideas and discuss freely, providing an important place for gathering and distributing non-governmental information and opinions, and the users' right of access to the media has reached a fairly high level.

New media is of positive significance to realizing users' right of access to the media for the following reasons.

First, new media breaks through traditional media's information access privilege. Second, new media enables powerful communication of personal views; third, new media puts the power of traditional media under control and supervision. Fourth, new media is realizing users' right of access to the media. Fifth, new media provides the information of the disadvantaged minorities a communication opportunity.

[1] Quoted from Zhang Guoliang: *The Principles of Communication*, p171, Shanghai: Fudan University Press, 1995.

Of course, the easy information access of new media has some negative impacts, the primary of which is low information reliability. Some people make trouble out of nothing and produce garbage information to confuse others, which weakens the influence of new media on the whole, and affects new-media attempts to realize better rights of access to the media users.

4.2 Analysis of Cybercitizens' Fundamental Characteristic—From Being Elite to Being Popular

In communication audience studies, the quantitative research method plays an important role. Famous audience theories in the history of communication were fundamentally developed on the basis of quantitative analysis and the study of a considerable amount of first-hand data. Today when new media is increasingly prosperous, it is urgent and important to carry out quantitative studies of cybercitizens.

Using the statistics in *China Statistical Reports on Internet Development*, which were released by the China Internet Network Information Center, and data from surveys performed by well-known network investigation companies and agencies like NetValue, Nielsen/Netratings, Jupiter Media Metrix and IDC, we studied cybercitizens mainly by the quantitative research method, supplemented by the qualitative research method, from which we discover cybercitizens' several characteristics and trends.

In the early days of development, the Internet was mostly a "province" of "the elite." "The elite" here refer to young single males, who are well-educated and handsomely-paid. This conclusion can be drawn from *China Statistical Reports on Internet Development* released by China Internet Network Information Center. Early research reports abroad also drew the same conclusion. General studies hold that in the early stage, cybercitizens had the following group characteristics: having great information demands, being young and well-educated, making handsome incomes, living and working in developed areas, and being mainly male white-collar workers.

However, by a comparative study of a great deal of past statistics and domestic and foreign data, we discover that cybercitizens have presented a widening audience trend, and the Internet is becoming more and more popular.

The growth of the population of Chinese cybercitizens follows the "S curve theory of diffusion," (see Fig. 4.1) and shows the China-specific "20 million phenomenon." It is a consensus in the communication field

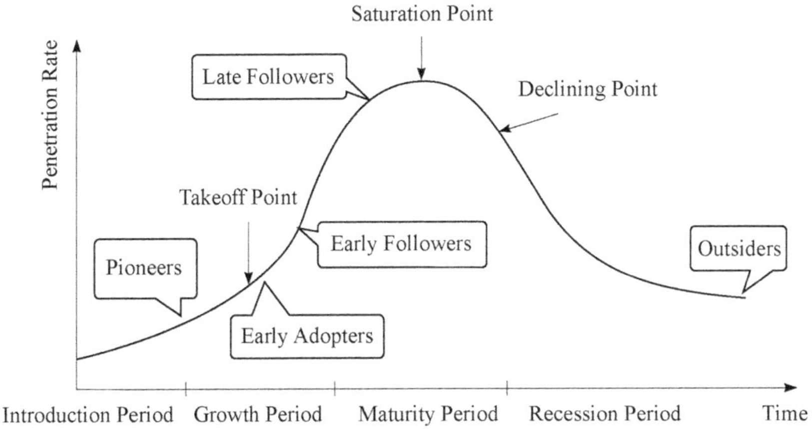

Fig. 4.1 S curve theory of diffusion

that, when the population of its users exceeds over 20%, that is, over one-fifth of the total population, a media surpasses the threshold of "popular." Take the United States for example. It took radio broadcasting 38 years, TV 13 years and the Internet only 5 years to meet the standard. According to the "S curve theory of diffusion" of the diffusion of innovations theory, when a new product or service holds a 10–25% shares of its potential market, its diffusion rate will rise sharply.

Mobile phones are a media tool that contributes to the rapid growth of the population of cybercitizens. In a short period of a few years, mobile phones have become popular in China, and their functions greatly enlarged. Mobile phones have developed from a single one-way voice communication tool in the beginning to a media information receiving end and a personal information initiating terminal. In particular, the improvement and popularity of the third generation mobile phone technology is changing mobile phones into an extension of the Internet. The development of mobile phone technology, the enhancement and expansion of mobile phone functions, as well as constant launches of new mobile phone products will increasingly highlight the characteristic of mobile phones as a media tool. Besides being a tool for people to access information anytime any place, the mobile phone is a sharp weapon that helps journalists deliver news in a timely and fast way. Given that the population of China mobile users is the largest in the world, the wide use of mobile phones that can surf the Internet will greatly promote the popularization of the Internet in China.

In the Chinese economic field, there is the so-called "20 million phenomenon," that is, color TV, 'fridge and air-conditioner all got popularized quickly after their user population reached 20 million. The popularity of mobile phones in China testifies to the view that "20 million users usually bring about an avalanche effect." After the population of cybercitizens broke through 20 million in China, the network in China has begun to lean toward low-income and female cybercitizens.

A conclusion can be drawn from the above statistics and analysis, that is, the Internet is being popularized quickly and presents a popularization trend. What's more, the more developed a country or region is, the more significant the popularized characteristic its cybercitizens will have; the less developed a country or region is, the more significant the "elite" characteristic of the network will be.

4.3 Analysis of New-Media Users' Psychology and Behavioral Characteristics

4.3.1 *Types and Mentality of New-Media Users*

New-media users can be divided into different types by different standards. Different types of cybercitizens have different psychologies and behaviors of surfing the Internet.

Different countries and regions have different climates, cultures and local conditions, which greatly influence cybercitizens' psychologies and behaviors.

Male cybercitizens and female cybercitizens are different in terms of their psychologies and behaviors of surfing the Internet. Male cybercitizens are rational and like searching science and technology news, military and similar information; female cybercitizens are emotional and like browsing fashion, cosmetology and similar information. More females chat online than males.

People of different ages will have different psychologies and behaviors of surfing the Internet. New media needs to release information with different content and use web-pages that are designed differently according to people's age differences in order to meet the psychological demands of cybercitizens of different levels to the maximum degree.

The ability to pay is an important factor that directly affects cybercitizens' motives and behaviors when surfing the Internet. It is hard to expect a person with a low income to spend more time chatting online.

Educational level also directly affects cybercitizens' psychologies and behaviors of accessing information online. The higher the education a person receives, the less the time that person will spend in entertainment and the greater the time spent reading news and scientific and technological information.

As well as all the above features, cybercitizens with different occupations and social statuses have different types of information demands.

4.3.2 *Analysis of the General Psychology of New-Media Users*

Different types of new-media users, although having different information demands, have a lot in common in terms of psychology. Generally speaking, ordinary users have the following psychological characteristics when using the media: pursuing novelty, being curious, pursuing truth, pursuing harmony, pursuing knowledge, making selections and being rebellious. Compared with the psychology of the traditional media audience, new-media users have the prominent psychologies discussed in the following three subsections.

4.3.2.1 *The Psychology of Participation*

Unlike the audience of traditional media, new-media users are more than just information recipients and onlookers, but participate more in the dissemination process. New-media users can put forward their demands for information, give their opinions on the dissemination content, or upload the information that they think is valuable for dissemination purpose. Participation does not simply mean a vague boundary between the disseminators and the users, or improvement of users' position, but also pluralism and complexity of the content of information online.

4.3.2.2 *The Psychology of Personalization*

Users can choose the websites, information or services they like more freely. More importantly, they enjoy greater autonomy in media consumption in terms of time and space. They no longer have to arrange their activities according to the schedule of TV and radio stations, or watch TV in fixed space. In the era of traditional media, especially of TV, people's rule of law was more affected by media programs. For example, to watch a TV program they were fond of, people might have to sacrifice other social activities. But in the network era people have greater right to decide their agenda.

4.3.2.3 Anonymity Psychology in a Virtual Environment

The anonymity psychology, in social psychologies, refers to the psychology that people may lose their sense of social responsibility and ability of self-control in an anonymous state without social restrictions.

Alongside, cybercitizens have the conformist psychology. Of course, since the network is concealing, cybercitizens may not have as large a conformist pressure as they had in the era of traditional media, and the conformist psychology is somewhat weakened.

4.3.3 Analysis of Cybercitizens' Purposes of Surfing the Internet

Domestic and foreign surveys all indicate that the primary goal of cybercitizens surfing the Internet is to access information, especially news information; and then to play games or seek entertainment. Commonly used tools include emails and search engines.

Results of past China Internet Network Information Center surveys show that cybercitizens' main purposes of surfing the Internet were in the following proper order: accessing information, learning new technology like computer skills, for work purpose, and seeking leisure and entertainment. The network services that are most frequently used by the cybercitizens are email boxes and search engines; and the main information accessed by cybercitizens online are various news.

Cybercitizens surf the Internet mainly to access information, especially news information. From the perspective of theories of new-media science, network news is less reliable and authoritative than traditional media on the whole. However, as reading news online has become a part of people's life with each passing day, network news is more and more believed by people.

4.3.4 Analysis of Cybercitizens' Motives for Surfing the Internet

Motive originally meant triggering (or starting) actions. In psychology, subjective factors that are expressed in forms like wishes, interests and ideals to encourage people to act are defined as motives. Motive is the forerunner and a condition of an action. Cybercitizens' main motives for surfing the Internet are discussed in the following subsections.

4.3.4.1 *To Pursue Knowledge*

The pursuit of knowledge, a motive that aims to get knowledge and information, is the cybercitizens' most popular and commonly seen psychological activity. Developing and improving themselves is a need that is popular in people, and the motive to pursue knowledge is exactly a psychological reaction to such need. Cybercitizens use the Internet to access external information and supervise the environment. Through new media, they understand the outside world, big events both at home and abroad and other people's opinions, and decide their own behaviors. In the process of pursuing knowledge online, cybercitizens seek information and knowledge on their own initiaive, which is entirely different from receiving information passively as the audience of traditional media does.

4.3.4.2 *To Be Entertained and Pass Time*

Entertainment is a motive to surf the Internet that aims at mental relaxation and enjoyment. Cybercitizens may know more and understand more, satisfy their curiosity, kill time, seek stimulation and happiness, relax themselves, get rid of worries and fatigue, and release the pressure and worries in daily life through new media.

4.3.4.3 *To Pursue Fame*

The pursuit of fame and gaining a sense of accomplishment are motives to surf the Internet. Many cybercitizens are happy to post their opinions on websites or in BBS to pursue fame.

4.3.4.4 *For Convenience*

Many cybercitizens shop online because it is convenient. When shopping online, cybercitizens require not only fast and convenient transactions but also home delivery.

4.3.4.5 *To Escape Reality*

In fact, to escape reality has become a reason why many people surf the Internet. Some cybercitizens seek consolation and relief in virtual network communities to escape from conflicts and contradictions in real life. The Internet has become a haven for some people. People who are dissatisfied with reality or have psychological problems find support and emotional comfort more easily in the virtual network world.

Cybercitizens have complicated motives to surf the Internet, and their surfing the Internet is a result of synthetic action of a number of motives. However, cybercitizens' main purposes of surfing the Internet are to access information, communicate with people, kill time and seek entertainment, and read news on the Internet.

4.3.5 *Analysis of Cybercitizens' Behavioral Characteristics—Cybercitizens' Attention Shows the "Matthew Effect"*

As investigated, cybercitizens' attention focuses more and more on a few well-known websites, and is an example of the "Matthew Effect."

The so-called Matthew Effect refers to a phenomenon where "the rich get richer and the poor get poorer." The term comes from "For to everyone who has will more be given, and he will have abundance; but from him who has not, even what he has will be taken away" Matthew 25, *Gospel of Matthew*, *New Testament.*

Robert Merton generalized the "Matthew Effect" as any individual, group or region—once achieving success or making progress in some aspect (e.g., money, fame, status)— would have an accumulation advantage and stand more chance to achieve greater successes and make greater progresses.

The term was later borrowed by the economic circle to reflect the phenomenon of unfair income distribution where the poor get poorer and the rich get richer and winners take all.

In the field of new media, the Matthew Effect refers to the phenomenon where cybercitizens grow in population, but the few websites they usually visit are more and more centralized.

PART III

Study of the Objects of New-Media Public Opinion—Platforms

CHAPTER 5

Network Forums

5.1 Dissemination Characteristics of Network Forums

Network forums serve as an important channel for cybercitizens to access information, unleash emotions and express opinions, and long held the hegemon position of network public opinion. Many public opinion events originated in network forums, got incubated before finally becoming important public opinion events with widespread influence. The decline in the rate of use of network forums is closely related to the development of microblogging, an emerging network application. The "first year of microblogging" has been accepted as 2010. By 2011, microblogging had become "the public opinion center of the network"[1] and the main battlefield where citizens supervised government exercise of public power and protected their own rights and interests.

5.1.1 Concept of Network Forums

Network forums, as places for online communication based on virtual Internet technology, is what people usually call "network communities" or "BBS." The term "network community" is the transplant of real-life community to online. Because network forums mainly function to facilitate

[1] Xie Gengyun, *The Report on Chinese Social Opinion and Crisis Management (2011)*, Beijing: Social Sciences Academic Press, 2011.

W. Kuang, *Social Media in China*, Sociology, Media and Journalism in China, https://doi.org/10.1007/978-981-13-0914-4_5

users' communication and interaction, they make the "global neighborhood" a reality. BBS, the abbreviation of Bulletin Board System, is literally translated into "cyberspace bulletin system," because it was first used to "put up bulletins" about share market prices and similar information, which was its main function.

The core function of network forums is discussion, and other functions include email, document transmission, online talking, bulletin and Internet access service. Actually, BBS basically includes most functions of the Internet. According to different classification standards, BBS can be divided into several big boards—letters discussion board, document communication board, information bulletin board and interactive discussion board. What is directly related to network public opinion is the interactive discussion board, the building of which requires three structural elements: cyberspace, account and posts.

From the first BBS that emerged in Chicago in 1978 up to now, BBS has had a history of over 30 years. The symbol of China's access to BBS was the building of "长城站" in Beijing in 1991.[2]

5.1.2 Development of Network Forums

The earliest BBS originated in Chicago, US, in 1978, and the then BBS system CBBS/Chicago could only be used on Apple computers and did not have most of the functions that network forums have today. Until 1983, RBBS-PC, the first ordinary PC-based BBS system, reputed as "BBS originator," emerged. It could support information discussion and questionnaires, that is, commonly used functions of the BBS system today.

China's first normal BBS station was Shuguang BBS station, opened by State Smart Computers Research and Development Center (now known as High Performance Computer Research Center), in May 1994, but it had limited influence at the time and has disappeared. In the history of network forums in China, the emergence of bbs.people.cn was a turning point. Formerly known as "BBS in Strong Protest against NATO's Savage Act," bbs.people.cn was a network forum opened on a specific public event.

After microblogging emerged in 2009 and became popular, the "hegemony" position of network forums in new-media public opinion had been gradually replaced by microblogging.

[2] Refer to Wang Haiming, Han Ruixia, Review of the status quo of the studies of BBS in China, *Journal of Lanzhou Petrochemical College of Vocational Technology*, 2004(4).

5.1.3 *Dissemination Characteristics of Network Forums*

For a long time, mankind lived in an environment that existed naturally or had been renovated by the ancestors, that is, "sinnenwelt," a natural world that can be keenly sensed and some artificial material world. Now, with the popularity of mass media and the arrival of the information society, people are able to expand their feelings of the outside world, and the imaginary world becomes more than extensive. Before they know it, people have become accustomed to accepting and operating information of the sinnenelt, which they can't access directly, and living in another world that goes beyond the sinnenwelt which they can sense keenly. This world is not about events, people, things or views that can be truly and directly contacted, but about replicated signs or imitation of them. It is a copy world, a symbolic world that co-exists with the sinnenwelt.[3]

With the information provided by various media, people can always build a virtual environment for them to survive by signalizing or labeling. Network forums open another virtual environment and interpersonal interaction model for the existence of human beings, playing an important role in people's building of a virtual world. As Marshall McLuhan said, we shape our tools and then our tools shape us. People's interaction in network forums is decentralized, beyond time and space, language-based, expansive and indirect.[4]

5.1.3.1 *Decentralized*

With the launch and application of Web2.0, cybercitizens are able to express their opinions on public events anytime anywhere, so information release is like "dialoguing" and information dispersion develops from one-way to two-way, even multi-way. In the era of Web2.0, public discourse turned from being monopolized by media elites or knowledge elites in the past to being shared by all. Theoretically, that is, all people can participate in discussions and express their opinions. In addition, given that people become more concealed on the Internet, they are bolder to express their opinions online and their opinions are more reliable. To a certain degree, the sense of critique of network news comments is even denser. Therefore, network forums to a certain degree become "free markets for opinions."

[3] Refer to Chen Lidan: *Public Opinion*, p65, Beijing: China Radio, Film and TV Press, 1999.

[4] Chen Xiaoqiang and Hu Xinhua: An analysis of virtual social interactions from the social sciences perspective, *Social Sciences Journal of Universities in Shanxi*, 2003(9).

Decentralization is the state of socialized relations and the form of content generation during the development of the Internet. It is the generation process of new-type network contents relative to "centralization." Compared with the era of Web1.0, the content of Web2.0 today is no longer generated by professional websites or specific groups of people, but is the result of joint creation by all cybercitizens through common participation with an equal-power hierarchy. All can express their views or create original content on the Internet to join information production.

5.1.3.2 Beyond Time and Space

American network prophet John Perry Barlow said that a space was being created for people around the globe to have a "new" kind of communication relationship where people wished they could fully interact with their communicative hearts.[5] It seems to be only a wish, but the Internet is indeed building such a "real" space—"cyberspace" for people. Cyberspace is the "material" being on which interaction in network forum relies. It is made up of "bit," something that does not have color, size or weight, and can travel at the speed of light. In this space, there is no "here" or "there," "now" or "then," so the scope of interaction in interpersonal communication actually goes beyond traditional boundaries of time and space.

5.1.3.3 Language-Based

In real social interactions, nonverbal communication is surprisingly common. Nonverbal communication proceeds with signs instead of language. Look, clothing and personal property may all become a form of nonverbal communication, of which body language and personal space are the two most important forms.

5.1.3.4 Expansive

Some worry that the Internet will become a force that estranges people. This is not necessarily a fact. An environment for virtual social communication benefits the expansion of interpersonal relationship more. That the Internet keeps its users anonymous gives interaction in network forums a communication environment that benefits the formation and expansion of weak bonds. Such an environment is better for the formation of weak

[5] David Gelernter, Glenn Reynolds, Eric S. Raymond, Jaron Lanier, John Perry Barlow, Jason Kuznicki. Internet Liberation: Alive or Dead?. Amazon Digital Services, Inc. Kindle Edition, p.45.

bonds with strangers, facilitates virtual communities to establish a model of equal interaction and makes communication smooth, and helps tens of hundreds of weak bonds to expand, some of which will develop into strong bonds. All this can't be realized with traditional means of interaction.

5.1.3.5 *Indirect*

Unlike direct interactions among people, the interactions in network forums are in the form of "indirect interaction between man—computer—man." Computer is actually the medium for realizing interaction in network forums. The Spanish network sociologist Manuel Castells called it "computer mediated communication," CMC for short. With the rise of the Internet worldwide in the 1990s, this communication form expanded to ordinary people, and "computers" then replaced "notes," indirect interaction became almost the only way to realize the interaction of its members (network forum members).

5.1.4 *Characteristics of Public Opinion in Network Forums*

Public opinion in network forums has all the characteristics of new media public opinion and some other characteristics.

5.1.4.1 *User-Generated Content*

The primary characteristic of network forums is the emergence of user-generated content (UGC), which is also the starting point where the Internet begins to be truly different from traditional media in terms of the way of information communication. From network forums up to the current time, UGC has gradually attracted people's attention. In network forums, apart from a small amount of content from network forum administrators for administrating the forums, the majority of posts and replies are from tens of millions of cybercitizens. The flat communication structure has replaced traditional media's top-down one-way communication. It is also because its content is directly from cybercitizens—the virtual doppelgangers of social public—that public opinion in network forums can vividly reflect the reality instead of being led.

5.1.4.2 *Instant and Interactive Opinion Communication*

"Human flesh search" is a byproduct of network forums. The first case of human flesh search, "the cat abuse event," occurred in mop.com, and its users, by "following clues" in a group of seemingly unconscious cat abuse photos, found the detailed location of the event and personal information of the cat abuser within six days, and forced the cat abuser to make a public apology. We do not comment whether human flesh search is right or wrong here but, seen from the realization of the human-flesh search process, opinion communication and interaction among cybercitizens played an enormous role. Network forums provide tens of millions of cybercitizens with platforms for exchanging opinions, where people piece up information fragments and help and benefit one another through such instant communication so that fragmented information gets superimposed like rolling a snowball before finally forming a panorama of information.

Human flesh search is just a special example. In day-to-day communication in network forums, people use instant interaction more often to give vent to their emotions, exchange information and express opinions. The fragmented posts, once encountering a sudden event that involves public interests, will develop a strong public opinion field to exert pressure on the real social event to push the settlement of it. Famous cases—like "South China tiger event" and "Zhou Jiugeng event"—could be reasonably resolved all because of the public-opinion spectacle created by public opinion in network forums through instant interactive exchange of opinions.

5.1.4.3 Public-Opinion Objects Are Both Fixed and Dispersed

Public-opinion objects more often than not point to specific public affairs. In the traditional public-opinion field, people's discussion about public affairs usually goes to an end, but in network forums, because of the network forums' concealing nature and the lack of restrictions over users in forums in general, public-opinion objects are both fixed and dispersed in network forums.

Given the great arbitrariness in network forums and the fact that the public affairs concerning the public-opinion subjects are ever changing, there is always the phenomenon of "switching topics" in an online forum. Sometimes, to joke on the topic or the objects involved in a network forum, cybercitizens "switch topics" purposefully. By frequently switching topics halfway, the public opinion objects decompose and dissolve the authoritativeness and seriousness of public affairs. The phenomenon is especially prominent in "necropost boards" of major network forums. Meaningless necropost gluts the screen and aggravates the decentralization trend of public opinion objects.

5.1.4.4 *Emotional Public Opinion Holds a High Proportion of Public Opinion*

What is emotional public opinion? Prof. Chen Lidan held that public opinion was a sum of public beliefs, attitudes, opinions and emotions toward the real society and various social phenomena and problems, so it was relatively consistent, intense and continuous, and affected social development and the progress of the state of affairs. There were rational and irrational elements therein.[6] Public opinion that concentrates on expression of emotion, we call emotional public opinion.

Before forums emerged, the mass media, as the "gatekeeper," would filter most emotional public opinion and replace it with even, rational, public opinion when giving selective feedback to public opinion. Emotional public opinion is highly relevant to people's instinct and unconsciousness. Network forums give ordinary cybercitizens the right to express themselves and people can express their opinions freely in network forums. Limited only by their education or knowledge level, and the fact that individual behaviors are the least restrained online due to the anonymity characteristic of the network, some of the public and cybercitizens express a fairly big selection of irrational opinions. Individual opinions gather and, pushed by the phenomenon of group polarization, can, on occasion, develop into irrational emotional public opinion.

The concept of group polarization was first put forward by Cass R. Sunstein, the contemporary American philosopher and professor of the University of Chicago Law School, in the book *Republic.com*. Group polarization refers to the social phenomenon that individuals, in an organizational group and being influenced by the group, will make more extreme decisions than those they make when they are alone.

Normally when one makes a decision, the person has a risk-aversion inclination. Ordinary rational decision makers will tend to avoid decisions that are risky and may cause them losses. However, when individuals are in a group, the inclination already existing in group members will be strengthened, enhancing a view or an attitude from the original average level in the group to a dominating position. The result is people treat things that do not exist at all as facts, thus producing unhealthy social influence.

Group members affected by group polarization have some deviation in opinion from the beginning. After discussion, people keep on moving in the deviated direction before finally forming extreme opinions. For example,

[6] Refer to Chen Lidan: *Public Opinion*, p11.

after discussion, feminists who used to be gentle will become radical; people who used to have race prejudice will show greater race prejudice; and people who used to be exclusive will show an even serious tendency of exclusiveness. Sunstein holds that group polarization is happening on the Internet. To many, the network is a hotbed for extremism because people of the same mind can easily and frequently communicate with one another online, but they do not listen to others' opinions, and will eventually walk to extremism, leading to the result of separation.

Such emotional public opinion usually appears in the early stage of a public opinion event when neither network media nor traditional media has sufficiently sought or presented relevant facts and information, which leads to too many changeable factors for event development, a large space for imagination and a low threshold for participation in expression. Emotional public opinion thus is diffused in high intensity under the role of group polarization. Even traditional media—due to pressure or a desire to capture social hotspots to improve ratings or sales—could join the diffusion of emotional public opinion.

5.1.4.5 The Pluralism Characteristic Is Even More Significant

Public opinion in network forums is plural, not unitary. Meng Chao believed that the main characteristic of network forums was "highly frequent one-to-one and one-to-many interpersonal communication management," and that network forums had realized "a plural space which no other media can possibly realize in reality or in technology."[7] That is why opinions in network forums are said to be like views and opinions in a free market.

In reality, people usually wear masks. *Flowers in the Mirror*, an 1818 work by Chinese author Li Ruzhen in the Qing dynasty, described a "land of two-faced people" where people all had two faces—a front face and a back one. The front face looked normal, but the back one ugly and malicious, ferocious and dirty, and was seldom revealed to others. Besides, the more righteous and awe-inspiring, handsome and highly esteemed, or naïve and unaffected the front face was, the more crafty and filthy and evil the back face would be. Each of inhabitants of the "land of two-faced people" therefore wore a special scarf, known as *Hao Ran Jin*, to cover their back faces.

[7] Meng Chao: Development direction of network media forums on journalism in China, *China Publishing Journal*, 2001(3).

But in virtual space, people can take their masks off. The plural speeches in network forums mainly emerge in the virtual space. The uncertainty of identities in the virtual space allows people to get rid of the restrictions of their roles in life.

However, in virtual space, there may be true voices, or uncommitted false information. People speak and act differently while playing different roles. A person who seems decent may be a nasty one in the virtual space, and an introvert person offline may become active and talkative on the Internet. Therefore, speeches in network forums are not totally consistent with those in real life, thus they can reflect cybercitizens' true ideas.

Although network forums form a noisy space, the interactivity of network forums will make public opinion in network forums the dominating public opinion.

5.1.5 Network Forum Administration

When major sudden events occur, the conflicts of remarks in network forums, to some degree, serve as safety valve for the society. According to Coser, social safety valves functioned to maintain social structure by manipulating potential conflicts so as to not destroy the whole structure.[8] Thus public-opinion conflicts and public-opinion supervision of network forums would greatly alleviate the possible social damages of major sudden events. Therefore, public-opinion supervision of network forums needs to be encouraged. In particular, in the case of major sudden events, the public-opinion environment may be even looser so as to let out more cybercitizens' real voices. Besides the opinions expressed in network forums, a virtual space, need to be made not virtual anymore, and able to develop a certain tension to effectively influence real life so as to enhance the influence of network forums and their attractiveness to the cybercitizens, and give full play to their role as a tool for supervising public opinion. Relevant departments need to face network public opinion correctly.

First, public-opinion supervision needs to be accepted actively and conflicts resolved reasonably. With regards to cybercitizens' news comments, blindly suppressing or labeling them helps little in settling the problem, and it cannot keep cybercitizens silent. Only by correctly understanding cybercitizens' opinions and pointing out the rational and irrational aspects

[8] Refer to Song Linfei: *Western Sociological Theory*, p335, Nanjing: Nanjing University Press, 1997.

therein can "news comments as a way of participating in government and political affairs" become possible and referential public opinion be accepted by competent departments, and functional departments' work be actually under supervision. In so doing, public power is placed under public opinion supervision of network forums, too.

Maintaining social stability and building an effective and orderly social structure is a normal need of every nation, but it never means prohibiting all fights and conflicts. "In the modernization process, it is inevitable to have some factors that affect social stability, but by institutional purification and absorption, all these factors can be resolved within the institution."[9] What the ruler needs to guarantee is the public's basic approval of the social environment. Allowing no opposition voice actually chokes the society. Disputes and different opinions are important factors for realizing general social goals.

Second, cybercitizens' opinions need to be faced squarely to prevent institutional ruptures. Cybercitizens' critiques do not target the established institution nor intend to challenge the legality of the established institution. Cybercitizens just expect to seek a fair and orderly social environment within the institution. Critiques or resistance for such purpose are not "great scourges," but can become a force and inducement to promote social dynamics.

In mass events on the Internet in recent years, each time the local governments did not fulfill or failed to properly fulfill their duties, network public opinion would bubble up, and critiques would be heard and shared. When the parties involved in the events were punished or information on the events was further disclosed, most cybercitizens accepted the conclusions. It is easy to show that many events occurred not because cybercitizens were irrational or lacked information, but mainly because functional departments and organs of public power failed to handle the situation in a timely and effective way.

There are rational and irrational elements in network public opinion. It is, therefore, especially necessary that the government *values* cybercitizens' opinions instead of just simply finding out cybercitizens' opinions. If leaving cybercitizens' comments unattended, it would inevitably cause an institutional rupture of the whole society when cybercitizens' negative opinions can't be expressed and develop to the level beyond the capacity of the existing system.

[9] Yu Jianrong: *Contentious Politics: Fundamental Issues in Chinese Political Sociology*, p5, Beijing: People's Publishing House, 2010.

In major network public opinion events, network forums still play an irreplaceable role. If not well administrated, they will easily become a base for producing and incubating rumors and unhealthy public opinion. Therefore, it is necessary to set great store by administering network forums.

5.1.5.1 *Developing Network Forum Ethics*

In the virtual space of network forums, it is hard to find out the identities of members of network forums. Once there is a major sudden event, false information will overflow easily in network forums. In addition, communication among cybercitizens in network forums is easily distorted. Under such circumstance, forum administrators may delete such information according to the administration regulations. However, deleting information alone only causes drainage of cybercitizens and misunderstanding in them. Therefore, it is crucial to develop network forum ethics.

5.1.5.2 *Reasonably Setting Topics in Network Forums*

Unlike the era of traditional media, in the era of new media, the success of agenda setting always depends on cybercitizens' active interaction. In the era of traditional media, there was no real-time interaction between the media, which held an advantageous position in the communication, and the audience and the audience's feedback was more than often ignored by the media. Whether something could become a topic for discussion in the public or not is no longer determined by whether it is set by traditional media or not, but by whether it has real news value or not. The setting of topics for discussion, which does not abide by the value of news events, will inevitably fail in the network era.

Network forums have changed the relationship between official-media agenda and the formation of public opinion. In major sudden events, the agenda setting by network forums is different from that in real media. If the public of a nation does not believe their media, they will turn to international media, even the media of an enemy nation. Therefore, global media and foreign media can affect a nation's agenda setting.

In network forums where information clusters, in the case of major sudden events, topics will no longer be set by the administrators at will. Instead they will be developed spontaneously by cybercitizens according to the news value of the information. Therefore, network forum administrators can no longer avoid hotspots that are much discussed by, or concern, cybercitizens, but carry out reasonable topic setting on the basis of fully respecting cybercitizens' interests. For example, "Recommended Discussion" set daily by "bbs.people.cn" was to, considering cybercitizens' interests in discussion, select quality original topics opened by the users or news topics that were much discussed, recommend such topics, and guide the users to express opinions on the topics before finally forming their own discussion.

5.1.5.3 Giving Play to Opinion Leaders' Active Role

Opinion leaders refer to people who are fond of disseminating information and expressing opinions in a group. They either contact the media or information source more than their partners, or are experts in certain fields, and their opinions usually affect those around them. Information often flows first from the media to opinion leaders who, according to their understanding of media reports, convey opinions to the audience around them. Relative to media reports, opinion leaders' opinions and views are more trustworthy to the general audience.

The same law applies to network forums. When major sudden events occur, there will be different views and opinions in network forums, but cybercitizens need to read in-depth opinions that carry weight, and opinion leaders' opinions play a role in steering the formation of public opinion in network forums.

Opinion leaders are able to always express opinions and views in a timely way to affect the other cybercitizens. For example, in case of major sudden events, network forums often guide the huge scale public opinion by inviting special guests to discuss the events in depth. When rumors appear, it would be better to have them clarified by opinion leaders. Meanwhile, using opinion leaders cannot be limited to the opinion leaders talking to themselves, but should aim at convergence of opinions in network forum interaction. Cybercitizens' opinions cluster in a short time. Although the pressure on groups in a virtual space is not significant, to maintain psychological coherence, people's opinions would normally form relatively centralized emotional and will directions in mutual communication. Opinion leaders can better steer public opinion in network forums as long as they use their unique statuses to influence and affect other groups in interaction and communication.

5.1.5.3.1 Classification of Opinion Leaders

C. R. Rogers (1902–1987), the famous American psychologist, professor and one of the founders of American applied psychology, summarized four effective methods to measure opinion leaders that is, self-designating/report techniques, sociometric techniques, interviews with key informants and observation.[10] These four traditional methods highlighted the screening of real opinion leaders. When screening proceedings in network forums, some method that is more appropriate for the network communication environment will be adopted.

Researcher Yu Hong, on the basis of the "influence diffusion model" built by Japanese scholars, developed a "network forum opinion leaders screening model."[11] The "influence diffusion model" mainly measures forum participants' activities quantitatively by extracting "words." Yu Hong extracted "influential active elements" from such model and then, with "positive and negative response values," screened "opinion leaders" from them. This study holds that cluster analysis is an original and effective method to mine data, which can realize the screening objective in a convenient and correct way with specific indicators like "the amount of posts," "the amount of replies," "the degree of diffusion" and "identity value."[12]

In actual work, different types and function setups of network forums may somewhat affect the selection of indicators. It, therefore, needs the administrators to make problem-specific analyses and adjust the indicators system according to the characteristics of the monitored objects and their own demands.

5.1.5.3.2 Management of Opinion Leaders

After differentiating opinion leaders, the administrators should establish a database to follow-up such opinion leaders and observe them. In crises, when opinion leaders appear as positive information providers, they can effectively alleviate the pressure brought about by information demand and play the role of pacifying critiques and appeasing cybercitizens' emotions. In addition, the administrators can also draw opinion leaders' social network structure charts through Social Network Analysis (SNA) so as to analyze their positions in the group, their interactions with the other

[10] Refer to [US] John Fiske, et al., *Key Concepts in Communication and Cultural Studies*, Beijing: Xinhua Publishing House, 2004.

[11] Refer to *Communication Statistics* by Ke Huixin, Zhu Jianhua and Sun Jianghua, Beijing: Beijing Broadcasting Institute Press (known as Communication University of China Press), 2003.

[12] Refer to A study of the communication model of influence of "opinion leaders" in BBS—'Yin Shui Si Yuan BBS' of Shanghai Jiao Tong University as an example" by Xue Ke and Chen Xi, *Jouralistic University*, 2010(4).

members, and the role they can play in guiding public opinion for the final purpose of assisting the administrators in making better decisions and judgments.

For opinion leaders in network forums, communication with them may be carried out online and offline. Besides, it is necessary to organize network safety education on a regular basis to promote the norms on network application and establish an effective mechanism for safety management of network public opinion. For network opinion leaders who have already become good examples, different methods shall be applied to publicizing them, and setting them as examples to encourage more cybercitizens to express their opinions.

5.1.5.3.3 Cultivation of Opinion Leaders in Network Forums

Besides positively intervening in and guiding the existing network "opinion leaders," another feasible way to build network opinion guidance is to cultivate more opinion leaders who represent the positive spiritual characteristics, ideology, speeches and social acts. To cultivate opinion leaders, the priority is to promote the shift of core members in some forums—like activists, forum administrators and forum leaders—into opinion leaders. It is a long-term undertaking to cultivate opinion leaders, but relative to rigid systems and regulations, steering public opinion through opinion leaders conforms more to the development characteristics of the new era, and better facilitates the maintenance of an open and harmonious network public opinion environment.

The positions of members, who have already become opinion leaders, have to be confirmed and highlighted. Their insightful and representative remarks may be highlighted by forum moderators or administrators within their purview or relevant mechanism of the forums in eye-catching fonts and colors at prominent places of webpages—top or bottom, or even recommended to the homepages of the forums so as to strengthen mainstream public opinion and isolate unhealthy speeches.

5.1.5.4 Application of Mandatory Regulations and Network Technology

Full use should be made of technology and software for controlling network information, for example, keyword-filtering technology. Posts containing obscene or derogatory keywords would be refused publication or shown as "**" or "□□." The application of such technology also plays the "gatekeeping" role in information selection. This is of course against the free and open nature of network forums, but it is a necessary measure to take in order to maintain normal and good operation of the entire "free markets for opinions." Meanwhile, a real-time network forum administration system should be built to attach great importance to information in network forums that reflects people's ideological dynamics, and the development direction of such information should be well guided.

5.1.5.5 Network Commentators with Chinese Characteristics

The Propaganda Department of the CPC Changsha Party Committee hired network commentators in October 2004, and this group made its debut in the media and was known by the public.

On January 23, 2007, the then Chinese President Hu Jintao requested "to strengthen the work of propagating public opinion and the building of an ideological and cultural front" in the 38th collective study of the Central Political Bureau. The General Office of the CPC Central Committee and General Office of the State Council issued a document to request each and every big website and the local governments in China to publish the speech by Hu Jintao, and select "comrades who are highly politically reliable" to each form "a team of network commentators."

5.2 NETWORK WATER ARMY

5.2.1 Concept of Network Water Army

5.2.1.1 Network Shuijun: *A New Word and a New Occupation*

Water army, formerly known as navy, was called 舟师 (Pinyin: Zhoushi) in ancient China, while online, it refers to people who make a lot of meaningless replies in network forums. It is a new job derived from network development and is remunerated by relying to hot topics online with meaningless posts. A water army—always hired by network PR companies—creates momentum by opening and replying to new topics, which usually needs to be completed by thousands of individuals together. Those who are hired temporarily from online to open topics are known as "water army." The administrators initiate topics which attract the attention of the most extensive "cybercitizens" before creating a hotspot. All network PR companies hire large groups of people to open and reply to topics for clients. Water army may be full-time or part-time occupation.

Events like "Jia Junpeng, your mum is asking you to go back for dinner," "Xiaoyueyue" who shot to fame like crazy, "3Q" battle, and then Meizu mobile phones being exposed to hype for going listed … were all investigated later and were found to have been manipulated by a group behind the scenes—a network water army. Besides playing publicity stunts on the Internet, some of water armies resort to slander, entrapment or defamation to attack their competitors, fabricate pseudo-events, and confuse the public. Before a hot TV series or movie is launched, a network water army will be invited to either attack or praise it.

A network water army, while playing the marketing role online, has obvious negative impacts. Many unscrupulous members of network water army, supported by agencies and capital abroad with ulterior motives, release and post aggressive information, rumors or provocative language, stir conflicts among cybercitizens, and conduct network cultural penetration in secret.

A network water army has the following characteristics: (1) scattered: network army spreads nationwide, gathers together when there is a task, and is dismissed after the task is completed; (2) uncontrollable: most of the water army are unidentifiable cybercitizens, who communicate with their employers undercover, so they are uncontrollable; (3) flexible: network water army may be selected by task.

5.2.1.2 Communication Mechanism of Network Water Army

Communication of network water army may be divided into the following two stages:

1. *Agenda setting.* New media is open and interactive and has an infinite information capacity that enables anyone to express his/her opinions. However, when some event goes through agenda setting by "network water army," it easily becomes a public topic. Different opinions and views become a strong power of public opinion in the communication and gaming process.

In agenda setting by "network water army," the most commonly seen "significant model" is to constantly insert the same information in the Q&A columns in network forums of big web portals, personal microblogging and mainstream websites like baidu.com to highlight a few questions in order to attract cybercitizens' attention. Their general communication model is starting topics and rumors on a large scale online and having them "topped" in network forums by "network water army" so as to attract the audience's attention.

2. *Information dissemination.* The emergence of new media has subverted traditional media's "gatekeeping" role and position. Through new media, information can be disseminated in multiple ways, responded to in a timely way and highly interactive, so cybercitizens may release, copy and post information like texts, pictures and videos any time, making information dissemination really fast. Information can thus be rolled bigger and bigger like a snowball. Therefore, it is hard to block information communication.

From the users' perspective, in new media, they are both disseminators and receivers who have the right to accept information and express opinions freely, and they are equal in theory. However, under the pressure from "the opinion of the majority," there will be the "spiral of science" effect in the users to some extent, and a "network water army" occupies the main field of public opinion.

5.2.2 Operation of Network Water Army

The network events hyped up by "network water army" roughly have the following forms of expression by type of manipulation and operational model.

5.2.2.1 *Making Topics to Attract Public Attention—The "Jia Junpeng event"*

The "Jia Junpeng event" refers to the phenomenon of a blank post online shooting to fame strangely on July 16, 2009. That day, a blank post—"Jia Junpeng, you mum is asking you to go back for dinner" in Wow Bar of tieba.baidu.com was replied to more than 750,000 times. The title of the post soon became popular online in China, and Jia Junpeng, a character whose real identity was unclear, became hot online, too, and caused many subsequent comments and effects.

At 10:59 a.m., July 16, a cybercitizen whose IP address was "222.94.255.*" opened a topic titled "Jia Junpeng, you mum is asking you to go back for dinner." Three minutes later, "Jia Junpeng" replied that he would not go back home for dinner, but cybercitizens found that the account of "Jia Junpeng" was registered at 11:02, and with a new ID. Jia Junpeng's "relatives and friends" almost all came out. Some cybercitizens took the chance to elaborate their own ideas and re-created it, for example using the sentence in hoax photos, or translating it into different languages, or even fabricating biography for Jia Junpeng. As of 7:48 a.m. the third day after that, if one replied to the topic on computer, he would see a notice that the replies had already reached the upper limit, and the topic had been clicked 7,818,740 times and had 302,259 replies. However, one could still reply to the topic on the phone, so replies to the topic kept rising.

Along with the phenomenon, Jia Junpeng, a disclosed name, shot to fame online. "Go back for dinner" became a new pet phrase online. It was another mystery in tieba.baidu.com. Many businesses discovered the business value of such phenomenon. Some businesses launched T-shirts with this slogan on them, while some embedded it into advertising slogans for the purpose of promoting sales.

After July 30, more and more marketing companies began to "claim" Jia Junpeng in succession. The manager of a Beijing media company claimed in his blog that Jia Junpeng event was solely planned by his company in order to create a momentum for some game (namely World of Warcraft), that the company hired over 800 people for marketing purpose, and that the company made a "six-digit" earning from it.

By creating public topics, replying to the topics and hyping the topics up, a "network water army" makes some character or event popular quickly on the Internet and the focus of discussion by the public, and such a character or event would always become widely influential and very famous. It is because such a character or event meets some characteristic of the present social culture—like being vulgar or ironic or funny or uniquely different—that they attract sympathetic responses to them from the people, and produce a great communication effect.

5.2.2.2 Promotion of Consumer Products—"The Wanglaoji Event"

According to statistics of China International Public Relations Association (CIPRA), the business of network public relations in China made strides in 2010, and most companies were involved in such service field. Of the forty (PR) companies on the list, fourteen (four more over the previous year) saw their network PR business exceeding 10 million yuan and seven saw their network PR business exceeding 30 million yuan.

Enterprises pay PR companies by demand and project. Normally, a PR company gets 60% and the network water army shares the remaining 40% of the payment.

After the Wenchuan earthquake in 2008, Jiaduobao, the producer of Wanglaoji herbal tea, donated a hundred million yuan to the earthquake-ravaged areas. In a few days that followed, almost all major websites and network communities had a report titled *Let Wanglaoji disappear from the shelves in China! Force it out!* The one who posted it said that "force it out" actually meant "buy Wanglaoji out from the supermarket! Drink only Wanglaoji in the future." The big contrast of it stimulated numerous cybercitizens to reply to the topic. A few words, very inciting, were not only crazily re-posted by cybercitizens, but directly agitated cybercitizens' enthusiasm in buying Wanglaoji. Wanglaoji herbal tea was sold out at sales terminals in many cities.

5.2.2.3 Deleting Posts—"Sanlu Milk Powder Event"

The "Sanlu milk powder event" in 2008 was a food safety event in China. It came into the open because many infants were found to have kidney stones after being fed with the milk powder products of Sanlu Group, and then Sanlu milk powder products were discovered to contain melamine, a chemical raw material. The event attracted great attention from other countries and led them to be concerned about the safety of Chinese dairy products. After the General Administration of Quality Supervision, Inspection and Quarantine of the People's Republic of China made public the report on melamine in infant milk powder products that were produced by domestic dairy companies, the event received great publicity; the milk powder products of Yili, Mengniu, Bright Dairy, Synutra and Yshily were all discovered to contain melamine. The event inflicted heavy losses on the reputation of commodities that were made in China. A number of countries began to ban Chinese milk powder products. On September 24, the General Administration of Quality Supervision, Inspection and Quarantine of the People's Republic of China showed that the milk event had been controlled and that melamine was not found in samples of yogurt, pasteurized milk or sterilized milk among other main types of liquid milk that were produced after September 14. In September 2010, many local governments in China gave an ultimatum to milk powder producers—if they turned in problematic milk powder products that were produced in 2008 before September 30, 2010, no punishment would be meted out. In 2011, CCTV *Weekly Quality Report* discovered in its investigation that 70% of the Chinese public did not dare to buy home-made milk powder products.

Where there is negative information unfavorable for the clients and where it has endangered the clients' interests, companies engaged in deleting posts would emerge to play their role. These companies can make posts disappear overnight. Generally speaking, the regular process of deleting posts is: the party involved submits an application to the website's customer service department, along with proofs. After approving the application, the customer service department would notify the person in charge of editing the content involved, and the website editor deletes the posts concerned according to instruction. The normal process of deleting posts is free of charge. However, if searching online, one would find that negative information on some enterprises disappeared overnight, because network-post-deletion companies did something. Besides regular business of deleting posts, a few post-deletion companies would open negative topics online on purpose, and tell the parties concerned in various forms, hinting that money could help solve it. In the "Sanlu milk powder event," the Sanlu Company kept the truth from consumers by deleting negative online posts. In the first few months after the event was exposed, the news that Sanlu milk powder caused kidney calculus in infants, even if appearing online, was soon shielded, even blocked. It was found out later that the Sanlu Company hired network PR companies to help it delete negative information. Thus, poisonous milk powder was able to remain on the market and harm many more infants and delay treatment once and again. Eventually, a national brand collapsed.

5.2.2.4 Repeated Voting Online

Online voting is thought to be a way to best demonstrate public will and a shortcut of public participation. Some contests began to adopt online voting in the hope of listening to cybercitizens' true inner voice with the openness and extensiveness of the network. However, a "network water army" is seen in more and more online voting activities.

In a network water army, there are special "network fighters." After receiving an instruction, tens of thousands of network fighters will use biased, radical and confusing texts against the same topic in network forums or blogs to defame competitors. Some websites—which want to improve their network flow—hire network fighters to leave aggressive messages on websites of the same type, expecting to introduce network traffic to them. Network fighters usually use exaggerated language to abuse and defame the targets. By continuing to open new topics or reply to topics, network fighters create a group effect before finally steering public opinion in society.

5.2.3 Control of Network Water Army

"People's clamor can melt metals, while accumulated defamation wears the bones." The network water army is suspected of manipulating public opinion and kidnapping public will, thus it has jeopardized the society, and will affect normal network order.

The dissemination characteristics of network information have facilitated the emergence of the network water army and made the Internet more bustling, but what's behind the network water army are lies, setups and the kidnapping of public will. From the marketing scheme of "force out" Wanglaoji in 2008 to "cat-abuse woman event" on mop.com to "the frame-up event" of Mengniu Dairy, it is safe to say that network water army has touched the edge of legality and attracted the attention of people in all walks of life and their reflection. How then can the network water army be controlled?

The acts of many members of the network water army are by nature online slanders, and they should be punished in accordance with the law. However, as the size of network water army grows, network slanders become increasingly professional.

First, network slanders became professional. As network PR companies and network marketing companies emerged and became popular, some network PR companies began to descend to "network fighters." They hired large-scale network water armies and, according to customer demands, established QQ groups of network fighters to organize network fighters to either lavish praises on the clients and their products, or defame others. In particular, "agency curse websites" that are built for benefits make network slanders increasingly professional.

Second, network slanders became clustered. The limitlessness and extension of the content of network slanders are based on the limitlessness and extension of network dissemination. The content of network slanders therefore are not confined by time or space, but can extend without limitation, which causes infinite magnification of the harms of the behavior of network slanders. Relative to the act of slander that is conducted with traditional media, the network water army greatly increases the victims of network slanders, and tens of thousands of network water army slander the victims randomly in cyberspace, and that has become one of the most important factors why network slanders have become more and more harmful to society.

The network water army jeopardizes society and affects normal network order, so it arouses dissatisfaction in people and needs to be brought under control. As regards the governance of network water army, some insiders propose to seriously punish websites that trample journalism morality underfoot, connive with web hypers, and provide breeding grounds for web-hypers' activities. For some forms of network dissemination that are easily manipulated by web hypers, timely studies of them need to be made to strengthen supervision. Websites, as providers of spiritual food online, need to strengthen self-discipline within the industry, take initiative actions, make a clear distinction from web hypers, and prevent web hypers from penetrating posts such as network editor and forum moderator.

We hold:

1. The network water army needs to be governed comprehensively. To govern the network water army, we need to make clear that the target is "the water army" and not "the network." Once there is a malignant marketing event, those to be investigated and punished include not only network PR companies but also forum moderators, editors, administrators and network supervisors because they are the objects of "PR."

2. Members of the network water army who are against the law must be punished in accordance with the law. China does not as yet have explicit and comprehensive laws or regulations to govern "network floods" specifically, but there are laws in the pipeline. Relevant laws and regulations can be referred to according to specific situations.

The acts of many members of the network water army are in nature network slanders. Both the "water army" who spreads false information or malicious rumors and PR "hypers" who are behind them need to face the corresponding criminal or civil liabilities. If one slanders or defames his competitors on the Internet, issues false propaganda or maliciously attacks a competitor's products, he may be subject to criminal liabilities according to the Law of the People's Republic of China against Unfair Competition and, if proven guilty, sentenced to a fixed-term imprisonment of five years at most; and enterprises have the right to claim compensation for economic losses. Under circumstances where troubles are stirred up or people are slandered or insulted, the victims may claim compensation for mental trauma. This compensation can reach up to 100,000 yuan.

CHAPTER 6

Blogs and Microblogging

Blogs and microblogging are parts of the social media network and have the characteristics of both group and mass information dissemination.

Blog is a blend word of Web Log. Microblogging or microblog is a form of blog that allows the user to update short entries (usually less than 140 Chinese characters in each entry) in a timely way and release them openly. It allows anyone or any group of people selected by the users to read the entries. Twitter and Sina Weibo are examples of microblogging websites. Unlike a traditional blog, a microblog has a smaller file (e.g., texts, videos or audios) capacity. Many microblogging sites provide short comments at a face-to-face level or news on products and services.

6.1 Blogs

Outside China, the history of blogs dates back to the 1990s. As a new form of online communication, it was much favored by cybercitizens.

Deep in the night of January 17, 1998, the American blogger Drudge was the first to expose the "Clinton-Lewinsky scandal," and it was thought to be the first successful political blog to lead the American political agenda for nearly half a year. It was a precedent in the history of journalism that an individual website set hot social topic for a long time and humiliated the mainstream media.

The "9/11 event" in 2001 was a watershed in the development of blog. It was that terrorist attack that refreshed people's understanding of

W. Kuang, *Social Media in China*, Sociology, Media and Journalism in China, https://doi.org/10.1007/978-981-13-0914-4_6

the fragility of life, the importance of interpersonal communication and the timely and most effective way to convey information. It is safe to say that the realest and most vivid descriptions of the "9/11 event" were in the survivors' blogs instead of *New York Times*, as were the deepest reflections on and discussions about the event.

After those two events, blogs became familiar to more and more people, and its team grew rapidly. Blog attracted extensive attention because it grew stronger day by day, and the mainstream network media began to attract blogs to join them in order to keep in the loop. Enterprises began to introduce blogs into their internal websites and company websites.

Since 2002, Fang Xingdong et al. have begun to vigorously publicize blogs in China. They translated blog into "博客" and established the first large-scale professional blog website in China—"blogchina.com."

6.1.1 The Concept of Blog

"博客" is the transliteration of English word Blogger, while Blog is the abbreviation of Weblog, that is, a blend of Web and Log. Weblog refers to a form of online journal records, shortened as "network journal." Blogger or Weblogger, referring to someone who is accustomed to making daily records and using Weblog, is widely translated into "博客" in Chinese. In fact, "博客" not only refers to someone who uses a Weblog but also the service or tool that provides Weblog. Often, people call the phenomenon of using the tool of Weblog, to establish a weblog website, or keep network journals the phenomenon of blog.

The blog concept is demonstrated by three aspects: frequent updates, being short and precise, and personalized. A more regulated and explicit formal definition is: the contents are aligned in the order of time, usually in the reverse order, that is, the latest is on the top of the page, while the oldest is at the bottom of the page; main contents of the web page are made up of many "posts" that are updated constantly and personalized; and the contents may be on different topics and have different looks and layouts and writing styles, but contents of articles must be expressed mainly in the form of "hyperlink."

6.1.2 Characteristics of a Blog

In real life, people say different words in different fields or scenarios depending on the social environment, their social roles, social statuses and social relations. They are accustomed to speaking and acting with masks, and more often hide their innermost thoughts or express their innermost thoughts only in their private domains.

A blog is different, because it provides a space without restrictions and with the possibility of real individual speeches: that the network is virtual allows individuals to hide their true identities and express their true inner thoughts and feelings without care; the openness of the network allows individuals to disseminate their articles, works and views at any time and to go around the globe in the twinkling of an eye; the interactive nature of the network allows individuals to communicate, exchange ideas and interact with people conveniently.

Blogs have realized personalization in the true sense: they are possessed by individuals, written by individuals, published by individuals and managed by individuals. Individuals may speak and make free comments in their blogs. Blogs meanwhile are open and socialized. As a media tool, a blog indicates that individual space becomes a public domain, and the threshold and restrictions over individuals' entry into the public domain disappear completely. An open blog group should be plural, tolerant and able to accommodate heterogeneity.

To a certain degree, blogs affect network public opinion. In China, the "Sun Zhigang event" was a typical case. In the evening of March 17, 2003, Sun Zhigang, a young man from Hubei Province who was then working for a company in Guangzhou, was caught by the police on his way to an Internet bar for not having a temporary residence permit and then sent to the Guangzhou detention and repatriation transfer center for people "without resident's ID card, temporary residence permit or proof of employment." The following day, Sun Zhigang was sent to a medical treatment center for detained people. There, he was beaten brutally by the staff and the other detained people and died on March 20. It was known as the "Sun Zhigang event." It aroused a big discussion about the detention and repatriation system in China. Later the Chinese government issued a new law to abolish the detention and repatriation system, a system that was widely thought to have disadvantages and loopholes.

Since their emergence abroad, blogs have shown an extraordinary social value. Matt Drudge was thought to be "incorrect and immoral" by the traditional journalism circle when he exposed Clinton's "zippergate event."

In May 1994, Paula Corbin Jones, registrar of the Governor's Quality Conference of Little Rock, sued then US President Clinton for "sexual harassment" of her in a hotel room on May 18, 1991, and claimed a compensation of 700,000 US dollars. On January 23, 1998, Monica Lewinsky, a witness in "Jones' sexual harassment case" and former White House fellow, was charged with having an affair with Clinton. Clinton denied having any relationship with Monica Lewinsky. On January 28 the same year, Janet Reno, the then Attorney General of the United States, authorized independent counsel Kenneth Winston Starr to investigate the relationship between Lewinsky and then US President Clinton. On April 1, Susan Webber Wright, Judge of the United States District Court for the Eastern District of Arkansas, denied all charges made by Jones in the sexual harassment lawsuit, but pointed out that Clinton was not to be exempted from investigation because of immunity for executive officers. On August 17, Clinton made a speech on TV to the country, admitting that he had a relationship with Lewinsky that was "not appropriate," that his relationship with Lewinsky was wrong, and that he was completely responsible for it. But he highlighted, "at no time did I ask anyone to lie, to hide or destroy evidence or to take any other unlawful action." On September 9, independent counsel Starr finished the investigation and submitted to the Congress a 445-page investigation report on the then US President Clinton and 36 boxes of appendixes.

However, in its pursuit of facts and explosion of truths, blogs exhibit extraordinary accountability. In the reports on the Iraqi war, blogs were objective and neutral, and found the principle of neutrality that the mainstream media lost in the war. In 2002, the racism speeches by Senate majority leader Trent Lott were exposed in a blog, causing Lott to resign.

Blog entries can be shared. Knowledge produced in the form of blog is disseminated by co-sharing. Each blog has a fixed URL, and all cybercitizens may read articles in the blog through this URL. It is like an open notebook that enables realization of maximum sharing of personal resources.

Blogs are interactive. Communication in blogs is done by leaving messages. The bloggers and the audience can have real-time interaction and become dialoguers in the true sense. Blogs break through the one-way communication in traditional media. Information releasers may also be receivers. This interaction can stimulate people's desire for active participation and their desire to realize communication in which they may not participate in real life.

Blogs are popular. At the technical level, blogs meet the "four zero" conditions (zero technology, zero costs, zero editing and zero form), and provides the simplest and most practical form to the users. Users can create their blogs just by selecting simple templates.

Blogs are entertaining. Many blogs are created for self-entertainment, not for economic benefit. The pieces of writing in blogs are from the authors' internal impulse, highlight the social attribute of sensibility, and are a way of free writing for experience. Articles in blogs are not limited in terms of genre, or length or quality. Bloggers are meanwhile journalists, editors and publishers. They write and proofread blog entries by themselves.

Blogs are friendly to the grassroots. Behind the openness of the Internet, there is the "elite" grouping, that is, entities made up of hackers, government departments and other technical elite—with their technical knowledge and operational skills—who have control of a specific scope. Blog is a super easy personal web page tool. Becoming a blogger does not require any technical content, any new technology, or registration of any domain name, or renting of server space, or many software tools, or knowledge on making web pages. Blog is a fool-safe tool, and can be used as easily as people can write and draw with paper and pen.

6.1.3 Blog's Influence on News Communication

Western countries see the emergence of a big population of "news bloggers" as amateur journalists. In the development of blog, Clinton's "zippergate event," the "9/11 event" and the "Iraqi war" reported in blogs were of landmark significance. On January 17, 1998, Drudge's blog website became the first to report Clinton's "affair" to the world; after the outbreak of the "9/11 terrorist attack," individual blog sites led by Dave Winer's Scripting News became important sources of information for the public.

The emergence of blogs as a new medium has affected the traditional mode of communication, and the established communication theories, with Kurt Lewin's "gatekeeping" theory one of them.

"Gatekeepers" are staff members inside mass media. Because all the information published by mass media needs to be filtered or screened by them before being made public, they are therefore "gatekeepers" of information dissemination. The "gatekeeping" theory was first put forward by Lewin,[1] an American social psychologist and one of the forerunners in communication studies. In his article *Channels of Group Life* (1947), he put forward the word "gatekeeping" for the first time. A "gatekeeper" may be an individual, like a source of information, journalist or editor, or a media organization.

In communication, "gatekeeping" is a prevailing phenomenon. The concept of "gatekeeping" has been universally acknowledged by mass media scholars, and the role and nature of "gatekeeping" have become important topics of mass communication. Between the disseminators and the audience, "gatekeepers" play a decisive role in continuing or discontinuing information dissemination. "Gatekeepers" may be individuals or collectives. From the perspective of society as a whole, the media is the "gatekeeper" of information circulation in the society; inside the media, different media have different "gatekeepers"; within traditional mass media like newspapers, broadcasting and TV, there are many "gatekeepers" in the process of news information provision, collection, compilation, editing and reporting, of which editing is the most important for the acceptance and rejection of news information.

The gatekeeping behavior of "gatekeepers" may be dredging or suppression. The former refers to the behavior of allowing circulation of news information; the latter refers to the behavior of prohibiting the circulation of some news information or putting it aside temporarily.

The zero technical threshold of blogs allows everyone to participate in news production freely and ad arbitrium. Although blogs can't match the power of mass media, they—as a source of supplements to news information, and re-processors, integrators and interpreters of news information—have increasingly demonstrated their unique value in news production. It allows grassroots blogs to gain large-scale popularity without the limitation of "gatekeepers." Therefore, someone put forward the concept of "citizen journalism."

[1] Kurt Lewin (库尔特·卢因, or 勒温 in Chinese, 1890—1947) was the founder of the gatekeeping theory in communication studies, and a famous social psychologist. His representative work was *Resolving social conflicts*, etc. A German-American Jew, he was born in Vienna on September 9, 1890, and attended famous universities like University of Munich and University of Berlin in succession. He fought in World War I. In 1921, he began to teach in the University of Berlin and established association with gestalt psychology before becoming an active advocator of such school. In 1933, he migrated to the United States and taught in Stanford University, Cornell University and Iowa State University in succession as a social psychologist professor.

The term "citizen journalism" emerged in the United States in the 1990s and expanded along with the arrival of the Web 2.0 era. We may understand it thus: citizens (not professional journalists)—through mass media or individual communication tools—release special and important information they access or grasp to the society at special times or in a special space. Put simply, "citizen journalism" refers to news that is accessed and written completely by "the readers" themselves from news interview, writing to news editing and release, without the help of professional journalists or editors.

"Citizen journalism" is the subversion of traditional news communication. It represents "news media 3.0" (1.0 refers to traditional media or old media; 2.0 refers to new media or trans-media; 3.0 refers to We Media or personal media that is led by the blogging trend). The first citizen journalist in the world probably was the American citizen Drudge who exposed Clinton's "zippergate event" in his personal blog in 1998.

6.1.4 Problems of Blogs

Blogs have brought a series of shocks to traditional ethics: its virtuality weakens the code of ethics, its information pluralism leads to the loss of moral faith, and its anonymity leads to the dissimilation of moral personality. A blog as a way of new media that carries forward personality should aim primarily to show individuals' social values, broaden individuals' knowledge horizons, give full play to the knowledge value of the network, and pursue the health, personality and spirit of the common people. But the weakening, loss and dissimilation of traditional ethics on blogs has become a social problem that should not to be ignored.

From the perspective of news communication, blogs have limits and cannot substitute traditional mainstream media. It deficiencies are demonstrated in the following sub-sections.

6.1.4.1 Blogs Still Need Mainstream Media and the Information Provided by Blogs Needs to be Verified

Although a blog is superior in its timeliness, pluralism and promptness, and even in its professionalism in some fields, it cannot match mainstream media in terms of news literacy. Bloggers just happen to report events around them, and are not conscious journalists in the real sense.

6.1.4.2 *The Audience (Users) Is (Are) Limited*

Despite the rapid growth of blogs, their audience is smaller than that of traditional media, which has developed for dozens of years. Even the most influential blog has a low readership.

All in all, blogs and professional media are mutually complementary.

6.2 Microblogging

Microblogging, the linking of "micro" and "blogging," is a user relationship-based information sharing, dissemination and access platform. Users with short entries (normally with less than 140 Chinese characters in each entry) update information and realize instant information sharing. The earliest and most influential microblogging site is Twitter in the United States. Sina Weibo and Tencent Weibo hold the biggest shares of the Chinese domestic microblogging market. However, microblogging is greatly affected by WeChat.

6.2.1 *Development of Microblogging*

6.2.1.1 *Development of Twitter*

Twitter, an American company established in 2006, was the first company to provide mobile social website and microblogging services.

Twitter ("推特" in Chinese) is a social network and a microblogging server that allows its users to each update up to 140 characters each time. This information is also known as a Tweet ("推文" in Chinese). Twitter is one of the ten most frequently visited websites.

In an English dictionary, Twitter has two meanings: first, "simple, little sudden information"; second, "the light chirping sound made by certain birds," which vividly demonstrates the characteristics of Twitter and endows the product with a beautiful visual image. The success of Twitter is inseparable from its tactical marketing methods.

Figure 6.1 shows a page of Twitter, from which we can see that people communicate more about daily experience on Twitter.

Since its emergence, microblogging has upheld the concept of cross-platform data interaction and communication.

The success of Twitter mostly depends on its open application programming interfaces (APIs). After a website provides APIs of open platforms, it attracts some third-party developers to develop business apps on such platforms, and platform providers will get more traffic and a greater market

Fig. 6.1 A Twitter page

share. Third-party developers don't need huge hardware or technical investment to start an undertaking easily and conveniently and realize the win-win purpose. Third-party apps expand the original functions of Twitter, and make Twitter more user-friendly, thus they greatly enrich the functions and entertaining nature of the Twitter platform. Currently over half of the traffic flow on Twitter comes from third-party APIs (See Fig. 6.2).

As Twitter has released more and more Open APIs, it exposes some problems in the operation process. The enormous visits to Open APIs have caused Twitter performance problems, and greatly reduced the stability of Twitter. As a result of supporting a lot of external APIs, Twitter has frequent crashes and shut-downs—a phenomenon that almost all Twitter users have encountered.

6.2.1.2 Development of Microblogging in China

Fanfou.com was the first website in China to provide a Twitter-like microblogging service. At present, the influential microblogging sites in China were all created under the domination of traditional web portals, and the one that is widely recognized to be the most influential is Sina Weibo.

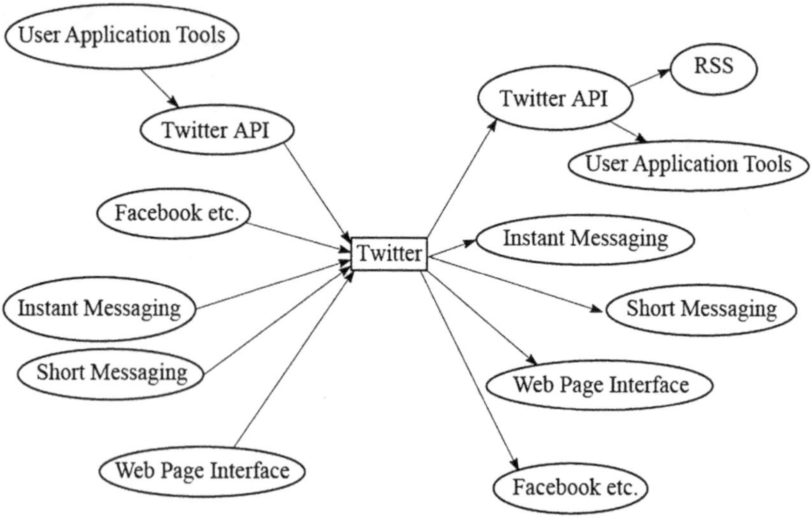

Fig. 6.2 Input and output interfaces supported by Twitter

That fanfou.com was forced to shut down demonstrates that microblogging's content is different from the content generated by users in Internet apps. Although a microblogging entry may contain fewer than 140 Chinese characters, hundreds of millions of cybercitizens together are mighty. All the voices that seem fragmented are enough to have great influence on real public opinion.

Unlike Twitter where, for most of the time, cybercitizens share "new things in life," microblogging, due to the cramped real public opinion environment, has undertaken the heavy task of "network public space" since its emergence. People expect microblogging to go further than past Internet apps in its intervention in public affairs.

The energy of public opinion that burst out after people access information on microblogging sites is tremendous enough to change the progress and direction of public events. Take, for example, the "Guo Meimei event," which started from microblogging when, within a week from June 21, 2011 "郭美美baby" "flaunting wealth in microblogging account" attracted public attention, microblogging entries on "Guo Meimei" on Sina Weibo rose violently to 530,000, and the event was then reported by traditional media before causing a great sensation online and in reality. Although Beijing Municipal Public Security Bureau and Red Cross Society of China denied the rumors, they failed to eliminate the event's real influence: since the "Guo Meimei event," social donations and donations to charity organizations dropped sharply. In July that year, social donations reached 500 million yuan nationwide, dropping by over 50% relative to that in June. The donations received by charity organizations dropped by 86.6% from June to August. The Red Cross Society of China, as a party involved in the event, received 2867 million yuan of donations from the public in 2011, accounting for 3.4% of total national donations, and down 59.39% year on year.

Besides subverting people's way of accessing news and building a new battlefield for people to respond to sudden public events, microblogging becomes a new platform for the construction of a civil society. The non-governmental self-help spirit is carried forward on microblogging sites, and that is exactly the core feature of a civil society.

It is safe to say that microblogging has taken over the network forums' role of as the main front of public opinion, and greatly affected the depth and width of public opinion on the Internet in China.

6.2.2 *Advantages of Microblogging*

Microblogging has a number of advantages, discussed in the following subsections.

6.2.2.1 *Simple and Easy to Use*

The contents of microblogging entries are simple words and sentences, so microblogging has a low threshold of technical requirements on users. Users may use mobile phones or PCs to instantly update their personal information.

6.2.2.2 *Timely*

Microblogging sites have a great instant communication function, and microblogging content can be written directly through QQ and MSN. In places where there is no computer, a mobile phone alone can help the microblogger update his microblogging entries instantly. Some major sudden events or events attracting global attention, if with microbloggers present, may be released via microblogging through different means, in real time, highly efficiently, and give the readers a strong sense of being on the spot. The convenience and multimedia provided by mobile terminals make microblogging users' experience more and more engaging.

6.2.2.3 *Highly Initiative*

When users simply click "Follow," they express their willingness to accept another user's instant information updates, which is of great value to business promotion and the dissemination of the entertainment "star" system, and to maintain interpersonal relationships.

6.2.2.4 *Open and Diversified Platforms for Publication*

Users may use mobile phones, IM software (gtalk, MSN, QQ, Skype) and external API interfaces to release news on microblogging sites.

6.2.3 *Influences of Microblogging on the News Industry*

6.2.3.1 *Microblogging Becomes an Important Source of Information*

Because microblogging supports multi-interface information input and output, especially the combination with mobile phones, it has become an important source of information.

A prominent example is the "Green Revolution" in Iran 2009, in which microblogging played an important role in information dissemination to the level that the movement was also known as the "Twitter revolution."

On July 12, 2009, Mahmoud Ahmadinejad, who ran for re-election, won the presidential campaign. According to the figures of the Election Committee, he won about 62% of the votes and his main opponent Mir-Hossein Mousavi, presidential candidate of the opposition faction and former prime minister, won nearly 34% of the votes.

However, Mousavi believed that the election was seriously fraudulent, and requested a re-run of the election. Early in the morning on June 13, large crowds paraded the streets to protest against the unfair election and the Ahmadinejad administration. Since Mousavi used green as his color in the campaign, most demonstrators were in green or wore green ribbons or scarves, or waved green flags—hence the name "Green Revolution."

The "Green Revolution" was the most serious riot since the Iranian Revolution. Meanwhile, it was characterized by the wide application of microblogging. Since the Iranian government carried out information control to block and expel the media, the Iranian domestic situation was unknown to the outside world immediately, but the Iranian people, with emerging network tools like Twitter, Facebook and YouTube and proxy servers, reported what was actually happening—the demonstrations and government suppression. Many people called it "Twitter revolution."

The Iranian "Green Revolution" is a typical case—in major political events—of accessing news with microblogging under the circumstance where normal ways of interview were hindered.

In some special environments, limited by technical conditions, journalists sometimes can't access information in a timely way. For example, in space exploration, if a journalist intends to interview an astronaut, the journalist will have to overcome many constraints and go through many procedures. Using microblogging to communicate with the astronaut will bring the journalist more firsthand information. In May 2009, astronaut Mike Massimino used Twitter to send the process of repairing and maintaining Hubble Space Telescope back to earth, and it was the first time that Twitter was used in the outer space.

In addition, more and more users released on Twitter the sudden events they personally experienced.

In January 2009, an American Airlines' plane collided with a bird and was forced to land on the Hudson River. Before the media reached the scene, a passenger on a rescue boat shot the scene of passengers being evacuated with the phone and put it on Twitter.

The above cases all illustrate that journalists in the era of new media, if ignoring microblogging, would lose an important information channel, even their competitiveness in the journalism industry in the era of media integration.

6.2.3.2 *To a Certain Degree Microblogging Affects the Development of Major News Events*

In major news events, microblogging is playing a more and more important role, and news workers are advised not to ignore it.

In the 2008 US presidential election, the United States had its first black President in history Barack Obama, who was known to be the first "Internet President." Obama sets great store by the Internet and he himself benefited from the Internet and social media (like Twitter) in the election. His campaign team created a social network to enhance his influence online, and made full use of socialized new media like Twitter, Facebook and YouTube to fully shape Obama's image in the era of Web 2.0, winning him many votes. Obama, a good learner, built a distinct image of himself as a young and refreshing candidate forging ahead through network marketing, bringing him closer to the other voters and making him more likeable and, therefore, competitive.

In the Democratic Party Primaries campaign, Obama attached great importance to the communication function of microblogging. As a matter of fact, his opponent Hillary Clinton also built a personal page on Twitter, but Hillary took Twitter simply as a one-way information publication platform instead of a communication tool.

In November 2016, Donald Trump was surprisingly elected US President. He showed that social media like Facebook and Twitter helped him all the way to the White House. Trump has as many as 15 million followers on Twitter, but Hillary Clinton, his opponent in the Presidential election, has only 11 million. Trump has 14.59 million followers on Facebook, but Hillary only 9.4 million. Each of his tweets and Facebook entries were forwarded between 20,000 to over 200,000 times.

6.2.3.3 Microblogging Is a New Way of Propagating Products by Media Organizations

Being short and precise makes microblogging an important source of real-time news. News agencies begin to use microblogging to send links to major news, release lead stories and short URLs.

News media organizations can also find potential audience with microblogging. In microblogging, if a group of nodes are more intimately and mutually related than they are to the outside, they can be generally called a "community," and such communities usually form as a result of having the same interests. Users may act differently in different communities. For example, in one community, a user may be an active source of information, but in another, he plays the role of information searcher.

With certain technical means, we can realize fixed-point dissemination of news by pinpointing some communities. Through data analysis, we can discover that a group of people communicate frequently among themselves, and keywords in their talks may include work, Xbox, computer and video games. They may be discussing the same interest—video games, while sharing personal feelings and experience through microblogging. News agencies can send the latest news on video games they collect to such group.

6.2.3.4 Network Word-of-Mouth Marketing of Microblogging and the Media Organizations

Word of mouth is people's mouth-to-mouth comments on something. The term "word of mouth" in the academic circle today originated from the science of communication. Since it is widely used in marketing, there is word-of-mouth marketing. Traditional word-of-mouth marketing means that enterprises spread their product information or brands through the consumers' communication with their relatives and friends. Many entrepreneurs discover that products with a good word of mouth will have a greater profit value. The most important characteristic of word-of-mouth communication is its high reliability, because generally word-of-mouth communication happens in groups of intimate relations like friends, relatives, colleagues and students. Prior to word-of-mouth communication, they have established a long-term stable relationship. Relative to pure advertising, promotion, PR, business recommendation, or recommendations of outsiders, word-of-month communication is even more reliable. In China, the Qingdiandian PR Company holds that word-of-mouth marketing is a means of propaganda with the power of public opinion. Insiders call word-of-mouth marketing "viral marketing." Marketer Ao Chunhua believes that it is because word-of-mouth marketing is highly influential. More and more marketers begin to study and use social media (e.g., microblogging, SNS-based word-of-mouth marketing).

In fierce intertype competition, to maintain a superior position or to survive, an enterprise must rely on and present a favorable enterprise image. Microblogging, as an important way of communication of network word of mouth, plays a role that should not be overlooked in the erection and maintenance of corporate images.

6.2.3.5 Application of Microblogging in Media Organizations

Microblogging is expected to become a new communication medium within organizations. In the past few years, with the development of telecommuting, communication inside organizations turns from traditional face-to-face communication to online network communication which relies more and more on emails and instant messaging. As the work pressure brought about by flat corporate governance and downsizing grows, email or instant messaging, although being convenient, may obstruct work. That explains why some companies explicitly ban their employees from using instant messaging tools during work hours.

As more and more users make public their recent situation through microblogging, microblogging may become an informal channel of communication among employees within media organizations to meet the members' information demand and social interaction and emotional demands. In terms of meeting their information demand, members of the media organization may share useful opportunity information, exchange their experience in career development, and jointly build and maintain their common interest foundation. In terms of meeting their emotional demand, microblogging enables them to share life experience by displaying their colorful life off work, and therefore becomes an emotional bond of the public inside the media organizations.

6.2.4 Microblogging and the Public Sphere

After the Internet entered the Web 2.0 era, the discussion of "whether the Internet can build China's public sphere" has become hotter. Especially when the real space for public opinion is restrained, people stake the hope of building the public sphere on the Internet. After microblogging appears as a new battlefield of network public opinion, similar judgments come out one after another.

After being put forward by the famous scholar Jürgen Habermas, "public sphere" became a hot term in social sciences. According to Habermas, the so-called "public sphere" refers to the time and space between citizens' private interests in daily life and the field of national rights, a discursive space where individuals can come together to freely discuss matters of mutual interests and, where possible, to reach a common judgment about them, and organize protests against assertive and oppressive forms of national and public power so as to protect overall interests and public welfare.

Chadwick pointed out that to build a public sphere, at least six conditions needed to be met: (1) autonomy after getting rid of national and economic power; (2) reasoning instead of assertion; (3) reflexivity; (4) ideal role play; (5) sincerity; (6) integration and equality without strata.

According to the conditions set by Chadwick, we now take the most representative Sina Weibo as an example to observe whether microblogging meets the conditions for building a public sphere. It not only helps us see the relationship between microblogging and the public sphere clearly, but helps us see the advantages and disadvantages of microblogging as a carrier of network public opinion.

Microblogging, as a carrier of public opinion, does not have any restrictive threshold, and cybercitizens are highly arbitrary in releasing information on the microblogging platform. This lack of a restrictive threshold also leads to the phenomenon of rampant restricted contents like rumors, violence and pornography on the microblogging platform. It makes public opinion on microblogging sites neither rational nor legal, and easily causes social problems like inducing crimes and corrupting minors.

In the Internet apps that have already emerged, microblogging is defined the most closely to public sphere. But after we observe it, we see that microblogging has not yet finished the journey of building a public sphere, which on the one hand is limited by the general domestic social environment and on the other, by the unfinished state of microblogging as a carrier of public opinion. Microblogging remains a "public sphere not yet finished," and completing the building of the network public sphere waits for the next-generation Internet products.

6.2.5 *Microblogging and Information Cocoons*

"Information cocoon" refers to the phenomenon that people will habitually be guided by their interests in the information field and then confine their life in silkworm cocoon-like "cocoons." Given that information technology provides even greater personal space of thinking and tremendous knowledge of any field, some people may possibly escape social contradictions further and become secluded isolators. Although communication in communities is even more efficient, communication among communities may not be as smooth and effective as it was in the era of information deficiency.

In the Internet era, as network technology develops and network information leaps, we can select topics of our concern from massive information at will, or customize papers and magazines totally as we like. It is possible for people to customize a "personal daily" for themselves. Such "personal daily"-type information selection will lead to the formation of information cocoons. When people are confined to a self-built information cocoon for long, their lives will be formularized or routinized. Exposed to excessive independent selection for long, they would become immersed in the contentment of their "personal daily" and lose the ability and opportunities to understand and contact different things and build an information cocoon before realizing it. To Sunstein, beneath the surface that the network information era brings more information and choices to people and seems to be more democratic and free, it contained the destruction of democracy. From the personal token of information cocoons, we can discover that information cocoons are demonstrated in the form of the "personal daily."

Microblogging filters the information, and may possibly cause microblogging users to split apart into smaller and smaller interest groups that do not have any common grounds with the other parts of society. Therefore, some researchers hold that microblogging exacerbates the "information cocoon" effect. But others hold that real-time updates of topics in microblogging open a window for people to pay attention to the external society, so it will alleviate the "information cocoon" effect.

6.2.6 *Calm Thinking of Microblogging*

As a new form of media after blog, microblogging has attracted wide attention from the academic circle and insiders. The academic circle holds a positive attitude to the phenomenon of "microblogging fever," even lavishes its praises on it. Some think that it brings a golden time of the Web 3.0 era to people; some think that the emergence of microblogging is a great leapfrog of the development of new media, a timely interaction that did not happen in the Web 2.0 era of microblogging and blog.

We believe that the social significance of microblogging is to advance social democratization, promote enterprise marketing and help build a civil society. However, microblogging is a double-edged sword. We retrieved all the academic papers on microblogging, only to find none that had gone deeper in comprehensively analyzing the problems of microblogging. We discover in our study that microblogging has passed through its development climax and the following disadvantages are restraining its development.

6.2.6.1 *Information Release Is Highly Arbitrary, and Information Truthfulness Cannot Be Guaranteed*

On microblogging sites, there is no "gatekeeping" role for information dissemination. Information on microblogging sites is not verified, and cybercitizens may release information arbitrarily on microblogging sites, so the truthfulness of information is unknown. A series of "microblogging events" in recent years like the "Guo Meimei event" have further cast into high relief the problem that information on microblogging sites is less reliable.

For voices and opinions that are expressed by individuals on microblogging sites, they may or may not be true. While expressing themselves, microblogging users are faced with the risk of moral disorder with their speeches. Microblogging further hastens the public desire to write and to express, but such writing is fragmented and segmented, and the contents are plural, fragmented and without titles. Texts are short, each just a few Chinese characters. Information on microblogging sites—released by the users themselves—is secret and open. Such information, which is neither verified nor screened, may even cause social panics and disturb the social order.

Microblogging users may release information through microblogging in an environment that is full of uncertainties and arbitrariness, so they may not deliberate it too much. What's more, microblogging sites do not have too many restrictions or requirements on microblogging users' information release, users' expression will become even more arbitrary, and frequently lack control.

The prevalence and wide spread of rumors on microblogging sites deeply hinder microblogging's role as an impartial recorder of the era. It means that to look for valuable news clues on microblogging sites is like looking for a needle in the ocean, and even if valuable news is found in numerous and jumbled and disordered information, it may not be true. It makes the information with fragmented content on microblogging sites even more fragmented.

There exist a considerable population of "zombie followers," which causes a crisis of cybercitizens' confidence in microblogging sites or channels and well-known microbloggers. According to a report of *Beijing Daily*, a cybercitizen selected ten celebrities on Sina Weibo as statistical objects, only to discover that about 17% of their followers were "zombie followers," of which Li Kaifu had nearly a million "zombie followers."[2] "Zombie followers" refer to users who are extremely inactive, and are mostly microblogging accounts registered for the purpose of increasing the population of followers or producing garbage microblogging entries. Three conditions may be used to define "zombie followers:" being revoked users, having less than five followers, or having less than five microblogging entries. Meeting any of the above three conditions make a "zombie follower."

6.2.6.2 *Microblogging Is User-Friendly for the Grassroots and Is by Nature an Entertaining Platform*

Given that each microblogging entry is limited to fewer than 140 characters, information dissemination will be fragmented. On the one hand, each microblogging entry is of a limited length, but in total, there is a tremendous amount of information on microblogging sites, presenting a sharp conflict between both. The conflict makes microblogging user-friendly for

[2] Refer to *Beijing Daily*, May 27, 2011.

the grassroots and entertaining. On microblogging sites, the limit of 140 characters of each entry lifts ordinary people to the same level as Shakespeare.

The most visited microblogging entries are written by entertainment stars, so microblogging is actually an entertainment-based platform. For example, Yao Chen's microblogging entries once ranked the third around the globe, and the first in Chinese microblogging accounts. If some not-yet-verified events are forwarded blindly by cybercitizens, they could easily mislead society and create microblogging users' collective view of the entertainment of public events.

Microblogging has become a "micro world" of the entertainment circle. Many microblogging entries pay too much attention to personal privacy, and even purposefully expose it, especially personal privacy of actors and actresses. As a private medium for public information dissemination, subtle personal affairs, especially celebrities' personal life or emotions may be exposed by microblogging users.

6.2.6.3 Microblogging Has Become a Tool for Commercial Speculation

It has become the norm on microblogging sites to promote popularity by speculation and fabricate false business news.

As a way of network communication, microblogging is different from traditional network marketing in that it reflects the plural ways of communication between companies and customers, and increases the possibility of mutual understanding between companies and customer groups. Since microblogging applies an anonymous login system, microblogging information is in a state of real-time updates, and it is hard to verify the truthfulness of microblogging information, microblogging sites finally become a manufacturing factory and a source of dissemination of false information. In the tremendous amount of information that is refreshed second by second on the network platform, it is unavoidable that some people with ulterior motives will intentionally distort facts.

Microblogging marketing has many defects. First, there must be enough followers to ensure the dissemination effect because popularity is the cornerstone of microblogging marketing. Second, microblogging content is updated all the time, so if the information released fails to attract the followers' attention in a timely way, it may be missed in tremendous flow of information. Finally, a microblogging entry usually has dozens of Chinese characters and limited communication power. Therefore, microblogging entries are disseminated only on the microblogging platform, and it is difficult for them to be forwarded greatly like blog articles. Therefore, microblogging marketing takes another road—speculation. Only by commercial speculation can microblogging realize the marketing purpose.

6.2.6.4 Microblogging Easily Causes Social Instability

Microblogging users can access information and update microblogging entries. Given information releasers' ideological inclination and possible errors of information that they access, microblogging—the public opinion pioneer—may very possibly disseminate a lot of inaccurate information, even false information while releasing correct information. Some microblogging users, for greater benefits, create rumors and troubles and arouse cybercitizens under the banners of justice. They even try to attract cybercitizen participation or tempt to rope in the minors by spreading pornographic, gambling and drug news, fabricating false news, disclosing privacy, and publishing games that are unhealthy for the brain in order to promote the communication power of their microblogging. Meanwhile the dissemination of rumors via microblogging cannot be put under timely and correct legal monitoring or social supervision. That microblogging is anonymous and open makes information asymmetry more serious in it than in traditional media, and conceals its lack of responsibilities.

The microblogging-based fast sharing and dissemination functions create convenient conditions for viral information dissemination. It is also because of such characteristics that microblogging becomes the source and distributing center of false news. Microblogging dissemination is a process in which both sides of communication constantly construct and deconstruct discourse texts. In the dissemination process, the sources of information are blurred. In the case of a sensitive event, cybercitizens usually do not have enough critical power, which may possibly contribute to the dissemination of rumors. Once the dissemination of rumors gets out of control, the consequences will be unpredictable.

In the election riot in Iran in 2009 and "the Jasmine Revolution" in 2011, Twitter played a significant role. Despite there being a number of reasons behind "the Jasmine Revolution," the primary reasons are government graft and economic crisis. However, an important characteristic of "the Jasmine Revolution" is that new media, led by the Internet, played a decisive role. Technological progresses often play a catalyst role in political events. When the network became the hero of that revolution, people were easily reminded of the audio tapes in early Iranian Islamic Revolution and Twitter and mobile phone media in the election riot in Iran.

Many people attribute the outbreak of "the Jasmine Revolution" in Tunisia and Egypt to the Internet, especially to new media and citizen media like Facebook and Twitter. New media was an important tool to gather the protesting forces in the revolution in Egypt. It effectively amplified the power and voices of the opposition faction and spread the riot around Egypt. Although Mubarak later took extreme measures, blocked Facebook and Twitter in Egypt immediately, and cut the nation's access to the Internet and mobile communication, it was too late like what had happened in Tunisia.

6.2.6.5 It Lacks an Effective Profit Model

At present, all microblogging sites in the world are in the red if accounted independently. Although Twitter user numbers grow at a surprisingly fast speed, Twitter made only 45 million US dollars in 2010, being in a state of loss. It makes money primarily from opening instant information for search engines like Google or Microsoft's Bing site to do instant information retrieval.

Chinese domestic microblogging sites now make money mainly by "no charge + ads marketing," that is, they are free of charge for the cybercitizens and collect marketing fees from enterprises. Also, some microblogging sites get benefits from winning more followers, forwarding microblogging entries, commenting and hyping topics up. For microblogging sites, authentication is a way to attract more attention. Some microblogging sites' authentication channels are not yet clear enough, so many people pay for authentication service at a price that ranges from dozens to hundreds of yuan and complete the authentication through "inside" connections. Nevertheless, the microblogging sites or microblogging channels in China are all currently trading at a loss.

Not having a clear profit model is a bottleneck against the development of microblogging in China. Microblogging also lacks an entry as a marketing platform. Despite the great ideas about the grassroots making money with microblogging, of all the microblogging sites, none is making money and most are still in the era of staking out their turf. On the one hand, microblogging is scattered, and microbloggers' interfaces are diversified and information there is highly fragmented, and microblogging sets higher requirements on marketing and propagation skills. On the other hand, microblogging information is less reliable. All these make it hard for the advertisers on microblogging sites to attract lasting attention, and it is very difficult to get money from providing information, because customers hardly get relatively attractive service experience from microblogging.

6.2.6.6 Management Plight

It is really hard to manage microblogging effectively because microblogging user numbers and information are very large and without national boundaries. Faced with the risky environment brought about by microblogging, the microblogging sites in China, in order to reduce risks, may focus on speeding up the shaping of the morality of microblogging users so as to effectively deal with global risks and the risks of institutional transition. Specifically, the priority is to strengthen microblogging users' media-literacy education. In the transitional period, if microblogging users are incapable of differentiating information, it will inevitably lead to information dissemination that is inconsistent with the facts and exaggeration even disorderliness of the entire social transition, making it a fuse for all possible social risks. To enhance the capability of microblogging governance, it is necessary not only to reform the microblogging governance structure and improve the level of supervision of microblogging by government or civil society but also to adjust the relationship between the government and microblogging and civil society and make it cooperative, complementary and benignly interactive.

Technical monitoring is also an important means to curb pornographic and fraud information. However, China has not yet introduced laws or regulations on microblogging, so the Chinese governments or competent law enforcement departments do not have any law to follow in the face of specific microblogging issues. However, there are heated disputes in theory and in practice as to whether it is necessary to develop microblogging laws and whether it would be effective to supervise microblogging through legislation.

Microblogging users, the population of followers and microblogging information are tremendous, so it is difficult to apply a real-name system in microblogging management. Besides, the Internet does not have any national boundaries, so monitoring microblogging is a thorny problem faced by the governments of many countries.

New regulations on a "microblogging real-name system" in China were put into effect by Beijing on December 16, 2011. The advantages of microblogging real-name system are: it provides a better environment for communication and makes cybercitizens more responsible for what they say; and it restricts websites or commercial companies from opening false microblogging accounts and produce "zombie followers" to seek popularity and gains by cheating for forwarding advertisements. But many believe that it will affect microblogging's function to supervise public opinion, and that "microblogging real-name system" may not be operable.

All in all, microblogging has already passed its development peak. According to the S curve of the diffusion of innovations theory that was put forward by Rogers, microblogging has passed the four stages of awareness, persuasion, decision-making and determination, and is at the declining stage.

6.3 Analysis of Microblogging Public Opinion

We call the new media public opinion that is formed and disseminated on microblogging sites "microblogging public opinion." In recent years, the most iconic event in the development of the Internet in China is that microblogging developed fast into the most attended network communication platform on the Internet. Microblogging, as an emerging technical platform for social communication and contact, has characteristics that are distinctively different from the past communication tools and platforms. As an emerging We Media platform, microblogging has attracted a big population of followers. With its advantages, for example, being instant, user-friendly to the grassroots, zero-access restriction, high interactivity, weak control and fission-style mode of dissemination, microblogging has gradually become cybercitizens' first choice to obtain information and express their opinions.

The most typical event would be the "July 23 bullet trains rear-end collision." Within a week, discussions on the event had reached over 300 million entries, in Sina Weibo and Tencent Weibo, respectively, and in total there were nearly 700 million information entries, posing an enormous public opinion pressure on the government.

After the event, the Ministry of Railways was doubted by people in all walks of life on such issues as whether the search and rescue ended too soon, whether it was way too fast to reopen the bullet trains to traffic, whether the locomotive was buried soon after it fell down, whether the government manipulated the media and the judicial system, and whether it was true that the earlier an agreement was signed, the more the compensation would be.

Microblogging is a special form of network media, in which network public opinion plays an important role. Therefore microblogging public opinion is a special form of network public opinion. Microblogging, with its technical advantages, plays a fueling role in the development of network public opinion and exaggerates the influence of network public opinion.

People use microblogging to meet different needs and purposes. Microblogging users form big and small communication circles mainly by "Follow." Each microblogging user has his interested objects to follow and is the object that's followed by others. Therefore, they are in the center of their own social circles, as well as a part of other people's social circles. In each social circle, the main activities are the same: releasing information, commenting and forwarding news. When people expose major news or sensitive information through microblogging, it immediately attracts other users in the same social circle to gather and comment and spread the information or news to their respective social circles. This explains microblogging's fission-type mode of dissemination. The process keeps repeating so that the news or information is spread rapidly. As participants constantly grow, the event would generally escalate into a sudden event on microblogging sites and become the center of attention. People comment on the event, and express their emotions, opinions and attitudes, and microblogging public opinion is thus formed.

6.3.1 Characteristics of Microblogging Public Opinion

6.3.1.1 Microblogging Public Opinion Is Formed Very Quickly

Public opinion dissemination is instant. As Internet technology develops and matures and mobile client businesses become popular, microblogging users may release and receive information anytime anywhere through the Internet, mobile phone, QQ and other instant chatting tools. The Internet and wireless terminals together ensure that users can always maintain a mobile online state. The low-threshold writing of fewer than 140 Chinese characters suits the general public more. Users do not need to make complicated creations or compilations, but just release details of their daily life.

Such function of instant information release breaks the situation that traditional blogging is limited by communication tools, layout and the literary expression ability, and advances the communication process of social events. Microblogging, in the form of "Follow" and "comments plus forwarding," builds the "bond" of the world and establishes for people an instant three-dimensional communication system with infinite connections.

The development of microblogging public opinion is fast and hard to control, posing challenges to the ability of governments—at all levels—to handle crises. Cybercitizens often broadcast live sudden events, like the "July 23 bullet trains collision event," through the platform of microblogging.

During the production and dissemination of microblogging public opinion, the disseminators and the audience, as the principal part, break the mode of communication of traditional media and shift it from the original one-way dissemination, to two-way dissemination to the present interactive dissemination. It is the cybercitizens who dominate the generation and dissemination of opinions. The dissemination groups that are organized by them independently gather many sources of news, dissemination channels and the audience, and become orderly media societies regulated by some mechanism. The agendas set by the cybercitizens are increasingly influential, too.

Microblogging is the object of public opinion dissemination. Microblogging public opinion is the integration of decentralized information flows in the generation and dissemination process, and even sees new differentiation or transformation and decline. The evolution of microblogging public opinion may be summed up into five stages "personal opinions—leaders' expression of opinion—integration and differentiation—expert guidance—differentiation and declining."

Microblogging dissemination is fast and its effect is fission-like. It breaks the linear news dissemination of traditional media and the networking news dissemination of network media, and forms a dissemination structure that combines chain-, ring- and tree-shaped communication structures. For its unique "information aggregation—critical point—information fission" form of information dissemination, after an entry is released, there are always many penetrating points and types of information. Such fission-like dissemination is unexpectedly fast and extensive.

6.3.1.2 Autonomy of Agenda Setting of Microblogging Public Opinion

In 1968, two researchers, Maxwell McCombs and Donald Shaw from North Carolina, investigated and analyzed the constituent influence of media reports on the 1968 US presidential election, and published an essay—*The Agenda-setting Function of Mass Media*—in *The Public Opinion Quarterly* in 1972. As a summary, they put forward the "agenda setting" theory for the first time, that is, the public get to know an event or problem through the media, and adjust their opinions on the importance of this event or problem according to the degree of media emphasis of the event or problem. In other words, the degree of emphasis that is placed by the media on something is in direct proportion to the degree of emphasis that is placed on the same thing by the public.

Microblogging dissemination can set an agenda autonomously. The "gatekeeping" role is weakened to the ultimate degree in microblogging, so microblogging public opinion is expressed more freely.

Microblogging public opinion is highly interactive. It completely breaks the "professionalism barrier" of traditional media and, while directly digging new topics for discussion, "scrambles" some agenda setting right from traditional media. Many news events demonstrate the trend.

The setting of agendas by microblogging is in fact different subjects' interpretation and dissemination of the core views on topics. The agenda-setting subjects develop from unitary to plural, and topics for discussion develop from top-down to parallel and intertwining. In the process of agenda setting, "the jungle rule" is demonstrated. After focal events or speeches take shape spontaneously, the media's "gatekeeping" role is filtered and users' opinions clash and get mutually integrated when forwarded and commented. Profound opinions will be placed high on the structural atlas of microblogging dissemination in such forms as being commented or discussed in depth. Opinions that are not accepted by the other disseminators will die out or be neglected in competition. It is like trees in a jungle—there will always be a tree that is the tallest and strongest and capable of absorbing sunshine, and trees that die for failing to get sunshine.

The so-called "law of the jungle" refers to the law in the natural world—natural selection, survival of the fittest and "eat or be eaten" in biological science. It has two basic attributes: natural attribute and social attribute. Its natural attribute is affected by the natural world, not humanity or social factors. The resources in the natural world are limited, and only the stronger get more. Plants generally demonstrate natural attribute, while animals demonstrate social attribute. Human beings, as higher animals, can change the natural attribute of the law of the jungle. It is also the law of survival to be followed in human society. The competition among countries, regimes, enterprises and people is all governed by the law of the jungle. As regards the competition result, it depends on their respective strengths, wisdom, means and ability to transform the world.

After an opinion is expressed on microblogging sites, the threads posted by some cybercitizens—as event participants, witnesses or informants—to expose social phenomena and dig social problems frequently become the sources of network public opinion. Topics that attract cybercitizens with the same interest facilitate mutual communication and improvement of such cybercitizens and help them develop the sense of a collective. Gradually, such topics become important to cybercitizens and, after being forwarded or commented, form a two-step or multi-step flow of information, and also cause cross flows of information.

The self-selection mechanism of microblogging public opinion plays an important role in the process of agenda selection. It can promote topics that are closely related to people's livelihood to the level of social concern at the first time, and hold domination over the selection of agendas. Microblogging is becoming a major channel for the public to release information, express opinions, comment on current political issues, and release emotions, and microblogging is having an increasingly significant influence on agenda setting by traditional media and the public.

However, the communication advantages of microblogging present new challenges for the management of microblogging. Microblogging is filled with a great deal of false information which the administrators are unable to distinguish, let alone eliminate. Microblogging may therefore easily become a tool for some people with ulterior motives to spread rumors, speculate maliciously and disturb the social order.

6.3.1.3 Microblogging Public Opinion Is Grassroots and Extensive

Microblogging is for the grassroots, which can be seen from three angles: first, the registration of a microblogging account is simple, and can be completed with an email box; second, microblogging is easy to learn and use, even for people who do not have fundamental knowledge of the Internet; third, information released through microblogging is short and vigorous, but has enormous influence. Public opinion in the past was only official or from the minority, but in the days to come, people can participate in the publication and supervision of public opinion more democratically through free, equal, real-time and interactive information dissemination on microblogging sites, and can access different versions and opinions that are completely contradictory or overlap in a more convenient and faster way. They access truth more conveniently, even create a public opinion momentum, lead the direction of public opinion, and participate in final decision making.

Opinions on microblogging are from common people, and microblogging entries mostly demonstrate people's daily behavioral norms and involve all life aspects. The huge information flow conforms to the logical structure of human nature—it not only includes current news events and information that concerns the cybercitizen, but also demonstrates people's feelings and views and individuals' state of existence. Through microblogging, the disseminators see ordinary people of flesh and blood and full of emotions. That's why microblogging content is disseminated to an even wider scope. As a result of this, plus the influence of people's independent feelings, public opinion supervision becomes more humanistic. The value of microblogging entries determines the depth and width of information dissemination. Supervision of social injustice and inequality becomes more and more valuable in public-opinion dissemination.

As shown by We Media, microblogging endows grassroots groups with a brand-new discourse right. While public affairs are disseminated through microblogging, in the process of being surrounded by onlookers on the Internet and the progress of public opinion, "opinion leaders" have new characteristics.

Microblogging public opinion has a decentralized characteristic. Microblogging communication blurs the boundary of information disseminators and information receivers, stimulates the general public's desire to create and express themselves, and turns the public from "onlookers" into "parties involved" and forms the pattern of "everyone is the media."

Decentralization is a form of socialized relations and a form of content generation in the development of the Internet, and a new-type process of producing network content relative to "centralization."

Relative to the early Web 1.0 era, content in the Web 2.0 era, represented by microblogging, is no longer produced by professional websites or specific groups of people, but is a result of equal participation by all cybercitizens with equal power status. Anyone may express their opinions or content they originally create online to produce information together.

After the rise of Web 2.0, the services provided by network service suppliers Wikipedia, Flickr and Blogger are all decentralized—any participator may submit contents, and cybercitizens make collaborative creation or contribution on the content and produce for or contribute to the Internet content in a simpler and more plural way, which encourages cybercitizens' participation and contribution and reduces the threshold of production of content. Eventually every cybercitizen will become a small and independent information supplier, and the Internet becomes even flatter and the production of content on the Internet even more plural.

The uniqueness of microblogging and the advantages of focused communication on the one hand tally with the information-based fast-tempo way of life in modern society and saved time cost, while on the other, affect information disseminators' mode of communication and acceptance habit, even the entire way of life in society and the tide of the method of interpersonal communication. The concept of equality has been further enhanced in information dissemination via microblogging blogs. As long as attracting enough attention, anyone may become the center of attraction. Unlike traditional mass media which is serious and authoritative, microblogging is liked because it is decentralized. Microblogging provides a platform for equal communication. It breaks authority, encourages innovation and publicizes personality. To a certain degree, it fills the dissemination blanks of mass media, reduces the cost and threshold of dissemination, reduces the discourse right of the elite class, and demonstrates its appeal to the grassroots and the common people.

From the perspective of psychology, the so-called attention refers to the direction to and centralization on certain targets by humans in psychological activities or in ideology. The basic function of attention is to select information. Faced with a great deal of information, people, to work and live normally, must select important information and exclude useless information. In this process, their motives, demands, emotions and feelings will all play a very important role. When the disseminated contents can meet people's motives and demands and give them pleasing psychological and physical experience, people will point to such content and centralize their attention to them. Given that individuals have different motives and demands, focus communication becomes necessary.

Microblogging public opinion is fragmented and plural. The biggest difference between microblogging and blog is its being "micro." Although information is condensed in microblogging entries, the quantity of information is increased, which contributes to the pluralism and fragmentation of information. In microblogging, information spreads rapidly and widely, and potential public opinion supervision topics ferment quickly. A seemingly ordinary microblogging entry may become the focus that's supervised by public opinion in a short time.

The word "fragmentation" vividly describes the dissemination context in the Chinese society at present. The so-called "fragmentation" originally means something whole is broken into pieces. Many understand "fragmentation" as "pluralism," while fragmentation in communication nature is the fragmentation of the whole society or a demonstration of pluralism.

6.3.1.4 Opinion Leaders in Microblogging Public Opinion and the Dandelion Effect

Although information on microblogging sites is fragmented, and on the surface opinion leaders' voices are easily covered by tremendous information and users disseminate information in a relatively relaxing and scattered environment, it does not mean that microblogging information is useless to the occurrence and development of an event.

On the contrary, in the environment of information dissemination through microblogging, opinion leaders are both authoritative and affectionate, changing the situation of the public looking up at opinion leaders in the traditional environment. Microblogging enhances the assembly and centralization of scattered information. Besides having the characteristics of network media, opinion leaders on microblogging sites also have the "Dandelion Effect" of information dissemination, namely people can all express their opinions and views and become opinion leaders in a hot social event.

The Dandelion Effect explains that a venture company or start-up will not disappear even if it fails, because its talents will spread with the wind like dandelions before falling on proper ground, rooting and sprouting. Information is like a dandelion that is blown—it will spread in different directions, adapt to users' demands and fall on the fittest ground.

Of the entire living nature, humans have the most extensive social connections. In past times, a person's social connections may have included as many as 150 people. However, the development of communication and traffic tools like mobile phones, computers and planes gives people more means and ways of expanding their social connections, and the biggest number of their social connections has now gone far beyond 150 people.

When disseminating information on microblogging sites, users may radiate more audience with the influences of their own chains of social connections. Before the emergence of social media, information dissemination in the past, through traditional media or the Internet, was one-way and took only one step. The connection chains of social media have opened up a convenient channel for interpersonal communication, and a simple "Forward" button helps the users share information with their friends.

The weak connection chains of microblogging give full play to the dandelion effect. Microblogging connection chains are relatively open, and information disseminates along instead of being blocked by the connection chains. Users therefore can easily find information in which they are interested. Meanwhile, equal discourse right and users' characteristic of loving to express themselves turn information A into information A + B after it is forwarded and commented by the users from different angles, even information A + C or completely unexpected information E.

When an opinion leader opens a topic, the topic will spread like dandelion seeds and radiate information to each and every corner in succession so thus enhancing the opinion leader's influence. If some topic meets agreeable soil and interests people, people may choose to comment and forward the topic independently through the forwarding and comment functions. Their followers will see the topic and comments. As long as a topic is sufficiently commented and discussed, the cycle would continue to extend and attract more and more people. The more fertile the soil for the growth of public opinion is, the better the effect will be. Microblogging entries that are forwarded will form a fission-type dissemination process to disseminate the topic to the maximum degree, and the information and views expressed by the person who first releases the topic will be forwarded to every corner of the world and promote the opinion leader's influence. If a topic, after being forwarded, fails to meet agreeable soil, that is, it fails to attract the attention of the opinion leader's followers other users, it will be buried in the enormous information on the network and die out.

Dai Lina holds that microblogging opinion leaders in China now are made up of the following several types of people: first, scholars and freelancers led by Lang Xianping, Yu Jianrong, Li Chengpeng, Fang Zhouzi and Zhang Ming, who have insightful opinions and are critical, and are highly recognized by their followers; second, entrepreneurs led by Jack Ma and Li Kaifu, who are highly active, but do not have significant influence in specific events, and whose topics usually do not involve politics and other sensitive fields; third, people in the media led by Rui Chenggang and Luqiu Luwei, who pay close attention to public topics in the society and have a sustainable will to participate; fourth, movie. TV and sports stars led by Yao Chen and Cai Yongkang, who, in a huge population, have a huge population of followers, and intervene less in public topics; fifth, right-safeguarding lawyers led by Xu Zhiyong and Si Weijiang, who together with the parties to some public events disseminate public appeals like right protection in the form of network public opinion, and greatly strengthen the vitality of right-safeguarding actions.[3]

Dai Lina combines the specific functions of Sina Weibo with social network analysis (SNA) to build an indicators system for identifying opinion leaders (see Fig. 6.3).

[3] Refer to Dai Lina: A study of the method of identifying microblogging public opinion leaders and the management strategy, *Shanghai Journalism Review*, 2012(9).

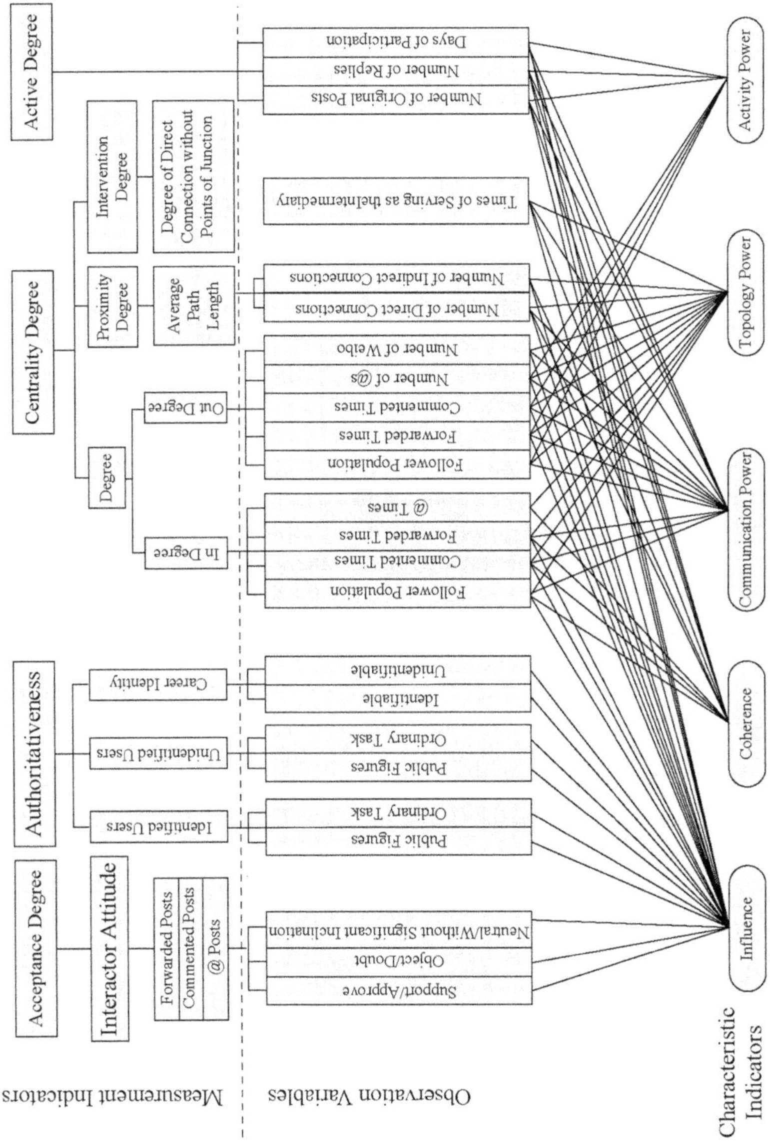

Fig. 6.3 (Sina) microblogging opinion leaders judgment indicators system

6.3.1.5 *Co-existence of Rationality and Irrationality in Microblogging Public Opinion*

Rationality refers to the trait of a man having confidence and courage, being able to keep calm in the normal mental state and being capable of comprehensive understanding and summarization and rapid analyses before properly applying one of several plans to handle the situation and then reach the desired effect. Rationality is a behavior that is based on normal mental results (otherwise, it would be irrationality). The significance of rationality is to take responsibility for self-existence and for social missions that go beyond self but are inborn.

Rationality is comparable to sensibility in meaning. It needs one to consider problems according to the development law of things and natural evolution principles, keep calm when processing things, and act based on fact not emotions.

In philosophy, rationality refers to man's ability to apply wisdom. Relative to the concept of sensibility, it usually refers to such a way of thinking that man derives a conclusion by reasoning after prudent thinking.

However, in real society, humans are a complex of rationality and irrationality. Within human mental attributes, there are rational and irrational factors. Rational factors are basic features specific to humans that distinguish human beings from animals. Humans' rationality develops along with social development. In general, human rationality is absolute. However, despite the fact that humans are conscious rational beings, thinking and rationality are by no means all that humans have. Human refers to the real individuals in social relationships where moral cognizance and moral will are combined. Irrational factors accompany humans. Each human has different irrational characteristics. Therefore, the irrationality of "individuals" is relative.

That humans' characters are a complex of rationality and irrationality is highly significant in microblogging public opinion. In the evolution process, microblogging public opinion easily has such problems as being emotional, inciting, highly destructive, personal and misleading.

Some cybercitizens' comments are far too arbitrary and not civilized enough, and there are even verbal attacks. Such comments hold a high proportion and are too emotional, demonstrating that some cybercitizens are emotional and irrational when thinking.

Cybercitizens have an increasingly bigger discourse right in the media. It is getting clearer that cybercitizens cause network vortexes, which then attract the attention of traditional media and affect government departments' day-to-day work. Some cybercitizens have elite consciousness, but a grassroots stance, and become important participants of such behavior. Many of their remarks are influential and capable of guiding public opinion views in the later stage. Of course, it is highly inciting, and many rumors cause enormous damage to the society exactly because of incitement.

Microblogging is a platform where a lot of users release information. Traditional news media is limited in number and has relatively centralized objects and content to study and judge. Microblogging has a big population of users, and public opinion supervision by well-known microblogging users will become hotspots, and some little known "grassroots figures" have the opportunity to accomplish a lot in microblogging public opinion supervision. For example, after the Beijing–Shanghai high-speed rail was introduced, many of its passengers released news of its failures on microblogging sites, and such microblogging entries, after being forwarded extensively, caused a great sensation on the microblogging platform, even became news clues for traditional news media and attracted the latter's attention.

6.3.1.6 Public Opinion Dissemination on Microblogging Sites Can Be Self-Purified

Besides the above characteristics, microblogging, more importantly, has the self-purification function of We Media in the dissemination process.

The term "self-purification" originated from "water self-purification." Self-purification of water goes in the following processes: physical self-purification, physical and chemical purification, and chemical purification. Physical self-purification refers to the process of purifying water by water turbulence, vortex, diffusion, volatilization, precipitation and filtration. Physical and chemical purification refers to the process of water self-purification by water oxidation, deoxidization, chemical combination, decomposition, neutralization, complexation, chelation, absorption and agglomeration through dissolved oxygen. Chemical purification refers to the process of purifying water by the dissolution effect of water microorganism on pollutants.

Since each microblogging account disseminates "self" information, the release, forwarding and comments of any news are selected independently, and true and false information can be differentiated in the process of interactive information dissemination, so is information self-creation. Wrong information can therefore be clarified. Microblogging's self-correction of mistakes is built in an environment that is full of open and plural information.

The self-purification of microblogging is phased. When a user releases information, the user's followers receive the information and perform the first-stage verification. The information verification ability at this stage is relevant to the population of the followers—the larger the population of followers is, the greater their knowledge base and their verification ability will be. However, at this stage, probably because the information releaser's high trustworthiness makes it more difficult to differentiate information, it is hard to distinguish wrong information in a big population of users. Then information is recognized in the first stage and forwarded extensively. During the process, it is further examined, as more and more people are involved, elements are plural, opinions from professional fields grow and help distinguish information. The information is forwarded for the third round, or the fourth round … the cycle goes on and on. Microblogging users participate in information creation when forwarding and commenting information, and looking on; forward more real information; seek further clues and enlightenment from cybercitizens' feedback; and remedy biases, even errors in past information, and try their utmost to put information fragments together for the information panorama. After information is expounded on by more people, other microblogging users and the parties concerned correct their mistakes in the process of information dissemination, constantly integrate microblogging entries that are being forwarded with commented and forwarded information, and gather information together to get more real and comprehensive facts.

6.3.1.7 "Tacitus Trap" in Microblogging Public Opinion Events

Publius Cornelius Tacitus (55 AD–120 AD)—a great historian in ancient Rome—carried forward and developed Livius's historical traditions and achievements. His position in Roman history was like that of Thucydides in Greek history. Tacitus was once the consul, tribune, aedile, quaestor, governor of ancient Roman. The so-called "Tacitus Trap," generally speaking, refers to the phenomenon when a department loses accountability, all its acts, good or bad, tell against it. The view later developed into one of the laws in Western political science—"Tacitus Trap."

The law of "Tacitus Trap" has been fully demonstrated in sudden mass events in the society in recent years. If the accountability system fails, the social order will become chaotic. When a department loses accountability, whether it tells the truth or a lie, it will be thought to be telling a lie.

Rome was not built in a day. The accumulation of social emotions is not completed overnight. The public does not believe the officially released figures because numerous reports in the past make the public more alert, because there were unsettled doubts in numerous mining disasters, earthquakes, even epidemics, and because the official data, which are so different from what the public see or hear, have confused the public about what China is really like. Rationalizing this, it will be easy to see that the public and the media that "do not understand the actual situation" are just forcing the truth out and defend justice and people's will in a rational and peaceful way.

In the microblogging era, along with changes in the mode of dissemination, the "Tacitus Trap" is becoming a challenge to be frequently faced in daily social management. Frequent microblogging public opinion events have made microblogging an important platform and channel for collecting and distributing public opinion. It may magnify rapidly as a result of the ignorance of public will and information stagnation, or gradually disappear following timely and rational responses. Ensuring the mass's right to know, right to participate, right to express and right to supervise is a guiding principle of social management in the network context.

As can be seen from the present social mentality and the phenomenon of network public opinion in China, more and more Chinese people are becoming upset, doubtful and critical about government acts—especially acts of local governments—in response to sudden events, or governments' professional quality in day-to-day work. People habitually blame the governments for repeated food safety, drug and medical treatment safety, housing safety and traffic safety problems, and "the chaos" caused by unscrupulous businesses and profiteers and some disordered market links. Popular wordings on the Internet such s like the people "do not buy [believe] it anymore," "You really believe it?" "You buy it or not, I don't buy it" interpret the "Tacitus Trap" of government accountability.

The concept of accountability, originated from English word "accountability," and refers to the responsibility for reporting, explaining or defending some event; taking responsibility for one's own acts and accepting inquiry. Accountability is a power of confidence in fairness, justice, efficiency, humanity, democracy and responsibility that is demonstrated by public power in the face of time disparity, public communication and interest changes in social public life. Accountability is not only the confidence in the social system, but also a true expression of public authority, so it falls into the category of political ethics. As an intangible asset, accountability is accumulated in the long development of the media, and demonstrates the authoritativeness, social reputation and public influence of the media.

It is an international proposition to build government accountability. On January 7, 2013, the Chinese Academy of Social Sciences released the *Blue Book of Social Mentality (2012–2013)* in Beijing, which showed that the total social trust index had declined to below 60 points, that is, the "pass line." According to the investigation of Beijing, Shanghai and Guangzhou citizens in the *Blue Book*, the total social trust index was only 59.7 points. Over the previous year, the social trust index in Beijing and that in Shanghai declined greatly and that in Guangzhou rose slightly.

According to the investigation, one of the characteristics of the declining social trust index was the expanded distrust among people. Only half of those interviewed believed that most people in the society were trustworthy. Another characteristic of the declining social trust index was the deepening and consolidating distrust among groups, as shown in many major social relationships like the relationship between officials and the ordinary people, that between police and the ordinary people, and that between doctors and patients, as well as the distrust among groups of people of different social strata.

As the *Blue Book* analyzed, the social trust level declined probably because frequent public events shocked public feelings about social trust. According to the investigation, the public's trust of government departments and political and legal organs was not high; and the public trust in advertising, real estate, food and pharmacy, tourism and catering industries was extremely low.

The *Blue Book* held that the Chinese society was transforming from a traditional one into a modern one when traditional interpersonal trust was broken and new system trust had not yet been fully built, causing frequent social trust crises during the transformation period. Social distrust led to intensified internal friction and conflicts in the society and became the culture medium of many social events.

Therefore, the *Blue Book* also suggested promoting the level of social trust in three aspects: advancing open and transparent operation by those in power, carrying forward information disclosure and public opinion supervision, and cracking down upon organizations and individuals that were in bad faith.

6.3.1.8 *Public Opinion Dissemination Through Microblogging Sites Has the "Group Polarization" Effect*

The so-called group polarization effect refers to the tendency for a group to make decisions that are more extreme than the initial inclination of its members. These more extreme decisions are towards greater risks if individuals' initial tendencies are to be risky and towards greater caution if individuals' initial tendencies are to be cautious. According to studies, the group polarization effect usually happens in informal groups' decision-making process, and microblogging's characteristic of being used by the grassroots serves as an objective factor for the effect. In microblogging public opinion, this group polarization effect more easily contributes to the formation of the public opinion effect. People may selectively accept, understand, focus on or memorize microblogging events. When a number of entities make choices on some event or phenomenon, such entities will build their respective microblogging circles, that is, informal group decision-making circles which may lead to the solidification of established cognitive structures.

There are many reasons for the group polarization effect. The development of network technology, while providing a great deal of information for cybercitizens, has also provided the search, filtering and screening functions and various personalized services. According to the audience's information selection psychology in information dissemination, the audience tends to select information that is consistent with what's in their impression or opinions, and information in which they are interested or which they think is right. Even if such information is different from what they think, the audience would understand it in their respective ways. The anonymity of the network leads to the lack of the sense of personal responsibilities, and cybercitizens thus are less scrupled when expressing opinions.

That network public opinion is free and plural meets most cybercitizens' demands and enables them to select information in which they are interested or which they think is right. In the network environment, the audience tends to visit websites that have similar views to theirs for a sense of belonging. Individuals in the same group are infectious to each other. For example, if the people around all use social networking like microblogging or renren.com, out of the psychology of communicating with them or being not isolated by them, one would choose to visit such websites, too. When communicating on such public opinion platforms, people access information on such platforms. Meanwhile, network platforms are open, so the audience can see other members' opinions on news events.

Public opinion dissemination through microblogging has a significant stereotype effect. Stereotype is always about prejudice. People have stereotypic impressions not only on those with whom they have contacts, but also on those who they haven't contacted according to indirect materials. They tend to classify people mechanically, and see a specific individual as a typical representative of a type of people; and view comments on a type of people as comments on a specific person, which affects them to make correct judgments. Because of the group polarization effect, people of a group easily label relevant persons or events negatively based on their impressions that are formed in daily life or online. For example, urban management personnel are always thought to be cruel and brutal. The group polarization effect keeps people from an objective and rational attitude on social events, and easily leads them to take a side, causing exponential growth of public opinion and magnification of the state of affairs.

6.3.2 *Microblogging's Public Opinion Generation Mechanism*

The development of the Internet, especially the emergence of microblogging, has changed the public opinion ecology—public opinion clusters on large scales, the dissemination of public opinion is more humanistic, and the rights to discourse nd expression right are further popularized. Although the content of microblogging information are scattered and fragmented, micro content, when accumulated, will have significant influence. Microblogging dissemination goes beyond the category of traditional interpersonal communication, and its public opinion influence has attracted the attention of traditional media and relevant government departments. Microblogging enables active discovery and settlement of problems in the process of public opinion dissemination and realizes a "bottom-up reflection of public opinion, top-down guidance of public opinion."

Microblogging upgrades the dissemination of network public opinion, and plays an important role in continuously deepening the pattern of discussion, attracting attention from the society and contributing to the settlement of events. Although microblogging participants are diversified and the public opinion generation environment is always changing, the generation of public opinion has its basic rules.

6.3.2.1 *First stage, the formation of public opinion*

After a public opinion event is exposed, microblogging allows the conveyance of fragmented information, and micro content will superimpose according to the event's social influence. Some micro content that have great social influence will soon get magnified. Anyone may become a microblogging user after registration and then release news according to independent choices. At this stage, the micro content on the event that are provided by the disseminator may be what users see or hear, or from other media. After the disseminator releases original information, such information may be covered by other elements of the huge information flow and end up not being widely spread due to the diversification and multiplication of microblogging information; or may be followed, commented on or forwarded by a great number of followers, spread like fission at a speed that is determined by the population of followers and followers' attention to the event. When users forward and comment the information, network public opinion begins to take shape.

6.3.2.2 *Second Stage, the Outbreak of Public Opinion*

As the event develops, the microblogging public opinion is in multiple forms and the coherence of public opinion gets constantly intensified along with the development of the event. Cybercitizens forward the information through instant messaging tools like network forums, blog, SNS and QQ, and public opinion begins to superimpose, followed by discussion and debates. Opinion leaders express their views and opinions on the event itself and forward the event. Traditional media interact and cooperate with one another and, through online and offline activities, seek and interview the parties that are involved in the event, investigate persons relevant to the event according to clues, and invite experts to comment on the event to try as much as possible to let more audience focus on the progress of the event, understand the truth behind it, probe into public attitudes and opinions in greater depth to push public opinion to a new height. Since the dissemination entities are huge in number, and individual cognition of the event is different, there are collisions and contests of opinions, and forces gather together to heat the event up till public opinion breaks out.

6.3.2.3 *Third Stage, the Crest of Public Opinion*

After the outbreak of microblogging public opinion, according to the typicality and significance of the event, there will be dissemination crests of public opinion in a long or short time. Generally speaking, the more important and complicated an event is, the longer the time from the arrival of crests to the occurrence of the event will be.

6.3.2.4 *Fourth Stage, the Ease of Public Opinion*

Competent departments give feedback on the event itself and the public opinion, then take measures to face the public opinion. Public opinion will therefore ease. As the event is further handled, public cognition of the event gradually becomes rational, and public feelings are pacified. Plus, with the emergence of new hotspots and events, some people's attention shifts, and public opinion declines from the highest point into the ease period of the event.

In this process, opinion leaders' role gets enhanced, because the public pays attention to the views—published by opinion leaders and network media—on the event. At this stage, public opinion will play a top-down supervisory role in government departments' activities. If the event is not settled properly, public opinion will rebound and trigger a second round of public opinion climax.

6.3.2.5 *Fifth Stage, the Pacification of Public Opinion*

Along with the settlement of the event, public attention on the event will fade and the public opinion field will be pacified. The disseminators shift their attention to other hotspots and form new public opinion. The generation and evolution of public opinion is different because the events are different in nature. Some hot events, for being instantly explosive and attractive, will generate public opinion in a short time, even directly enter the public opinion outbreak period. At this stage, the public opinion on the original event will ease gradually.

6.3.2.6 *Sixth Stage, the Reappearance of Public Opinion*

As public opinion is pacified, public attention on the event will be shifted, but when new facts or evidence appear, public opinion on the whole event will break out once again and form a public opinion chain, which then forms the next-round microblogging public opinion on the event, attract users' attention and discussion till the event is figured out. The environment for the growth of microblogging public opinion is featured by being wavy. The chain of public opinion that is built in the development of the event affects the structure of social life, advances reasonable settlement of social events, and guides the orbit of social ideological trend.

The role of microblogging in the formation of network public opinion can be described by some models, as shown in the Figs. 6.4, 6.5 and 6.6.

Microblogging events usually follow this rule: first, they are exposed on microblogging sites by public opinion entities, and then followed and discussed by opinion leaders and looked on by the mass; and the public opinion more or less affects decision-making and game rules. It indicates that microblogging has gone far beyond the category of dissemination means or neutral tools, and has social force, even political attributes. At present, microblogging—with its advantage of being short and efficient—is forming its unique "microblogging public opinion field." Microblogging's dissemination characteristics accelerate the formation and diffusion of public opinion; the real-name identification system has made microblogging public opinion more authoritative and reliable; and the huge group of users gives the field of microblogging public opinion a scale effect. From individuals' life trifles to sports events to global disasters, microblogging has become an important channel for cybercitizens around the globe to express their opinions and will, and its influence should never be ignored.

A significant characteristic of the topics for discussion is that microblogging public opinion declines with the scattering of topics for discussion, and enters the "long tail" stage, that is, at the final stage, opinions that constitute public opinion reduce gradually, but are always in a fading state instead of reaching an end. Sometimes, they rebound, but they will never become zero. There is evidence to prove that it declines naturally in the evolution process.

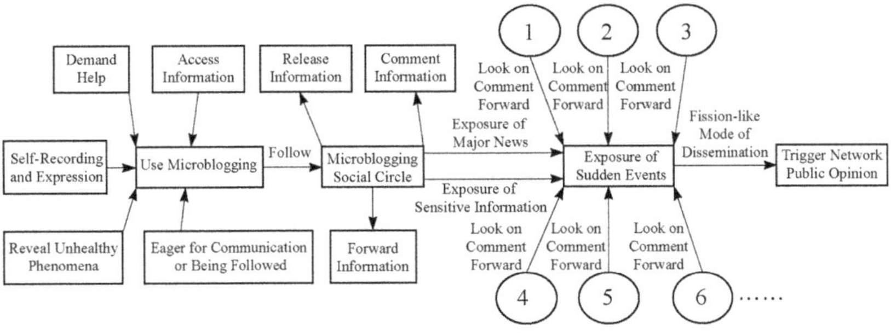

Fig. 6.4 Role of microblogging in the formation of network public opinion

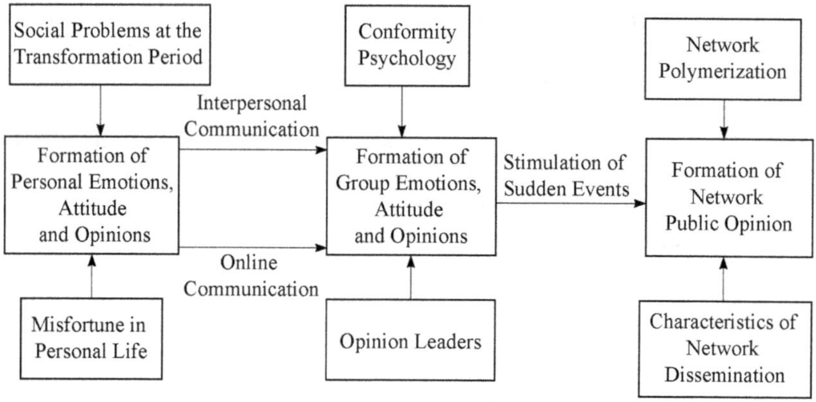

Fig. 6.5 Influencing factors for the formation of network public opinion

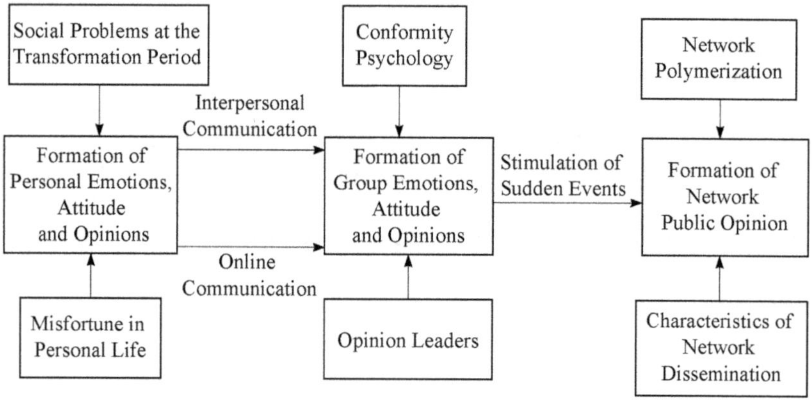

Fig. 6.6 Formation of network public opinion

First, along with constant developments of the media technology, the media team grows bigger, and follow-up reports on some events have grown in recent years. The public not only needs news on recent events, but investigation and follow-up reports of past facts.

Second, after an event occurs, it reminds people of similar old topics, with which a new topic for discussion is introduced. The part—of such new topics—on old topics naturally becomes the "long tail" of the old topics.

Finally, after occurrence, many events give birth to "topic nouns" or "topic genres" and other residual cultures. They often appear in network topics and become network expressions that are much favored by the public. All these residual cultures become a part that lasts long and spreads widely in the "long tail" of network topics for discussion.

6.3.3 Expansion Mechanism of the Influence of Microblogging Public Opinion

6.3.3.1 Combination with Mobile Phone Media

Mobile phones have become an important media tool. Today, it has become normal that mobile phone users spread news and express demands through mobile phone media. Mobile phone users have exceeded 1.3 billion in China, and users surfing the Internet on mobile phones have exceeded those who surf the Internet with PCs. Given the huge population of users and convenient mobile interconnection channel, mobile phones are becoming an important tool for people to participate in news and public opinion.

The combination of microblogging with mobile phones is an extension of the interactive behaviors on the Internet, and it allows cybercitizens to keep a mobile state online. At any time anywhere, they can access others' comments on an event or express their opinions on the event. More importantly, microblogging users may become instant reporters with mobile phone media to simply and rapidly report ongoing events, and may very possibly surpass traditional media in terms of reporting speed and width, which can enrich public opinion participants' understanding of the reality and expression of their opinions.

6.3.3.2 Multipoint Release and "Synchronization"

Microblogging attracts users because it is simple, free and interactive. Users may release information simultaneously with instant messaging tools like QQ, MSN, Fetion and WeChat or with the help of other plug-ins. Meanwhile, if a user has microblogging accounts on a number of websites, the user may select one as the main address to update information, and "synchronize" the updated contents to the remaining microblogging accounts. This operation allows users to update their microblogging content any time anywhere. "Synchronization" maximizes the influence of users' public opinion and allows them to disseminate information on a number of websites. It was rarely seen in past Internet dissemination, and is a new characteristic of microblogging that affects the generation of public opinion.

WeChat is a quasi-instant messaging software product that was launched by Tencent on January 21, 2011. It supports Windows Phone, Android and iOS platforms. WeChat users may share words and photos with their friends through smartphone clients. WeChat is a chatting software product for smartphones that supports group chatting, voice and visual talking. The software itself is free of charge, so are its functions.

6.3.3.3 Chain Reaction and Circulating Reposts

A chain reaction exists in the updates of microblogging content. The content released by one user may be instantly seen and forwarded by the user's followers or friends, and then seen and forwarded by the latter's followers or friends. Therefore, information dissemination is no longer one-to-one or one-to-many, but a chain reaction of one being multiplied by many and then multiplied by many more. Such information dissemination, which inflates instantly and rapidly, enjoys an incomparable dissemination advantage relative to the other media.

The concept of "chain reaction" originated from the science of physics, and exists in all flaming combustion. When some combustible is heated, it will not only evaporate, but its molecules will conduct pyrolysis action and produce free radicals. A free radical is a highly active chemical speciation which can act with other free radicals and molecules to continue the combustion. That is the chain reaction of combustion.

Microblogging's information updates have a very interesting phenomenon of "circulation of replies": when a hot topic is opened, it will be forwarded by a number of the microblogger's good friends, and re-posted by the microblogger till some point, and be re-posted and re-posted, during which process the microblogger may appear many times in the chain of re-posts. It is like rolling reports in chat rooms. The above two actions may influence public opinion as follows: when a piece of important news attracts attention or an important comment is much followed, it will soon have a chain reaction, and spread rapidly among microblogging users; when the news or comment is highly recognized, it will form the circulation of reposts, and continuously appear on the top of personal page or sharing pages and attract continuous attention or reaction of public opinion.

6.3.3.4 *Interaction with Traditional Media*

All in all, the generation of public opinion is inseparable from information dissemination, and microblogging may be seen as a form of information dissemination that newly appears with the development trend of individual media. That microblogging supports multipoint release of information, information synchronization, combination with mobile media, chain reaction and circulations of replies is the basis of microblogging's enormous influence on the generation mode of network public opinion in the past.

6.4 Comparison of Public Opinion in Network Forums and Public Opinion on Microblogging Sites

Although both are important forms of new-media public opinion, network-forum public opinion and microblogging public opinion have different characteristics in terms of opinion generation and diffusion, for which there are various reasons.

6.4.1 *Comparison of the Differences Between Network-Forum Public Opinion and Microblogging Public Opinion*

6.4.1.1 *Network Forums Put Hot Topics High on the Page, While Microblogging Focuses on Reposts*

In terms of user-interface characteristics, the homepage of a network forum presents clear-cut boards to the users, thus allowing the users to decide independently which board to participate in. After entering a sub board, users do not access all contents, but independent threads under different titles. Titles condense the contents of threads, so users can click to read them according to personal interests. After a thread is read, the clicks and the replies determine its popularity. Hot threads will be placed at prominent places of the forum automatically or by board managers. Microblogging presents a completely different way of participation in public opinion. Users first need to "Follow" the producer of the content they are interested in, not the content itself. After following an account as its "followers," users will receive content from the account. If users feel it worth to share or repost the content, they may forward the content and their followers receive this content. The process goes on and on like this.

It is because the two ways of participating in public opinion are different that the impact factors in these two public opinion fields are different.

The influence of contents in a network forum comes from the participators' comments. Of the impact factors of microblogging public opinion, the role of reposts is greater than that of comments. Even if a microblogging entry has tens of thousands of comments, its influence is limited to the releaser's personal webpage. Once the butterfly effect is triggered, followers drive followers before finally contributing to the "fission-like" exponential growth of the influence of a single microblogging entry.

Besides, hot topics in some network forums are to a great extent determined by the managers who may grant topics different levels of importance. In microblogging, the managers' role is greatly weakened, and public opinion entities have greater power to make independent decisions, and the dissemination and diffusion structure of public opinion is even flatter and decentralized. It is safe to say that they are two different incubation forms of public opinion.

6.4.1.2 Network Forums Are Professional, and Microblogging Does Not Have Many Classifications

Network forums can roughly be classified into comprehensive forums and professional forums. Professional forums stand out with delicate positioning and classified boards, but even comprehensive forums have professional classified boards. Unless a board is defined as "a hodgepodge," it has relatively distinct boundaries with the other boards, and postings different in nature are effectively integrated. Users may have reasonable expectations for the content of such board, and public opinion with specific nature may be incubated and diffused in a specific board.

Microblogging is different. All the content a user follows are presented on the user's single web page. Usually users are reading some opinion leader's views on public affairs when they suddenly skip to anti-jokes that are launched by a marketing account. Contents are separated and irrelevant, weakening the acceleration of the diffusion of public opinion. Relative to network forums which discuss a topic "from the beginning to the end" in a centralized way, reposts make microblogging influential, while decentralizing the attention of microblogging public opinion and making people's discussions on public affairs more and more fragmented.

Of course, there are changes. Microblogging operators and participators are working hard to sew the fragments together. That microblogging launches the search function is an example. Users search specific contents in disorderly microblogging fragments with constantly improved search technology, and realize the restoration of the causes and results of public affairs by way of artificial integration. The grouping of content also plays a role, and users can initiatively put microbloggers with different natures into different groups. In so doing, it can roughly avoid the aforesaid passive thinking jumps. Another example is the length of microblogging entries, which to a certain extent subverts the definition of microblogging because microblogging entries may not more than 140 Chinese characters each, so complicated logical reasoning can be carried out on the platform of microblogging. Multiple third-party apps have realized effective suture of fragmented microblogging information. All in all, microblogging public opinion needs to overcome its weaknesses and enter the public sphere. It is the general trend to realize effective information integration.

6.4.1.3 *Network Forums Are One-Way, but Microblogging Is Interactive*

The "one-way" we mention here refers to one-way interaction between both sides of public opinion in cyberspace. Specifically, in the past public events that started in network forums, the side with power to which public opinion pointed rarely responded to public opinion directly in network forums in cyberspace but was forced to make concessions or change at the later stage as a result of public opinion. Take the "Chongqing nail-household event" for example, the event broke out, developed and ended in network forums. Although it was eventually resolved, neither the party involved nor the side with power realized interaction with the public opinion initiator in the same field of public opinion. In this sense, although network forums conducted effective public opinion supervision over public events, they failed to bring the parties involved in the event to the network platforms to build a platform for the communication of both parties. Being effective on sudden events only, but ignoring daily interaction, the split of public opinion subjects and objects in the public opinion field also weakens the long residual action of network forum public opinion—these are the limits of network forums as a public opinion carrier.

6.4.2 *Reasons for the Differences Between Network-Forum Public Opinion and Microblogging Public Opinion*

6.4.2.1 *Evolution of Technical Form*

Network forums and microblogging are Internet products of two different generations—network forum is a typical application of the Web 2.0

era, which truly initiates the interaction function of the Internet; while the emergence of microblogging is sublimation of the idea and application of Web 2.0 technology, and is known to be the beginning of the Web 3.0 era.

True news information is often where public opinion starts. In network forums, due to the operators' restrictions on boards and the managers' control of content, the release of firsthand news on current politics is confined. On the other hand, even if network posts releasing news information, the releaser's characteristic of being completely anonymous makes it difficult to confirm news information and people have to wait until they are reported and verified by traditional media in order to incubate further public opinion storms.

Relative to network forums, microblogging has obvious media attributes: on the one hand, a big number of traditional media have realized a perfect change in the way of information release on microblogging, and short and valuable news contents for the grassroots are first reported by traditional media, which have a content advantage, through their microblogging accounts; on the other, even if with individual accounts, microblogging users are less restrained than before, so they can directly release news information that they have already known, the effect of which is equal to media microblogging accounts. In particular, identified individual accounts are more accountable than anonymous IDs in network forums. Free and responsible remarks are partially realized on the microblogging platform, and the attribute of microblogging as a "We Media" is so obvious.

Although microblogging, as the technical form of We Media, can't match traditional professional news agencies in terms of professionalism, it has speed advantage and immanence advantage in sudden events which are unmatchable by traditional media. The era where "everyone is the media, and everyone has the microphone" has begun since the moment microblogging emerged, which to a great extent attributes to the convenience brought about by the unique technical form of microblogging.

6.4.2.2 Differences of User Characteristics

Network forums flourished at the end of the twentieth century and start of the twenty-first century and 2010 was known as "the first year of microblogging." Although network forum users and microblogging users overlap, general user characteristics have changed. Users, as entities of both public opinions, profoundly affect both public opinions and the differences of public opinions with different characteristics.

It is in an era where the social environment is becoming increasingly open, people's overall living standards are constantly improving and people's minds are more and more liberated that microblogging replaces network forums and becomes an important battlefield of new-media public opinion.

6.4.2.3 Change of the Management Style

With progresses of the era, social management departments that are intimately related to social public opinion are seeing changes, too. For most of the time, such departments are just new-media managers. They are facing new-media public opinion with an even and open attitude, which is so evidently demonstrated by the phenomenon that tens of thousands of Party and political organs and political cadres have opened microblogging accounts. The change is driven by the initiative reform of the governance concept on the one hand; and on the other, in today's society where public events are frequent, open power has become a result of the push of social public opinion.

When network forums dominate new-media public opinion, the management departments have only a few methods to handle public opinion, the most commonly seen of which is "deleting posts," a word which has been in use up to now. On the platform of microblogging, such management style still exists and is becoming fiercer and fiercer, but its effect is not as good as it was in the past. The dissemination hierarchy of microblogging is flatter and more decentralized than network forums, and traditional deletion of posts can delete only a node of the whole dissemination structure. "Network commentators" do not disappear completely, but because the population of the followers determines influence and microblogging content determines the population of the followers, the microblogging content of "network commentators" are no longer followed initially, and their influence on public opinion has been weakened dramatically.

Therefore, a new management style has been taken into consideration by the managers, that is, to meet public opinion demands initiatively, respond squarely to public opinion doubts on the same platform, and be at an equal position as public-opinion entities. Whether initiative or reactive, such change enlarges the real influence of microblogging public opinion, so it facilitates more the advances of the government and society as a whole.

6.4.2.4 Forums and Microblogging in the Mobile Internet Era

If the Internet has changed human society in the past decade, mobile phones will change people's life and the media industry in the next decade. Mobile phones on the one hand have almost all the functions of PC-based network media, and are an extension of network media, while on the other hand make up for the disadvantages of general network media with its characteristics of being portable and capable of spreading information instantly. The mobile Internet represents the development trend of new media. Under this trend, network forums and microblogging perform differently. But in terms of its attributes as a public-opinion carrier, microblogging can better adapt to the changes that are brought about by mobile Internet than network forums.

Compared with microblogging, the way of participation in network forums in nature excludes portable participation, and microblogging positions co-sharing of "short and valuable" micro content for the grassroots from the beginning, and the emergence of mobile phones just corresponds to such positioning in time. Microblogging disseminates fragmented contents, while mobile phones use segmented time. Such fragmentation and segmentation "chime in easily" and generate the speed advantage and scene advantage of microblogging on mobile phones as a public opinion carrier. It also explains why in many public events, especially sudden public events, microblogging on mobile phones plays a crucial role.

CHAPTER 7

Mobile Phone Media and Its Public Opinion Management

7.1 Concept and Characteristics of Mobile Phone Media

Media, also known as "媒介" or "媒质," is an information carrier. According to *Xiandai Hanyu Cidian* (meaning *Modern Chinese Dictionary*), media refer to "tools for communicating and disseminating information like newspapers, broadcasting and advertisements."[1]

As mentioned earlier, the mobile phone media has emerged and has profound social influence. We believe that the so-called mobile phone media is a tool for information dissemination with the help of mobile phones. As communications technology and computer technology developed and smartphones became popular, mobile phones are no longer "mobile telephones" anymore, but mini computers with a communications function; and mobile phone media is the extension of network media (see Fig. 7.2). Mobile phone media has to become a new part of network media where information is tremendous, or it will face the problem of a lack of information.

Mobile phone media is an important member of new media. It has to be specially highlighted that short messaging is just a form of existence of mobile phone media, but not all, and it does not represent the direction of mobile phone media in the future. In China, many people mistake mobile

[1] *Xiandai Hanyu Cidian*, compiled by Dictionary Editorial Office, Institute of Linguistics, Chinese Academy of Social Sciences, 5th edition, p928, The Commercial Press, 2005.

W. Kuang, *Social Media in China*, Sociology, Media and Journalism in China, https://doi.org/10.1007/978-981-13-0914-4_7

phone short message service (SMS) for mobile phone media and call SMS "the fifth media." As a matter of fact, SMS is enormously demanded and a short message culture has been developed in China because of China's specific telecom management system and charging model.

7.1.1 Characteristics of Mobile Phone Media

Mobile phone media has the basic characteristic of being digital, and its most essential dissemination characteristic is being interactive and its biggest advantage is being portable and user-friendly. Meanwhile, as the extension of network media, mobile phone media is featured by high interactivity, fast information access, fast dissemination and fast updates of network media. All these features enable mobile phones to penetrate all walks of life in the human society and profoundly affect human dissemination activities.

7.1.1.1 Advantages of Mobile Phone Media

7.1.1.1.1 High Mobility and Portability
Mobile phone media is highly mobile and portable and realizes extremely convenient information dissemination. Mobile phones have become a part of people's daily life. That mobile phone media is highly portable makes it highly personalized, private and next to skin. Mobile phones are "a media with body temperature," and are really close to people's life. It requires that mobile phone media disseminators provide personalized information according to user demands, that is, to truly realize focus dissemination.

7.1.1.1.2 Instant Information Dissemination
Mobile phone dissemination is digital. Information dissemination through mobile phones is fast and highly timely, covers a wide range and is less restrained. Given the huge number of mobile phone users, the audience for mobile phone dissemination is enormous.

It is obvious that mobile phone media has the advantage of being instant. Without the need to turn on their computers or TVs, many of the audience can access, through mobile phone media, real-time news, scene pictures or videos of the scene that are provided by authoritative media agencies. Mobile phone media realizes instant information receipt and dynamic information dissemination. In particular, when there is a sudden event, mobile phone media can also realize dynamic dissemination of news like websites.

Information dissemination via mobile phones is updated frequently at a low cost. The update cycle of information that is disseminated through mobile phones can be counted in seconds, but that through TV and broadcasting by day or hour; the publication cycle of newspapers by day, even week; and the update cycle of paper journals and books is even longer. That mobile phone dissemination is instant improves the timeliness of news. Meanwhile, mobile phone dissemination realizes "asynchrony of information receipt." For example, if one receives a short message, one may read and reply to it whenever one has time. The asynchrony of information receipt exempts the audience from the restriction of the time of media dissemination, and allows the audience to receive and use information anytime as needed.

7.1.1.1.3 Interactivity

Mobile phone dissemination is a form of open and interactive dissemination. The dissemination mode of traditional media is usually one-way in reality, that is, the disseminators and the audience can't realize two-way communication any time anywhere. Mobile phone dissemination may be one-way, or two-way, even multi-way. Mobile phone dissemination is highly interactive.

Mobile phone media has an incomparable advantage over traditional media in terms of "interactivity." An important characteristic of traditional mass media is one-way information dissemination, which causes audience feedback to be always behind time, untimely and indirect in most cases. Mobile phone media not only releases news that the users need, but has functions such as tracking, collection of materials, investigation of readers and readers' comments. It provides more and more convenient services for the readers and the newspaper offices and realizes more extensive and faster interaction.

Mobile phone dissemination highlights personalization and humanity and stresses user participation. Relative to traditional mass media, mobile phone media is significantly diversified in terms of dissemination forms, and integrates interpersonal dissemination, group dissemination, organization dissemination and mass dissemination into one. Mobile phones in themselves are tools for interpersonal communication. Forums, chat rooms and mobile QQ, with the help of mobile phone media, further enrich the channels for interpersonal communication. Group dissemination can be realized conveniently on mobile phone media. Many mobile phone websites focus on building themed BBS, thematic forums and mobile phone communities for the communication of users with the same hobbies or demands.

Mobile phone dissemination is humanized. Mobile phone media is small and portable, so it meets individuals' demands more. Mobile phone media is a media that can be "mastered" and controlled by people instead of separating people from the media—as do traditional media—or "submerging" people, as happens on network media. It further demonstrates the mainstay status of mankind. The mobile phone, as a media "that constitutes a part of human body," is organic in nature, and vividly interprets "media is the extension of mankind."

7.1.1.1.4 Rich Audience Resources

An important indicator to measure if a media is competitive or not is the real and potential audience population. For mobile phone media, the least worry would be the users. Mobile phone users in China have broken through 1.3 billion, far greater than the population of cybercitizens and newspaper readers. Relative to newspapers and magazines with the biggest circulation, the websites with the highest click-through rate, and outdoor media in stations and subway stations with the biggest traffic of passengers, mobile phone media has an even bigger audience that covers an even wider range of types.

A mobile phone is more than just a simple tool of communications. Its rapid development is changing people's way of life. A mobile phone is becoming a device for disseminating and integrating information, even a digital entertainment center for individuals. In the future, the main development goal of the mobile communications industry will shift from expanding the population of users to maximizing the profits per capita. Although in many mature markets, the mobile phones possession has reached saturation point, using mobile phones for information dissemination and profiteering purposes is still at the initial development stage.

7.1.1.1.5 Multimedia Dissemination

Mobile phones have an increasingly stronger function to process information. Surfing the Internet, taking photos, recording sounds and filming have become the basic functions of a lot of mobile phones, and multimedia mobile phones have gradually become popular. The operational platform of mobile phones has seen great changes, and the computerization trend of mobile phones has become reality. Some newly launched mobile phones have also integrated the latest applications like mobile blog and instant messaging, and the information processing and dissemination functions of mobile phones are constantly enhanced.

7.1.1.1.6 A Mobile Phone is Also an Important Tool for News Interviews

In July 2005, in a few seconds right after the serial bombings in London, a dozen subway passengers and pedestrians near the bombed bus shot the terrifying scenes at the first time with their mobile phones. Some shot the scene of the bombing at a subway station (see Fig. 7.1). According to the photos, there were thick smoke everywhere and passengers had to cover their mouths. Another photo captured a nearby man who was taking photos with his mobile phone, too.

The video clips and photos on TV and news websites presented the scene of desperate subway passengers running for their lives. There were also photos indicating unconscious passengers lying on the ground after the bus bombing. They clearly captured the situation of passengers with black ash on their faces fleeing for their lives. A woman curled up in pain on the sidewalk. There was spattered blood on the buildings around.

The rapid rise of mobile phone media technology has enabled almost all ordinary people in the world to shoot sudden news and put them on the Internet. The way that the world witnesses history is changing, and celebrities have no chance to hide their embarrassing moments. Some Western scholars call this phenomenon “grassroots journalism” and “grassroots journalists.” With a mobile phone, anyone can become a journalist.

Fig. 7.1 Mobile phone photos of London subway bombing

7.1.1.1.7 Privacy

The mobile phone media is a highly personalized media. It is not like TV, which families watch together, or newspapers, which can be passed around for reading. It is a distinctively personal information dissemination tool with personalized labels, and it is highly private. Every mobile phone terminal corresponds to a specific audience, allowing it to follow user information and behavior more accurately than Internet IP addresses.

7.1.1.1.8 Conformability

A mobile phone is an important platform for medium integration. Mobile phone media can integrate diversified media forms, carry the content of traditional media like newspapers, broadcasting and TV, and fully display all the dissemination advantages of network media.

7.1.1.1.9 Organic Unity of Synchronous and Asynchronous Dissemination

Mobile phone media organically unite synchronous and asynchronous news dissemination, that is, users with the news dissemination tools provided by mobile phone media can receive information from the disseminators in real time and have real-time communication with other users, or access the information disseminated by the disseminators and communicate with the other users at any selected time. It is like the dissemination model of network media.

7.1.1.2 Disadvantages of Mobile Phone Dissemination

The biggest advantage of mobile phones as a media is their portability. Mobile phone media is a digital new media. As mobile phone media extends network media, many characteristics (including defects) of network media are extended to mobile phone media. At the present stage, mobile phone media has the defects discussed in the following sections.

7.1.1.2.1 Dissemination of False and Unhealthy Information

Some rogue elements release false information, and bluff and deceive wantonly. Obscene information and rumors spread through mobile phones, jeopardize social atmosphere, mislead the public, and cause chaos in the social order.

7.1.1.2.2 Infringement of Individual Privacy

More and more rogue elements take stealthy photographs with mobile phones or other electronic products, and the legislation organs in some countries and regions are only slowly beginning to intervene.

7.1.1.2.3 Information Garbage

Spam emails received by Chinese cybercitizens are now equivalent to normal emails, and there are countless spam messages too.

7.1.1.2.4 Information Security

Some mobile phone hackers design special mobile phone software viruses to attack the vast number of mobile phone users. Some viruses utilize the loopholes or defects of the programs of mobile phone chips to spread virus codes through SMS and cause damage. The mobile phone viruses in the past could cause automatic power-off or failure of mobile phones, even damage mobile phone chips. Some viruses even caused mobile phones to call the police automatically, or automatically forward the contacts in them.

7.1.1.2.5 Mobile Phones' Inherent Technical Defects: Small Screen, Insufficient Battery Capacity

A small screen is an inherent defect of mobile phones. However, in recent years, mobile phone screens are getting bigger and bigger. Before 2011, 3.5 inches was the mainstream size of mobile phone screen, and in 2009, many mobile phone manufacturers had begun to manufacture 4.0-inch or bigger mobile phone screen. In September 2011, Samsung launched the 5.3-inch Galaxy Note and made an enormous success. After 2012, big screen mobile phones have become the mainstream.

However, battery life remains a factor that restrains the development of smartphones. People are more and more reliant on smartphones, but the development of battery technology can't meet the demand. The solution now is increasing battery capacity, but it is far from being enough. Brand-new charging technology (e.g., charge with kinetic energy, fuel cell technology) is the future development direction.

Despite the defects of mobile phone media, mobile phone, as a new media, has realized a breakthrough, and is becoming an information system that people carry with them. As a new terminal for information dissemination, the mobile phone, being efficient, convenient, timely and interactive, provides more colorful and personalized information services for people any time anywhere. It will be a brand-new form of cultural production and an information dissemination channel that is different from the past and challenges traditional media.

Seen from its characteristics, mobile phone media is completely different from traditional media, and is similar to the network in terms of dissemination characteristics. It has integrated functions. For example, when calling people, it is mobile phone; when texting messages, it is a text medium; when surfing the Internet, it is a network media. It is safe to say that mobile phone media is the extension of network media.

The big population of mobile phone users has constituted a tremendous, but scattered audience that is necessary for mass dissemination. As their functions grow stronger, mobile phones are turning from a communications tool into an information platform.

Mobile phones are mobile and personalized. On the one hand, real-time rolling news allow the users to read some important and brief news anytime anywhere on the road; on the other, the information collection network, media brands, advertising operation and social accountability that have long been developed by traditional media like newspapers, broadcasting and TV remain insurmountable thresholds for the other emerging media.

7.2 Problems Caused by Mobile Phone Media

Mobile phones, as mini computers, used to be a mobile means of communication, but have become mass media now. Mobile phones are changing the dissemination pattern in Chinese society rapidly and reshaping people's habit of information dissemination. They promote social communication and interaction and bring to people unprecedented convenience and freedom of information delivery. Mobile phone media, as a newborn thing, has relative superiority over the other media, but there are inevitable defects in its development and negative impacts that can never be ignored. In particular, if the dissemination of abundant and diversified information is left unchecked, it will easily pollute information dissemination and deteriorate the dissemination ecology. The defects of mobile phone media are discussed in the following subsections.

7.2.1 Illegal Short Messages

The priority in the administration of illegal short messages is to check the behavior of sending short messages through mobile phones illegally, specifically sending short messages for fraud purpose in the name of

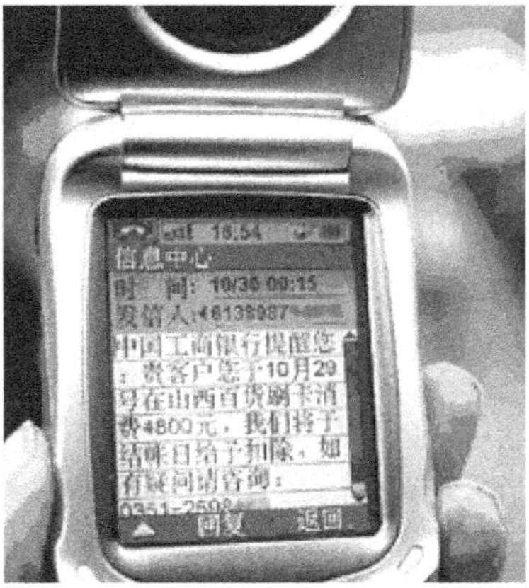

Fig. 7.2 Harms of short messages

banks (see Fig. 7.2); spreading pornographic, gambling, violence and frightening content; selling guns, explosives, smuggled cars, drugs and fake banknotes illegally; releasing false information about winning lotteries, marriage introduction or recruitment; or seducing or introducing others to prostitute.

Some rogue elements release false information, and bluff and deceive wantonly. Obscene information and rumors spread through mobile phones, jeopardize social atmosphere, mislead the public, and cause chaos in the social order.

7.2.2 *Garbage Information Disseminated Through Mobile Phones*

Dissemination of false and harmful information and floods of garbage information are two of the thorny problems in the development of mobile phone media.

According to a research done jointly by the University of St. Gallen and International Telecommunication Union, over 80% of the European mobile phone users have received at least one piece of garbage information in the form of a short message.

The research result also shows that 83% of the interviewees believe that receiving spam information will become a serious problem to haunt them in the next one or two years.

The United States and the Republic of Korea require consumers to present their resident's ID cards when buying mobile phones so that the sellers can input consumers' ID numbers and addresses into the telecommunication operators' central databases. When a mobile phone user sends information, the memory unit of the telecommunication system will have the sender's mobile phone number, with which the sender's name or address can be accessed.

Some countries allow advertisers to send advertisements through mobile phone SMS, but with conditions. For example, advertisements in short messages must be clearly indicated, and advertisers are not allowed to send advertisements in short messages between 21:00 at night and 8:00 the next morning.

7.2.3 *Security Problem Brought About by Mobile Phones*

Since the mobile communication network uses mobile phones—made up of hardware and software—as the terminal devices, some overseas companies try to change the software or hardware in mobile phones to turn mobile phones into devices for eavesdropping and taking stealth photographs. Such devices resemble ordinary mobile phones on the outside, and have the normal communication function. Some altered mobile phones, even if powered off by the users, can be activated by others and got through without ringing so that sounds around them can be heard stealthily. The mobile phone operational system also has some "backdoors." Some mobile phones which can surf the Internet will pass mobile phone viruses or be implanted with eavesdropping programs through the Internet, and have functions of illegal eavesdropping and remote control.

Mobile phone dissemination also causes national security problems.

In Russia's Chechen war, the Russia Air Force discovered traces of the head of Chechen separatists through electronic reconnaissance and easily killed him.

In March 2002, Abu Zubaydah, Bin Laden's capable assistant and No. 2 figure of Al Qaeda, was seized because he exposed his hideout after using a mobile phone.

Therefore, mobile phone communication is an open e-communication system. With corresponding receiving equipment, the conversation of anyone any time anywhere can be intercepted.

Even if in a standby state, mobile phones can keep uninterrupted signal exchanges with the communication network, and the electromagnetic spectrums can easily discover, identify, detect and follow targets with detection and supervisory technologies, pinpoint the targets and get valuable intelligence from them.

Even if a mobile phone is powered off, experts can still turn its receiver on remotely with special instruments for eavesdropping purpose. Therefore, as long as users put their mobile phones beside them, they have no secrets at all. During the manufacturing process, mobile phones have been implanted with receiving and delivery functions in their chips. Even if they are powered off, such mobile phones, as long as they have batteries, will receive voice information and deliver such information anytime. Through the repeater station on the geostationary satellite, such information will be delivered to a ground processing system. Mobile phone users are suggested to take batteries out of their phones when necessary to completely cut off the power of their mobile phones; or put their mobile phones far away from where they talk to avoid being eavesdropped.

The intelligence departments, important military and government departments in some developed countries all forbid the use of mobile phones in office areas, even mobile phones that have already been powered off.

Also, cases of terrorists setting off bombs with mobile phones happens from time to time.

China is the country with the most mobile phone users in the world. If it fails to fully recognize the double-edge sword effect of mobile phones, the security of its national defense intelligence, economic intelligence and science and technology intelligence will be seriously threatened.

7.2.4 Problem of Citizen Privacy Protection Brought About by Mobile Phones

Smartphone cameras are getting increasingly popular. Some mobile phones have unique designs oo special functions—like the pick-up lens installed on the back which can be hidden. Therefore, even if one pretends to be talking on the phone, he can easily take stealthies of secrets or infringe privacy.

7.2.4.1 *Mobile Phones Have Multiple Functions, and Their Filming and Sound Recording Functions Are Worrisome*

The most influential and controversial issue at present is mobile phone cameras' function to take stealthies. It is worrisome that mobile phones support filming, and it is even terrifying that mobile phones support sound recording. In the past, a recorder was needed to stealthily record other people's talk, which would easily be discovered no matter how small it was. It is unlikely to cause suspicion using a mobile phone. Many ignore mobile phones' sound recording function. A few buttons alone can help record the talks at both ends of the line. In daily chats, mobile phones can record what others say without being noticed by the latter. In the era of the third-generation mobile phones, even facial expressions can be filmed by mobile phones.

7.2.4.2 *Different Countries Legislate Laws and Regulations to Ban Taking Stealthies with Mobile Phones*

In recent years, there have been events of individuals being stealthily photographed, thus their privacy being infringed in different countries. In particular, the popularity of mobile phones with cameras makes it easier to take stealthies, and the places of taking stealthies have gone from bathroom or bedroom in the past to public places like fitness centers and hotels.

Mobile phones with cameras may also become tools to steal business secrets. Given that mobile phones with cameras are highly concealing, a company's important drawings and samples may be stealthily shot and leaked in a few seconds. It has almost become an unwritten rule in the retailing industry that shopping malls forbid photo-taking. However, in the face of mobile phones with cameras, the rule has become almost powerless.

To promote sales, mobile phone manufacturers compete against one another on mobile phones' photographing technology. On the one hand, the photographing technology of mobile phones is becoming increasingly improved, while on the other, it makes taking stealthies more convenient. First, cameras are more and more hidden. They may be on the back of mobile phones at the beginning, but they are now on the clamshell or the axis; secondly, according to market surveys, consumers are more and more interested in mobile phones with the photographing function. Manufacturers therefore highlight mobile phones with the HD photographing function.

It is very difficult to investigate or collect evidence on the infringing or illegal, even criminal behavior of taking stealthies. It is suggested to restrain the scope of use of mobile phones with cameras. In some places, mobile phones with cameras have to be regarded as cameras. Therefore, in places where photography is prohibited, the use of mobile phones with cameras should be prohibited, too.

7.2.4.3 *Analysis of the Motives of Taking Stealthies*

7.2.4.3.1 For Excitement

Seeking excitement has become a big motive of taking stealthies. More and more photos, which claim to be "photographed secretly" and involve privacy, attract cybercitizens who also seek excitement, and are searched much more. The malicious cycle has caused more and more habitual offenders or lechers who do it.

7.2.4.3.2 For Blackmailing and Extortion

Taking stealthies for blackmailing or extortion purpose will cause great harms to the parties involved. As smartphone cameras are becoming more capable, the phenomenon of taking stealthies with smartphone cameras for blackmailing and extortion purpose is popular on mobile phones.

7.2.4.3.3 Psychological Problems

The motives of taking stealthies can be classified into three: blackmailing, psychopathy and aimless curiosity. If the aims is blackmail, taking stealthies is the same as kidnapping in nature, only they are two different means. Taking stealthies can be explained from its motives to the behavior itself, but is against the widely acknowledged moral standards. If it is metaphrenia, we have to see if one takes stealthies for sexual purpose, that is, for sexual satisfaction with some improper means like taking stealthies of others' private body parts with a mobile phone. It is difficult to define the third motive.

As for the ones who are stealthily photographed, they mainly have two reactions: to make concessions to avoid troubles and be unwilling to make it public; or to bravely report it to the police and bring the criminal to justice. In the psychological perspective, the former ones believe in external control, and feel that events are mainly determined by external factors, but can't be affected by themselves; and the latter ones believe in internal control, have a great sense of self control, and believe that, with efforts, they can resolve problems, so they are usually optimistic and active.

In China, anyone who takes stealthies of people's privacy will be detained by the public security organ. The Law of the PRC on Penalties for Administration of Public Security, which was put to practice on March 1, 2006, clearly provides, a person who peeps or secretly takes photos (including with mobile phones) of another person's bedroom, bathroom or any other private places, or eavesdrops the privacy of another person shall be detained for not more than five days or be fined not more than 500 yuan; if the circumstances are relatively serious, he shall be detained for not less than five days but not more than ten days and may, in addition, be fined not more than 500 yuan; if one is secretly photographed in public by another person with a mobile phone, the one may request the person who takes stealthies to delete the stealthies, or the one may dial 110 to report it to the police.

7.2.5 Mobile Phone Viruses

Computer viruses are so familiar to us, but mobile phone viruses did not appear until recently. We may define mobile phone viruses as a new type of viruses which—by infecting mobile phones on the platforms of mobile communications network and computer network and in the form of short messages with viruses—work as computer viruses to attack mobile phones and cause mobile phone failures. As a matter of fact, mobile phone viruses are even more harmful than traditional computer viruses. Mobile phone is an instant messaging tool that integrates the functions of emails, individual multi-functional information management tools and instant chat software. The trust among mobile phone users is greater than that among cybercitizens. Therefore, if a virus on the Internet has a mobile phone version, it is far more disastrous than network viruses.

7.2.6 Other Problems Brought About by Mobile Phones

7.2.6.1 Mobile Phone Ringtones or Mobile Phone Talk May Cause Noise Pollution in Public Places

Mobile phone ringtones are becoming new sources of noise pollution in urban life. In China, a country of ancient civilization and etiquette, mobile phones usually ring out suddenly in libraries, theaters, music halls, classrooms and other public places. Some people answer their phones loudly without any consideration of those around them, which is really intolerable.

7.2.6.2 *Mobile Phone Addiction*

China now has 1.3 billion mobile phone users. A recent survey by CCTV indicates that 76% of the interviewees showed that they would feel at a loss, even "at a great loss" without a mobile phone.

7.2.6.3 *Road Safety*

It has become widely known that using mobile phones may affect road safety.

7.2.6.4 *Environment Protection Problem that Is Brought About by Mobile Phones*

As people's living standards are increasingly improved, a mobile phone has become a communications tool that is integral in people's day-to-day life. However, the rapid and constant upgrading of e-technology and continuously updated and expanded social demands for mobile phone functions enable people to discard or eliminate old mobile phones more frequently. If the discarded or eliminated old mobile phones are not properly disposed of, they will cause great damages to human health and environment security. The cadmium in the battery of an old mobile phone can pollute 60,000 liters of water, an amount that can fill three standard Olympic Games swimming pools.

7.3 WeChat

7.3.1 Development of WeChat

WeChat is a free application that was launched by Tencent on January 21, 2011 to provide instant messaging service for smartphones. It enables the users to send texts, pictures, video and audio clips rapidly through smartphones, tablet PCs and web pages. WeChat also provides public platforms, moments, and information push functions. Users may shake their mobile phones, search numbers or people nearby, scan a 2D code to add new friends or follow public platforms. WeChat shares contents in the form of WeChat moments.

WeChat is not the first mobile Internet instant messaging tool in China, and its concept of design wasn't original, either, but it learned from Kik, an instant messaging software product launched by Canadian company Kik Interactive.

Users may contact their friends through WeChat in various ways similar to short messaging or multimedia messaging. The software of WeChat is free of charge, and not a dime will be charged for using any of its functions, and the network traffic fee will be collected by network operators.

7.3.2 Dissemination Advantages of WeChat

WeChat is a representative product of the mobile Internet. Mobile Internet (MI) is an emerging form of business to get businesses or services through smart mobile terminals and via mobile and wireless ways of communication. It combines mobile communications with the Internet.

WeChat is changing the way of interpersonal communication quietly and has incomparable advantages over the other media. It is free of charge and, relative to short messaging, its voice and video dissemination functions make both information disseminators and receivers more direct and real, and highly reachable than QQ or email. Communication is more private relative to the microblogging platform. Specifically speaking, WeChat has the dissemination advantages discussed in the following subsections.

7.3.2.1 Human-Oriented Design, Convenient Operation

On the official website of Tencent, the advertising slogan is "Speedy, novel, convenient—brings to you new experience of thumb communication." It points out the first convenient place of WeChat: "Short messaging that speaks." It is not complicated, and it simply requires the users to press some button on the mobile phone screen when dialoguing, and say what they want to say. Simple operation wins the users and greatly extends the base of WeChat users.

7.3.2.2 Multimedia Dissemination

WeChat supports real-time delivery of texts, pictures, audio and video clips, and displays the contents disseminated in an omnibearing and three-dimensional way to make the information forms and structure change substantially and satisfy the audience with different habits of reading or watching.

That smartphones develop and soon become popular gives mobile phone media, which takes the smartphone terminal as the main carrier, enormous development space. WeChat has diversified modes of dissemination like voices, texts, pictures and video clips, providing technical supports and serving as a dissemination platform for media dissemination.

7.3.2.3 *Open System for Free Use*

WeChat is almost free of charge, so it is cost-effective.

7.3.2.4 *High User Stickiness*

WeChat can be bound to QQ, QQ mailbox and QQ Music. Users can log in QQ directly and add QQ friends to WeChat friends, and receive offline information. All these advantages increase user stickiness and popularize WeChat to a wider scope.

7.3.2.5 *Two-Way and Interactive Dissemination Entities*

From the communication perspective, WeChat dissemination is mainly point-to-point interpersonal dissemination, and is two-way and interactive.

The dissemination entities of WeChat, namely the user groups, are accurate. WeChat mainly relies on the smartphone mobile platform and, based on the platform of Tencent, mobile phone QQ users are the main force of WeChat. Besides selecting information receivers from QQ friends, users may also select information receivers from mobile phone contacts. Two-way communication easily occurs between WeChat information disseminators and receivers.

Given that WeChat information disseminators and receivers are mainly from QQ friends and WeChat users' mobile phone contacts, WeChat information disseminators and receivers are close. The main function of WeChat is making voice calls, which are kind of like phone calls. From the angle of users' psychology and habits, chatting verbally will make the relationship between the disseminators and the receivers more intimate. WeChat information disseminators and receivers are mainly relatives, close friends, friends and colleagues, determining that both sides are even more interactive in conveying and feeding information back through the media.

7.3.2.6 *Disseminated Content is Private and Instant*

Given the intimate interpersonal relationship between information disseminators and receivers, the contents of communication through WeChat are even more private. WeChat integrates the functions of QQ and micro-blogging, and its release of contents is instant. As long as a user is online, he can rapidly receive and respond to news. Besides, WeChat supports offline QQ information receipt, so it is more rapid in messaging.

7.3.2.7 *Dissemination Channels Are the Integration of Multimedia Platforms for Co-sharing*

WeChat maximizes the use of all functions of smartphones. As an advantageous platform for co-sharing, it basically covers all communication tools that people use daily.

7.3.2.8 *WeChat Builds an Omnibearing and Three-dimensional Social Network for Its Users*

WeChat takes close interpersonal relationship as the main social relationship. As mobile phone-based communication software, it is cored with individuals' interpersonal relationships and produces and conveys information through close and weak relationships. The social circles of WeChat users can be divided into acquaintances, 1000 m-circle friends and strangers. Acquaintances mean close-quarters social circle and a close interpersonal relationship, while 1000 m-circle friends and strangers represent medium-distance and long-distance social circles. These three social circles indicate that WeChat's moments are delivered from acquaintances to strangers. WeChat build an omnibearing and three-dimensionsl social network by fully covering three cross-sections. People can allocate their energy in social interactions in a more accurate way as needed.

However, the scope of WeChat users is narrow. Since the most basic relationship in WeChat is based on "friends," "relatives" and "colleagues" in real life, the frequency of online social interactions tends to be the same as that of offline social interactions in the real society. On the whole, acquaintances have more frequent interactions than strangers. However, the two-way interpersonal relationship inevitably leads to a narrow scope of users of network public opinion, and the scope of social interaction of an ordinary person is basically kept at a size of hundreds. What's more, WeChat also limits the functions of public platforms, so it restrains large-scale dissemination, making the scope of users even more restrained.

7.3.2.9 *Diffused and Accurate Dissemination Effect*

The simple diffusion ability of one-to-many dissemination: First, the WeChat public accounts have the basic broadcasting ability, and WeChat provides its users with the function to follow WeChat public accounts. Some "big WeChat public accounts" may have tens of thousands of followers and can realize simple broadcasting function. Second, WeChat moments have gradually become new platforms for sharing. Different from the open information sharing of microblogging, WeChat moments are information that is shared among acquaintances, and a fully consolidated relationship chain. Information that a WeChat user sends to WeChat moments can be shared by all of such user's WeChat friends, thus it realizes one-to-many information diffusion.

The point-to-point accurate dissemination ability: WeChat mainly supports point-to-point interpersonal dissemination, which makes the information arrival rate almost 100%. WeChat's main functions of voice chat and point-to-point communication are like live broadcasting. Expressing feelings verbally helps better understand the mind of both the disseminator and the receiver and bring mutual relationship closer. In accurate WeChat social circles, both sides of communication have a close interpersonal relationship, and the information conveyed and responded to is true and accurate.

All in all, WeChat has changed people's way of life.

There is the advertising slogan on the official website of WeChat, which reads "WeChat, a way of life." The emergence of new information dissemination media led by WeChat has changed people's way of life and existence, built an omnibearing and three-dimensional social network for the users which covers people from acquaintances to strangers, while meeting people's emotional demands.

7.3.3 Problems of WeChat

7.3.3.1 Information Overload

WeChat information overload mainly refers to the problem of junk information that may be caused by information release. Information is released on WeChat through real-time push so that WeChat users do not miss any information. However, like spam, if WeChat information push is abused, it will weaken user experience and unavoidably harass the customers. Meanwhile, many traditional media expect to expand their influence through WeChat, so they try WeChat public accounts. However, if a WeChat user follows a number of WeChat public accounts, and the media push highly similar content every day, it will make the user impatient, even disgusted. For WeChat users, overloaded information becomes junk information.

7.3.3.2 Privacy Protection

Although WeChat protects its users' privacy by setting functions such as supporting the approval of requests for adding friends and visibility of WeChat moments to different groups, there are cases of using WeChat to conduct illegal activities in the society. WeChat involves users' personal data and privacy which may be leaked if not properly protected or managed. For example, contacts and backup files in the phone may not have safety setting or be properly protected. Besides, when WeChat users use LBS functions to extend their interpersonal relationship, there is the problem of possible leakage of personal information.

7.3.4 *WeChat Diversifies Opinion Leaders*

In daily life, there are people who can influence others by disseminating information, and they are known as opinion leaders. Studies show that opinion leaders' access frequency and intensity to newspapers, magazines, TV programs and broadcasting are far greater than those of ordinary people. Therefore, in mass dissemination, information does not "flow" directly to the general audience, but needs to pass the intermediate link of opinion leaders, that is, "from mass dissemination to opinion leaders, and then to the general audience." That is two-step dissemination.

After the emergence of new media, the "opinion leaders" no longer need the aid of mass dissemination. It provides more convenient means of dissemination for the "opinion leaders." It is safe to say that new media contributes to the emergence of We Media. As long as one has the discourse say and information, he is a media that attracts followers and then has influence. WeChat, as a good We Media platform, attracts more We Media people to join. Equal discourse right, simple operation and an open platform contribute to the emergence of more and more "opinion leaders" with different occupations from different social strata. Opinion leaders are even more diversified.

7.3.5 *WeChat Integrates Interpersonal Dissemination, Group Dissemination and Mass Dissemination*

The original mode of information dissemination was one-to-one. It is typical interpersonal dissemination. Interpersonal dissemination, as the original and typical form of human dissemination activities, has the following prominent characteristic: in the dissemination process, both the disseminators and the audience are individuals, not the masses, and they don't involve organizations or groups. Interpersonal dissemination is in nature an activity of individuals exchanging spiritual information. The quality of the exchange of spiritual information to a great extent depends on its media.

WeChat dissemination integrates instant mass dissemination, group dissemination and interpersonal dissemination into one. WeChat dissemination mostly covers good friends in mobile phone contacts, so it is group dissemination. Personalized dissemination gives WeChat the advantages of mass dissemination and interpersonal dissemination and enables it to break through the limitations of the two combined. WeChat at the mobile terminal not only makes communication more instant, its multiple ways of communication make information dissemination accurate, profound and extensive. Information release and receipt among phone contacts turn from static to dynamic, and contacts have the ability of one-step information diffusion, and the forms of dissemination are even more personalized and automatic.

7.3.6 Comparison of WeChat and Microblogging

Although microblogging and WeChat are both representatives of We Media, they are different.

7.3.6.1 Mode of Dissemination: WeChat Highlights Interpersonal Dissemination and Group Dissemination; Microblogging Highlights Mass Dissemination

WeChat highlights interpersonal dissemination and group dissemination, that is, WeChat is "one-to-one" and point-to-point dissemination and the target groups are more targeted. WeChat involves roughly three modes of dissemination: dissemination among good friends, dissemination through WeChat moments and information receipt. "Dissemination among good friends" refers to point-to-point two-way dissemination between users who add mobile phone contacts and QQ friends as their WeChat friends. The relationship between both sides of dissemination is stable in such mode of dissemination which is kind of like mobile phone messaging.

"Dissemination through WeChat moments" means that WeChat users receive their WeChat friends' moments, or send their own, and simply comment the moments on the mobile phone. The scope of dissemination is relevant to the number of their good friends. WeChat "moments" are defined as private picture sharing and are limited to mutually followed "WeChat friends." Because of their privacy, WeChat moments may receive "Thumb up" or "Comment," but WeChat does not support the forwarding of WeChat moments. So it is difficult to form large-scale dissemination.

"Information receipt" means that WeChat users receive news from the website of Tencent or information from WeChat public accounts, and may forward them to their WeChat friends or share them in their moments. However, the fact that the system releases two pieces of news everyday greatly limits the dissemination capability of WeChat. After receiving information, individuals share the information with their WeChat friends, and that is point-to-point mode of dissemination. After information is shared as WeChat moments, it may be simply commented or thumbed up, but can't be forwarded. Therefore, WeChat dissemination can't form multi-layer chain dissemination like microblogging.

Microblogging highlights mass dissemination and the dissemination objects are usually the majority of the uncertain strangers. Microblogging, as a completely open information platform, can realize one-to-one, one-to-many, many-to-one and many-to-many interactive dissemination, and information releasers can't predict information release and receipt.

7.3.6.2 Users' Network Social Interaction: WeChat Stresses Interpersonal Relationship, Microblogging Does Not

Seen from users' network social connections, WeChat takes close interpersonal relationship as the main social relationship. WeChat, as a mobile phone-based communication software product, is centered on individuals' interpersonal relationship, and produces and conveys information through close and weak interpersonal relationships. Seen from the close interpersonal relationship of WeChat, the most fundamental relationship network is based on such relations as "relatives," "friends" and "colleagues" in real life. Both sides exchange information in a point-to-point way. Seen from the weak interpersonal relationship, WeChat provides a number of functions and can expand the scope of social interactions. Information conveyed through weak interpersonal relationship can be classified mainly into two types: users' personal information and information that is released by strange users via apps or public platforms. The scope of WeChat users' social connections can be divided into three levels: acquaintances, 1000 m-circle friends and strangers, extending from acquaintances to strangers.

Relative to WeChat, microblogging highlights the weak interpersonal relationship, and helps agglomerate people. It is very easy to realize social interactions through microblogging: by clicking "Follow," one can become a microblogger's follower, and microblogging's functions like "Forward, Private Message" also promote mutual communication. What is built after the behavior of clicking "Follow" is an asymmetric interpersonal relationship. Microblogging simplifies social relations, and users can follow other microbloggers at will. They do not need to be identified or approved by the latter as friends. The process therefore facilitates the agglomeration.

7.3.6.3 Dissemination Effect: WeChat Information Is More Reliable than Microblogging Information

Since the dissemination objects of WeChat are acquaintances, friends and relatives in mobile phone contact, while microblogging highlights mass dissemination and the dissemination objects are usually uncertain strangers, information on WeChat is more reliable than that on microblogging sites.

WeChat and microblogging have completely different genetic attributes—microblogging has more intense dissemination and media attributes, while WeChat has better adhesion and communication experience, and is a private bond of communication.

WeChat dissemination is mainly point-to-point interpersonal dissemination—the dissemination is based on individuals' social ties and WeChat friends are mostly people whom one contacts in real life; WeChat accounts can be bound to QQ numbers or mobile phone numbers; users make friends in their true names, so the contents disseminated are personal and private in true names. Seen from basic product functions, WeChat, as a product for individuals' communication for social interaction purpose, naturally highlights close relations. It is mainly a chatting and communication tool for acquaintances. Therefore, users' privacy is strictly protected. WeChat focuses on point-to-point accurate positioning, which determines that WeChat limits information sharing in terms of product functions. All these lead to WeChat's poor capability of mass dissemination.

Relative to WeChat, microblogging's characteristics of being an instant individual media and mass dissemination mechanism are even more prominent. The behavior of "Follow" in microblogging leads to an asymmetric interpersonal relationship, and the process easily expands interpersonal relationship from acquaintances to strangers, and therefore greatly expands individuals' scope of social interaction. "Followers" may reach hundreds of thousands, even tens of millions. Loose social relationships enable microblogging to conduct one-to-many group communication on a large scale and realize mass dissemination. The one-to-many mode of information release on microblogging sites exponentially magnifies the influence of microblogging, wins it the scale discourse right, and further reacts to traditional media (Table 7.1).

Table 7.1 Comparison of Microblogging and WeChat

	Microblogging	*WeChat*
Dissemination Type	Mass dissemination Microblogging is more like a personal web portal, and has the characteristics of mass dissemination.	Mainly interpersonal dissemination and group dissemination WeChat is mostly point-to-point communication and information dissemination among friends and acquaintances. WeChat dissemination belongs to group dissemination.
Dissemination Objects	Mainly uncertain "strange audience"	The dissemination objects are "acquaintances," that is, a few familiar audience, and have the characteristics of individual communication, interpersonal dissemination and group dissemination
Dissemination Speed	Instant and delayed After microbloggers release information, their followers can check the information immediately or at some later time. Receivers initiatively receive information, and determine the timeliness of receiving the information.	More instant WeChat is a kind of instant dissemination. After individuals or groups send some information, the information will immediately be received by the receivers. While receivers receive the information sent to them, online disseminators' information synchronically reaches online receiving terminal.
Dissemination Contents	Public Contents disseminated on microblogging sites are mainly public topics and mostly involve politics, economy and people's livelihood. Microblogging is open diffusion-type dissemination. Information dissemination is public.	Private Information disseminated on WeChat is mainly about private personal life. WeChat supports closed-loop communication in private space, and the information disseminated is private. WeChat is like a private network where people share information with their friends, relatives and acquaintances. For valuable information in WeChat, it will be disseminated from close relationships to weak relationships. The more valuable the information is, the narrower the scope of its dissemination will be.

(*continued*)

Table 7.1 (continued)

	Microblogging	*WeChat*
Information Type	Less than 140 Chinese characters for each entry, pictures, texts, links.	No length limit, and may be multimedia dissemination; pictures, texts, links, voices, video clips
Dissemination Effect	Having a strong effect in society, but a weak effect among individuals Microblogging is mass media in nature, and information disseminated via microblogging easily poses a public opinion pressure in the society after it is forwarded on a large scale, and the effect is strong. However, the dissemination effect of microblogging contents is weak among individual users. Given functions such as forwarding and commenting, a great number of replies to the information can be seen, of which there are rumors or meaningless replies that dilute or confuse the true information disseminated. ID is tradable, and there may be a great number of zombie followers. "Opinion leaders" have relatively weak marketing influence.	Having a weak effect in society, but a strong effect on individuals WeChat provides private space, and the dissemination objects are all "acquaintances," increasing the degree of participation and interactivity. WeChat belongs to information sharing among acquaintances. Information disseminated is highly reliable, and the effect of information dissemination among individuals is great. In the process of disseminating and commenting information, information releasers and receivers are friends or acquaintances, and there are a few participants, which greatly increases information reliability to users. The percentage of meaningless replies is low and the dissemination of harmful information is reduced dramatically. ID is untradeable. "Opinion leaders" have greater marketing influence. The "close relationship" among good friends makes opinion leaders in WeChat very possibly opinion leaders in real life. Opinion leaders' opinions may even possibly influence group members, and more acceptable.
Dissemination Structure	Radioactive The dissemination structure of microblogging is radioactive around users.	Loops plus dotted lines The dissemination structure of WeChat is an integrated chart of loops plus dotted lines, and is asymmetric.
User Relationship	Microbloggers' followers are mostly strangers who have never met one another, and do not live or work together.	WeChat users' friends are mostly small groups like their relatives, classmates, colleagues.

(*continued*)

Table 7.1 (continued)

	Microblogging	*WeChat*
Degree of Openness	Highly open A microblogger's social connections are open. The number of the followers a microblogging user has, or the microbloggers a microblogging user follows are open to the public.	Less open WeChat users' social connections are private and secret, and no one can check their friends' social connections.
(LBS) Location Based Services (LBS)	Microblogging does not support location check.	WeChat supports location check.
Product Carriers	Computers, smartphones among all smart terminals	Mobile phone is the main platform of WeChat.

7.4 Management of Mobile Phone Media

With the development of mobile phone media around the globe, many countries have realized the necessity to develop and manage mobile phone media. Mobile phone media has such advantages as spreading information fast, being highly portable and interactive, which are unmatchable by paper media, broadcasting or TV. Like the Internet, mobile phone media, as a new media, has had social influence. The "PX" event in Xiamen was typical. In December 2007, Fujian provincial people's government and Xiamen municipal people's government decided to respect people's will and stop the building of a paraxylene (PX for short) factory by Taiwan-invested Xianglu Group in Haicang District, Xiamen, and moved the project to Gulei Peninsula in Zhangzhou. In "PX event" in Xiamen, new media, including mobile phone media, became a new way and platform for the expression and agglomeration of public will.

However, it is difficult to supervise mobile phone media.

7.4.1 Difficulties in the Supervision of Mobile Phone Media

7.4.1.1 Massive Population of Mobile Phone Users

The population of mobile phone users and the pieces of information disseminated through mobile phones are counted by billion. It is impossible to realize comprehensive and timely control of mobile phone media or limit or prohibit the dissemination of some information. Social control seems pale and weak for mobile phone media. The dissemination of SARS-related information through messaging was a very typical example.

7.4.1.2 *Challenges of Cross-Region Dissemination*

Mobile phone dissemination is cross-region, it even goes beyond national boundaries. Mobile phone users may easily log in the websites, BBS, microblogs or chat rooms of any country or region in the world through the Internet. So Internet users are extremely scattered in different regions. Illegal and criminal activities online usually affect many countries and regions. When handling such illegal and criminal activities, there are always thorny problems in terms of jurisdiction.

7.4.1.3 *Policies, Laws and Regulations that Lag Behind*

The law always lags behind scientific and technological development, and the rapid development of mobile phone dissemination forms a sharp contrast with the less-developed policies, laws and regulations and management. Meanwhile, the management authority does not have sufficient management experience in managing mobile phones, a brand-new media, so management means and methods are updated more slowly than the emergence of new problems. In laws and regulations that are newly introduced, some systems are not operable in reality and will cause conflicts, or they are hard to be realized in execution.

7.4.2 *Problems of Mobile Phone Media in News Dissemination*

Relative to traditional media and network media, mobile phone media has natural advantages in news dissemination, and provides the vast user population with more convenient, faster and richer mobile information services. Since mobile phone media is interactive, open and private, and the gatekeeping mechanism is not yet sound, as are the corresponding management policies and system measures, mobile phone media has a lot of problems in the process of disseminating news.

The main problem of mobile phone media in the dissemination of news is that it spreads false news and unhealthy information, which has negative impacts on the development of mobile phone media that cannot be ignored, and may even jeopardize social stability and national security.

Mobile phone media has the problem of disseminating false news. Such news is generally disseminated in two ways: mobile phone websites edit and forward false news from traditional media or network media and disseminate such news; traditional websites send false information to mobile phone users—who subscribe their news information services—through short messaging, and mobile phone users forward and disseminate before diffusing such false information. A lot of false news can cause a sensation in society and, with the great power of interpersonal dissemination, usually would have great social influence.

Take mobile phones for example, in January 1997, the State Council of China promulgated *Regulations on Publication Administration*, requesting publishing entities to apply the publishing editor system to ensure the legitimacy of publications. The state administration organ in charge of the publication industry allocates book numbers to realize overall control of book publication, which is obviously effective for traditional publication. However, it is challenged when it comes to mobile phones or network publication. The current *Regulations on Publication Administration* are basically preventative legal regulations, which request the adoption of the publishing editor system to ensure the legitimacy of publications. Besides, the state-level administrative organ in charge of the publication business, by allocating book numbers, realizes overall control of book publication—a publication rule that is highly administrative and well planned. Despite the disadvantages (e.g., the book number allocation system indirectly leads to prevailing trading of book numbers), in the network field, the original set of "game rules" for publication becomes meaningless.

First, the Internet and mobile phones enable people to skip the intermediate link of publishing houses or magazine offices and directly express their opinions (publish their works) on the Internet (including mobile communications network). The network saves the procedure of "editing, printing, binding, transportation, issuance" that is necessary in traditional editing and publication, and users can publish their works conveniently and quickly.

Second, there is no such thing as a book number in online publication, so online publication can fully get rid of the restriction of book numbers. Book numbers have lost micro control of publications. It is a huge shock to the publishing departments that highlight book numbers.

Third, in online publication, the authors do not need to be examined by the editing and publishing department in order to publish their works, so it poses a challenge against the existing publishing editor system.

Fourth, everyone can publish works because there is no threshold of network technology. It becomes extremely difficult to monitor and manage the quality of the published content.

7.4.3 *Problems of Mobile Phone Media Management in China*

China is at the fumbling stage regarding the management of mobile phone media. Given its special telecommunications charging system and implicative Chinese culture, the short messaging culture is highly developed in China. Therefore, the management of mobile phone media including mobile phones in China at the present stage is mainly demonstrated by the control of negative short messages.

Mobile phone media can be classified by different standards. According to its relationship with traditional media, mobile phone media can be classified into two types: mobile phone media that rely on traditional media and mobile phone media that do not rely on traditional media. The latter are hard to manage, but represent the mainstream and direction of the industry, while the former may adopt the management mode of traditional media and are less difficult to manage. However, seen from the development of digital new media, the former—restrained by the established management mode, personnel structure, ideological ideas and capital operation—will find it difficult to become the principal part of the emerging industry.

Mobile phone media, as a product of high technology, develops where different industries—including the media and communications—superimpose. It spans a number of industries and has a complicated industrial chain. Its rapid development and the complexity of the problems it causes have surpassed the present cognition and management level. There are therefore problems like unclear management responsibilities, insufficient management references, and weak management capability, as well as problems such as the development of the industry is significantly driven by interests, IP protection is weak, and the ecology of the industry is deteriorated.

The management responsibilities are unclear, and there are supervision blanks. The management of mobile phone media involves different industries and industrial departments, so there are a lot of uncertainties in management.

The management references are insufficient and it lacks laws, regulations and policies. Take mobile phone newspapers for example, what qualifications are needed in order to run a mobile phone newspaper? Does the current print media automatically get such qualifications? Are new entities allowed to run mobile phone newspapers? How to master and guide the contents of mobile phone media? How to ensure copyright of mobile phone media? Mobile phone news websites, mobile phone TV programs and mobile phone novels also meet similar management problems. Laws, regulations and policies on such problems are not yet clear enough, and the system and measures are not yet complete. It is an urgent problem in order to guide healthy development of mobile phone media.

The industry is significantly driven by interests; there are a lot of consumption traps; and unhealthy information flows. Copyright protection is inefficient, and infringement and piracy are serious. Business models are similar, and industrial ecology is deteriorated.

7.4.4 *Policies and Laws on the Management of Mobile Phone Media in Developed Countries*

Currently, there are laws and regulations on the mobile communications industry and mobile phone users' behaviors, but not any law or regulation on the management of mobile phone media.

At present, the country with the most developed mobile phone media in the world is Japan, but Japan relies on industry self-discipline to manage mobile phone media. The nongovernmental industrial associations on mobile phone media in Japan play a crucial role. Given Japan's special self-discipline culture, its experience in managing mobile phone media would be difficult to transplant to China.

In the United States, Europe, Singapore, the Republic of Korea, and Hong Kong of China, management laws and regulations on the mobile communications industry are complete. However, the whole world is at the initial stage of managing mobile phone media by legislation.

As for noise pollution in public places, which is caused by mobile phone ringtones or phone calls, it is completely a problem of the users' habits of use and sense of social morality.

The control of mobile phones with cameras—which infringe the right of privacy or steal secrets—actually targets the problem of disseminators' self-discipline and heteronomy. It is not the mobile phones, but mobile phone users who infringe privacy. Therefore, mobile phone users need to be effectively restrained and controlled in heteronomy. Some countries have realized the seriousness of the problem, so they are restraining the scope of use of such "concealed cameras."

7.4.5 *Management Measures of Mobile Phone Media*

A mobile phone is not only a carrier of person-to-person communication, but also mass media in nature. It involves different industries and industrial departments. It disseminates huge amounts of diversified information, and has high technical conditions and standards and requirements. The release, dissemination and disposal of information through mobile phones are random, short and widely influential, and hard to be controlled by information releasers, disseminators and receivers. Not only enterprises of different categories, but also news media participate in the business of news dissemination through mobile phones. Regarding such emerging media, there have not been relevant domestic management systems or laws or regulations. A major topic to be studied and settled is how to strengthen the supervision and management of mobile phone media businesses, especially the content and information therein, respect and protect intellectual properties, and prevent the dissemination of illegal and unhealthy information on the Internet.

7.4.5.1 *Ways of Management of Mobile Phone Media*

In the development of mobile phone media, the significance of the government cannot be ignored, because the government not only manages mobile phone media, but also promotes the development of new media. The government has the responsibility to purify the content of mobile phone media and ensure the security of mobile phone network so as to promote vigorous development of such emerging media.

Control and freedom are inseparable, like both sides of a coin. But when developing the control strategies, the reality of mobile phone media must be taken into consideration and the measures for controlling traditional media are inapplicable here.

That the mobile phone media is portable, open, free and interactive, and costs less makes "noise" dissemination technically possible. The characteristic of mobile phone media breaking through region and time constraints makes it more difficult to control mobile phone media. For traditional mass media, laws, regulations and policies can be developed to control media stance, and ensure that it serves the mainstream ideology of the nation and people's interests. For mobile phone media, some visible means of control are hardly workable, and it is difficult for a nation to supervise the huge amount of information and large number of users in a comprehensive and timely way.

At present, mobile phone media may be controlled and regulated in the following three aspects.

7.4.5.1.1 Strengthening the Development of Laws and Regulations on Mobile Phone Media

At present legislation on mobile phone media has just been initiated in countries throughout the world. Legislation is just an issue of form, and the greater difficulty is the fact of obstacles against law enforcement. How to monitor information dissemination in mobile phone media, investigate and collect evidence on facts that are against the law, how to maintain coordination among different departments are new tasks to be resolved by the law-enforcement departments.

7.4.5.1.2 Strengthening the Code of Ethics of Mobile Phone Media

Ethics plays its role through public opinion, customs and beliefs, while laws play their role through deterrence and punishment. As the second space of survival for modern people, mobile phone media should have its own system of ethics.

7.4.5.1.3 Technical Management

To overcome effectively the negative effects produced by mobile phone media, besides strengthening government supervision and the control of mobile phone media, conducting legal management of mobile phone media and advocating civilized network ethics, there are also technical measures, that is, technical control can be further intensified with technology.

7.4.5.2 Respecting the Special Development Rules of Mobile Phone Media, Innovating on the Principles of Management of Mobile Phone Media

7.4.5.2.1 Respecting the Special Rules of Mobile Phone Media, and Establishing Correct Legislation Principles

Mobile phone media has its special industrial development rules and technical characteristics. Ostrich policies have to be avoided when developing mobile phone media-related policies, laws and regulations.

When managing mobile phone media—the extension of network media—by legislation, China's experience in and lessons learned from network media management may be referred to. Mobile phone media goes beyond regional and national boundaries, so we should take into consideration international conventions, and learn from past experience and lessons.

The principle of policy development and legislation should meet and promote the development of the mobile phone media industry, and put equal emphasis on regulation and development. Mobile phone media can be classified by different standards. According to its relationship with traditional media, mobile phone media can be classified into two types: mobile phone media that rely on traditional media and mobile phone media that do not rely on traditional media. The former are hard to manage, but represent the mainstream and direction of the industry, while the latter may adopt the management mode of traditional media, and are less difficult to manage. However, seen from the development of digital new media, the latter—restrained by the established management mode, personnel structure, ideological ideas and capital operation—are hard to become the principal part of the emerging industry. China's policies, laws and regulations should not restrain the former's development.

One problem China is facing now in the supervision of new media is that China highlights "regulation," but ignores development. Laws, regulations and policies should promote the development of the media industry, but in fact, many policies, laws and regulations are restraining its development.

There are no national boundaries on the Internet. Excessive supervision of local video websites may push some cybercitizens to overseas websites, dragging down the development speed of domestic video industry. Obviously, simply transferring the methods of managing traditional media like TV and films to digital media does no good to its development.

Mobile phone dissemination does not have any threshold. Of the hundreds of millions of mobile phone users, anyone can become the disseminator. Therefore, it is difficult to manage mobile phone dissemination with the traditional publication examination and approval system. Given the special rules of mobile phone media, it is suggested to separate enterprises' and individuals' behavior in mobile phone media, and adopt the "registration system + investigation and punishment system" to manage mobile phone media.

Since the new-type digital mode of publication led by network media and mobile phone media is the development direction of the entire news publication industry, it is a progress and an inevitable thing that paper media declines. Therefore, in legislation, traditional publishing houses should be encouraged to use new media technology, and actively devote themselves to network media and mobile phone media activities to promote the upgrade of China's publishing industry.

7.4.5.2.2 Paying Attention to Intellectual Property Protection

There are unsatisfying places in present network dissemination legislation and law enforcement, like network copyright protection. On the Internet (including mobile communications network), intellectual property (IP) infringement cases are common. An author needs to pay a high time and economic cost to protect his/her legitimate rights and interests on the Internet, and faces a high risk of losing the lawsuit, because IP infringement on the Internet is costless, concealing, rapid and global, and it is hard to collect criminal evidence. In short, infringement is easy, but right safeguarding is really difficult. In mobile phone media, if the problem of copyright is not properly solved, it may completely destroy the mobile phone media industry.

7.4.5.2.3 Enhancing the Operability of Policies, Laws and Regulations

Everything has two sides. It pays a price to manage the mobile phone media, and the stricter the management is, the higher the cost will be. Cost here refers to social cost in the broad sense. Therefore, the cost and efficiency of management of mobile phone media need to be balanced.

As a result of modern science and technology, mobile phone media in itself is neutral. Both the good effects and the negative effects are "made" by people who participate therein. Mobile phone media can change people, and vice versa. We just can't stop using mobile phone media or deem it as monstrous only because it has defects.

PART IV

Hot Topics of Studies of New-Media's Public Opinions

CHAPTER 8

Studies of New Media's Rumors

8.1 The Evolution of the Rumor

8.1.1 Studies of the Concept of the Rumor

Rumors have been around since the birth of the human being. Ancient Greeks and Ancient Romans regarded the rumor as the "oracle" and worshipped Fama, the Goddess of Rumor, with tangible constructions and intangible literatures.

In Chinese, the word "rumor" (谣言) is read as Yao Yan, which referred to singing without music accompaniment in the first place. According to *Mao's Commentaries on the Book of Songs*, the rhythmical language accompanied with music was a song, while without music, it was Yao. Derived from this word, the verbs Zao Yao (create a rumor) and Chuan Yao (spread a rumor) and so on were produced. This is a neutral word on the whole.

In the article *To Scholars*, Xunzi warned the men of noble character that "The man of noble character should be alert to the gossip, statement, strategy, reputation or complaint without foundation that is often heard but not from appropriate means."

Being loyal but suffering from doubts and slanders, Qu Yuan sighed in *Li Sao*, "Those women were jealous of my graceful figure, slandering that I was licentious." We can see how accumulated defamation destroys a man in this poem.

W. Kuang, *Social Media in China*, Sociology, Media and Journalism in China, https://doi.org/10.1007/978-981-13-0914-4_8

As emphasized in the story of "Zeng Shen has killed a person" recorded in the *Strategies of the Warring States, Qin's Strategies II* and the adage that "three people spreading reports of a tiger make everyone believe there is one around" described in *Han Fei Zi Inner Part Upper Left Volume*, repeated rumors exert a great impact on people's mind.

Springs and Autumns of Master Lu, Be Cautious concisely explained the misrepresentation of the content during rumors spreading, "They say a dog looks like an ape, an ape looks like a female monkey, and a female monkey looks like a man, but a man is so different from a dog."

After two thousand years of evolution, in the contemporary Chinese language "rumor" equates to the "lie" produced and spread "maliciously." In other words, the modern Chinese language abandons the meaning of "singing without music accompaniment" and only preserves the meaning of "cooking up a story and defaming somebody" for the word "rumor."[1]

Though the concept of rumor has existed since ancient times, Western scholars started to discuss and study it as an academic issue earlier than China according to the research literature. The German scholar Hans-Joachim Neubauer, American sociologist Knapp, French scholar Jean-Noël Kapferer and American scholars Gordon Allport and Leo Postman have conducted a great number of studies and discussions on this topic. There follows an introduction to the studies of Chinese and foreign researchers to help sort out the development course of rumor studies.

8.1.1.1 From the Perspective of History

The German scholar Hans-Joachim Neubauer believed that a rumor was a product of historical development. Neither a baseless creation nor an incarnation of evil, it is a part of history that shows a nonnegligible impact on the progress of human civilization. The rumor "is firstly a custom changing along with historical development that is described by people, which consists of all different phenomena. Moreover, the rumor is also a message communicated in a group through listen and talk or a similar way. What everyone is saying is not a rumor. A rumor comes into being when everyone allegedly is saying so. The rumor is incompletely quoted from someone nobody knows by someone nobody knows."[2] It explains that a rumor is spread through interpersonal communication, though the communicator cannot be determined.

[1] Jin Ping, *The Rumor: Reflection on the Concept and the Enlightenment for Modern Society*, from the *Journal of North University of China (Social Science Edition)*, 2011(1).

[2] [GE] Hans-Joachim Neubauer, *Fama*, Page 10, Beijing, CITIC Press, 2004.

8.1.1.2 From the Perspective of Social Psychology

The *Social Psychology Dictionary* defines "rumor" as: "the hearsay without a factual basis and the message deliberately fabricated and spread from mouth to mouth, including partly the defamation and partly the exaggeration."[3] When analyzing the SARS incident in *The Aberration of Communication—a Psychological Analysis of the "SARS" Rumor*, Zhou Xiaohong stated that rumor had always been a common social psychology either in traditional society or in modern society, or had been a collective behavior characterized by information communication. According to Francoise Reumaux from France, "The history of a rumor is firstly the history of a group capable of internal communication, while the collective memory, experimental social space and opportunity constitute the tools to create rumors in different ways."[4] In other words, a rumor is more easily made and spread in case of challenges against social stability and threats to people's life, as a psychological projection of people's insecurity.

Furthermore, Gordon Allport believed that a rumor was derived from human needs, "Any human need may drive the force. The sexual interest gives rise to many lies and slanders; anxiety contributes to the horrible and threatening rumor often heard; the hope and desire produce the daydream rumor; and hatred causes the rumor of accusation and defamation."[5] Therefore, a profound social psychological cause can be seen behind every kind of rumor.

8.1.1.3 From the Perspective of Social Public Opinions

The Chinese scholar Liu Jianming held that a rumor, being a social public opinion, was a libelous idea without factual basis, so the rumor was an offensive and negative public opinion rather than neutral hearsay.[6] At the same time, Francoise Reumaux from France considered there was a complicated relation between a rumor and public opinion. "In view of the whole structure, the public opinion can be easily represented by a concept, but the rumor keeps changing and is easily incorporated in a model of

[3] Shi Ronghua, *Social Psychology Dictionary*, Page 243, Chengdu, Sichuan People's Publishing House, 1988.

[4] [FR] Francoise Reumaux, *The Black Widow—the Meaning and Spreading of the Rumor*, Page 125–126, Beijing, The Commercial Press, 1999.

[5] [US] Gordon Allport et al., *Rumor Psychology*, Page 18, Shenyang, Liaoning Education Publishing House, 2003.

[6] Liu Jianming, *Principles of Social Public Opinions*, Page 211.

image or metaphor. This kind of model is a changing or predictive concept where various new concepts and/or presentations are processed and produced."[7]

He also thought that "the rumor is a response to social imbalance or unrest."[8] The Chinese scholar Chen Lidan proposed a similar idea, "The rumor is the stress state that the public handles social life and an inevitable form by which the public solves problems."[9] Both Francoise Reumaux and Chen Lidan inclined to the view that the rumor was a product of the special social status and emphasized its sociality.

Then, Hu Yong laid further stress on the rumor's role as public opinion and put forward the idea that a rumor was a kind of social protest. As the new media are constantly emerging, any group is able to publish its ideas in this way and challenge society at any time. "In the vast intermediate region between silence and vigorous resistance, the rumor is playing as a powerful tool. Though the weapon of rumor held by modern rebels is not as strong as those used by revolutionaries in previous times, it is playing a greater role compared to the 'weapons of the weak' as once discovered by James C. Scott."[10] This view was proposed upon the basis, "the rumor is a social phenomenon and meanwhile a political phenomenon," which was first put forward by Jean-Noël Kapferer. He also pointed out the relation between the rumor and authority, "The rumor reveals the secret, suggests a hypothesis and forces the authority to break silence, and also raises the objection against the exclusive authoritative role of the authority."[11] Therefore, the rumor constitutes an anti-power to check the power.

8.1.2 The Evolution of the Communication Form of the Rumor

Owing to the constant development of information technology, science and technology have altered the operating mode of the whole of society and new forms for communication between human beings have emerged.

[7] [FR] Francoise Reumaux, The Black Widow—the Meaning and Spreading of the Rumor, Page 182.

[8] Ibid., Page 125.

[9] Chen Lidan, *Studies of Public Opinions—Research on the Orientation of Public Opinions*, Page 102.

[10] Hu Yong, *The Rumor as a Social Protest*, from the *Communication & Society*, Hong Kong, 2009(9).

[11] [FR] Jean-Noël Kapferer et al., *Rumors*, Page 14, Shanghai, Shanghai People's Publishing House, 1991.

Therefore, the rumor, established upon interpersonal communication, is exposed to constant changes of the communication form. Compared with previous network rumors, Weibo rumors have become the new favorite. In virtue of the constant updates of advanced Internet technologies and portable terminals, the rumor is always in a race with human beings. Here, the associations and differences among the traditional rumor, the network rumor and the Weibo rumor are organized and listed, to help people understand the communication of rumor in the new media.

8.1.2.1 *The Relation Between the Traditional Rumor and the Network Rumor*

The traditional rumor and the network rumor make up a pair of relative concepts. The traditional rumor, created upon interpersonal communication, spreads among people through listen and talk, particularly among acquaintances. As the traditional rumor is subject to the limit of time and space, a rumor at one place may be old news or even new news at another place. In this way, the traditional rumor features information lag, which conversely restricts the range and depth of the influence of the traditional rumor. Meanwhile, people will be confused as to the traditional rumor and are unable to judge whether it is true merely relying on their own strength.

As a kind of network communication constructed upon the computer technology, the network rumor is disseminated from one ID user to another ID or other several ID users, going beyond the range of acquaintances and communicating with a virtual society across time and space. Free from any time or space constraint, the rumor will be known to the world in a very short time, so it presents the feature of communication immediacy. Moreover, the network rumor often has complete details, including the time, place and event, thus to make the netizen believe and raise social public opinions. Under certain circumstances, the netizen may combine their wisdoms and apply their knowledge to examine the rumor from all different aspects and actively crack down on the rumor, as strongly proved by the "Zhou Tiger Incident."

8.1.2.2 *Similarities and Differences Between the Weibo Rumor and the Network Rumor*

Featuring both properties of interpersonal communication and mass communication, Weibo is a product of Web 2.0. Weibo 2.0 adheres to the idea of "decentralization," focuses on user construction, user participation and user orientation and has transformed the mode from the passive reception of information in the era of Web 1.0 to active creation of Internet information, typically represented by the blog, Wiki and BBS. Weibo is derived from the blog, so the Weibo rumor, as with the rumor in the network communities, falls into the category of network rumor.

As a result of the development of the mobile Internet and reform of mobile phone functions, Weibo has attained rapid development and currently become the most popular new media. People are increasingly expecting to get rid of the constraint of the fixed network during the information-oriented transformation of society, while the mobile Internet exactly satisfies people's need in going on-line at any time anywhere. Responding to the infinite development of the mobile Internet in the future, the mobile phone is constantly updating its operating system, widening the screen, making the machine thinner and developing from the smart phone to a mobile platform. The mobile Internet and the smart phone are promoting the development of each other, laying the foundation for the birth of Weibo.

8.1.2.3 The Mobile Weibo Rumor and the Network Weibo Rumor

Though Weibo also applies to the computer, the Weibo rumor on the mobile phone is still distinct from the network Weibo rumor. The Weibo rumor spreads and disseminates at a higher rate owing to mobility of the mobile phone. Also, Weibo information can be followed (subscribed to) and forwarded, and thus realizes real-time communication through the mobile phone. However, both share the similarity that no complete verifiable details can be provided within the word limit of 140 characters.

In a word, while widely welcomed by people, Weibo is also the rumor's favorite platform owing to its communication characteristics. The rapid, real-time and global communication of the Weibo rumor based on mobile media has become an issue that should be studied and solved urgently.

8.2 The Rumor Communication and Dissolution Model in the New Media

By analyzing previous research on the rumor, we put forward the idea that the importance and ambiguity of the incident and information asymmetry give rise to rumor communication, and we further establish the model of rumor communication, spreading and dissolution on this basis, so as to theoretically support and practically guide how to correctly deal with the rumor.

8.2.1 Gordon Willard Allport Model

In 1947, the American psychologist Gordon Willard Allport et al. proposed the two basic conditions for generation of the rumor: first, the story must be somewhat important to the one spreading or listening to the rumor; and second, the true fact must be covered by a certain ambiguity.[12] Upon the two basic conditions, they put forward the basic law of the rumor: the importance and ambiguity of the incident is associated with rumor communication, and then presented the formula:

$$R = i \times a$$

In this formula, R = rumor, i = importance, a = ambiguity. R represents how popular and how wide the rumor has been spread; i suggests how important this incident is to a certain group; and a indicates the ambiguity of this incident or evidence. A rumor is only made based on both conditions, i and a. According to the formula, when the incident is more important to a certain group and is more ambiguous, it is more possible to create a rumor and the rumor will be spread more intensely and widely.

In 1953, the communication scholar Kroos tried to improve this formula in introducing the factor of communicator, that is, people, and proposed: $R = i \times a \times l/c$, where c means critical ability, that is, "man's judgment."[13] This formula states that the rumor communication is inversely proportional to "man's judgment," since a person mature enough is able to resist the rumor's influence and even prevents further spreading of the rumor. In addition to the importance and ambiguity of the incident, whether the public hold a rational understanding and appraisal of the incident also determines whether the rumor spreads or fades. Though Kroos noticed the important role of people in rumor communication, it became more difficult to establish the formula: how to evaluate man's judgment and which criteria should be applied. As is known to all, man is the subject to understand and transform the world, and many factors are affecting a person's judgment, such as the cognitive ability, social background, social status and influence from others. Therefore, it is a very complicated course to measure man's judgment. Accordingly, this

[12] [US], Gordon Allport et al., *Rumor Psychology*, Page 17.

[13] Wang Canfa, He Wen, *The Rumor Communication System of the Public Emergency and Its Process Analysis*, from *Young Journalist*, 2009(33).

rumor formula proposed by Kroos is not feasible but adds to the difficulty in essentially dissolving a rumor.

On the basis of previous researches, we improve the rumor law here by adding the factor of information asymmetry. The rumor formula should be:

$$R = i \times a \times ia$$

The *ia* here means information asymmetry. In other words:

$$\text{Rumor} = \text{Importance of the incident} \times \text{ambiguity of the incident} \times \text{information asymmetry}$$

The more severe information asymmetry is, the quicker rumor communication should be; and, conversely, the less severe information asymmetry is, the slower rumor communication should be, or it might even be stopped. The importance and ambiguity of the incident and information asymmetry are directly proportional to rumor communication, while the three are all indispensable to create a rumor.

Here we will explain it with the rumor caused by the "7.23 rear-end collision of bullet trains" as an example.

First let's talk about the importance of the incident. China's high-speed railway plays an essential and strategic role in economic construction and the development pattern of China in the future. Any major incident of the high-speed railway will undoubtedly draw the nationwide and even worldwide attention due to people's doubt about security of the high-speed rail and concern for the lives of people on the train. It is a matter of individuals' life and safety, but, more importantly, it also concerns how a state respects and assures the life of all citizens.

The second is about the ambiguity of the incident. The incident of the "7.23 rear-end collision of bullet trains" was a completely true fact, which was not made up or fabricated by people. However, the ambiguity of the incident increased as the Ministry of Railways did not publish relevant information after the incident quickly enough. Information such as how they performed the rescue, what measures they took and why. As a result, the public raised a storm of conjecture and rumors on Weibo, some of which were fabricated and widely spread. Within 26 hours of the incident taking place, while no information about the incident had been published by the government, the picture of "the secret hand" triggered the rumor of "the buried alive," which created quite a stir among the netizens and in the whole country. The rising voices of doubts, questions and blames flooded the network. In the subsequent press release held by the Ministry of Railways, the opportunity to calm the rumors was lost when Wang Yongping, the spokesman of the Ministry of Railways, answered "Whether you believe it or not, I do." This arrogant explanation showing no care for life could not relieve people's questions for the rescue, but, instead, aroused public anger. Hence the ambiguity of the incident was intensified again, leading to increasing rumors and the consequent chaos.

Finally, why did this incident give rise to as many as eight major rumors? Information asymmetry is considered to be the reason. The information asymmetry was mainly between the government and the public. Responsible for social administration, the government has access to much more information than the public being managed, and particularly holds many first-hand sources. In general, if not published by the government, this information will be never known to the public. However, citizens have the right to know pursuant to the *Constitution* of China, so the government is required to disclose all information except that which may endanger national security. From this point of view, the information asymmetry between the government and the public could be eliminated. In this incident, the government's information on the accident conditions, accident rescue and handling was asymmetrical to the information known to the public, and the information published by the government failed to satisfy the public's hunger for the truth of the incident. More profoundly, the rumors incurred by this incident were essentially an outburst of the public's resentment and even antipathy towards the Ministry of Railways, which had accumulated over a long period, and reflected their strong distrust of the Ministry of Railways.

8.2.2 The Communication, Spreading and Dissolution Model of the Network Rumor

In light of the law of the rumor after supplement and the case analysis of Weibo rumors caused by the "7.23 rear-end collision of bullet trains," the importance (i) that determines the rumor cannot be decreased. An incident, particularly a major incident, often concerns human survival or social stability, so its importance can hardly be artificially lowered and is almost invariable within a certain period. Meanwhile, people cannot give accurate judgment on the causes of the incident or agency background within a short time after the incident takes place, so ambiguity (*a*) always exists in the incident. Theoretically, the ambiguity can only be lowered upon in-depth investigation of the incident and acquisition of true and essential information. Lowering ambiguity can be achieved by constantly introducing information. However, it should be noted that ambiguity about the incident may increase instead of decreasing if the information acquired brings about more doubts. It is a complicated course to remove the ambiguity concerning and incident. Information asymmetry, the imbalance of information held by the government and the public, tends to create the public's misunderstanding of the incident and their distrust of the government, and thus give rise to more rumors. Therefore, the rumor may find no foundation for existence if information symmetry is achieved between the government and the public. A conclusion can be drawn from the above examination of the three components of the rumor: as the importance of the incident cannot be changed and the ambiguity can hardly be confirmed, information asymmetry (*ia*) is regarded as the key factor to dissolve the rumor. Since the Weibo rumor is still a kind of network rumor, the communication, spreading and dissolution model of the network rumor focusing on elimination of information asymmetry established here is called the "communication, spreading and dissolution model of the network rumor". (See Fig. 8.1).

First of all, this model explains the formation conditions and the communication and spreading path of the network rumor.

The birth of the rumor is closely associated with people's pursuit for security. Any incident involving people's lives and living security, such as an earthquake, nuclear radiation or traffic accident may give rise to people's doubts or puzzles. Busybodies may unveil their psychological insecurity and guesses to the whole world, while sympathizers may widely spread the guesses as good advice, and then the rumor is created. People may easily believe the information delivered by the rumor owing to their instinctive fear of death and high level of concern regarding personal security, which indirectly promotes rumor communication. The emergence of the network further accelerated the rate of spread of the rumor. The network here covers not only the Internet and the mobile phone, but also a larger scope of social networks, including Weibo and the rest.

Secondly, this model proposes the idea of dissolving the rumor relying on the strength of three parties—the government, the media and the

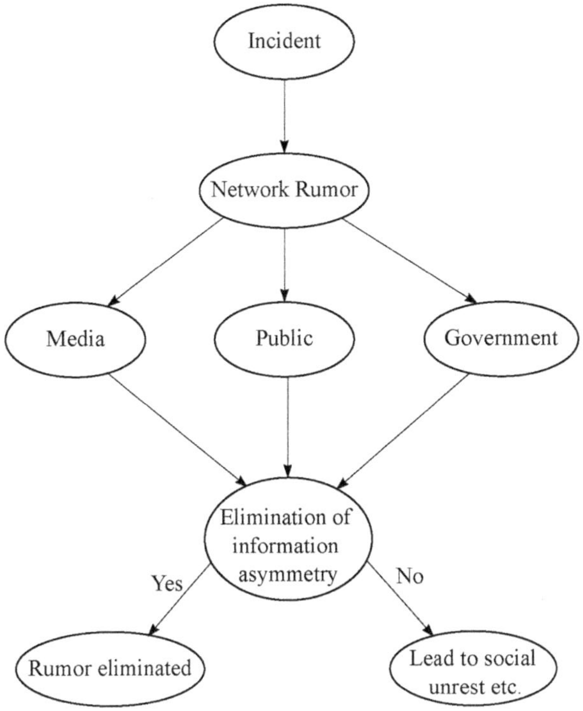

Fig. 8.1 The communication, spreading and dissolution model of the network rumor

public. The government and the public are the two subjects of information asymmetry, while the news media provide the channel to realize information symmetry between the government and the public. Hence the key to dissolving the rumor lies in whether the three parties are able to eliminate information asymmetry during rumor spreading. If these three parties succeed in eliminating information asymmetry, the public will not lose themselves in the rumor or do things blindly; instead, they will take the initiative to spread the true information and gradually dissolve the rumor.

The panic of the "salt rumor" in March 2011 was a typical case where the rumor was communicated at a higher rate due to information asymmetry.[14]

[14] In March 2011, the nuclear power plant explosion in Japan gave rise to the panic of "nuclear leak" that was widely spread in China. Many residents of coastal cities in Jiangsu and

According to science and professional knowledge, the iodine content in salt was too low to play a role in protecting against radiation. Also, the extremely small quantity of radioactive substances leaked by the nuclear power plant in Japan, particularly having been exposed to the dilution process before arriving at the coastal area of China, only exerted negligible impact and caused no pollution of sea salt at all. Nevertheless, since the vast majority of people had no professional knowledge about nuclear radiation, the rumor communication had been accelerated by the panic owing to the asymmetry of professional information.

Finally, this communication, spreading and dissolution model of the network rumor is constructed on the basis of communication studies on the information system and its laws and relying on the network. Distinguished from the traditional model, this model fully respects the principle of freedom and equality of the network world and emphasizes and stresses on guiding the dissolution of the rumor, without setting any channel or variant for how to prevent communication of false information. The free flow of information in the network can hardly be blocked by any power, while the block would only incur more problems and more severe effect. The netizens have their own judgments against the popular rumor. Even if they are misguided for a short while, the truth will be unveiled through various channels because of the real-time information communication. Therefore, the focus should be placed on how to rationally dissolve the network rumor.

8.2.3 Strategies for Dissolution of the Network Rumor Based on the "Communication, Spreading and Dissolution Model of the Network Rumor"

8.2.3.1 The Government Should Enhance Its Credibility, Publish Information Based on Facts and Lay the Foundation for Dissolution of the Rumor

Currently China is undergoing an important transformation period. Despite periods of rapid economic development and social prosperity, social conflicts are intensified. Government credibility is challenged by the

Zhejiang, such as Shaoxing, Ningbo and Fuzhou, rushed to supermarkets to purchase salt, preparing against the nuclear radiation pollution from Japan. They did this for two reasons: firstly, it was said that iodized salt could protect people from radiation; and secondly, sea salt was rumored to have been polluted by nuclear leak.

widening gap between the poor and the rich, peasants' land issue, officials' corruption and unequal distribution of resources and so on. Under the circumstances, if the government continues to disclose information selectively, it will descend to a passive position and see inestimable consequences, which has been demonstrated by the large-scale disturbance raised through the new media such as Twitter and Blackberry mobile phones in London, UK. Hence a foundation for dissolution of rumors is to enhance the government's credibility and publish information based on facts.

The effective approach for the Chinese government to enhance credibility is to make use of its advantages in information, observe the principle of seeking truth from facts, publish information through Weibo and other media in an open, transparent and timely way, try to explain the issue in the first place and dissolve the crisis of the rumor.

8.2.3.2 Pay Attention to the Impact of the "Tacitus Trap"

Technologies are relative, and are never absolutely mature or immature. This is the case with the high-speed rail technology in China. An accident is actually a probability event. Owing to the nature of the "natural monopoly" of the railway, the railway management system is evidently characterized by administration monopoly, without a clear line between the government and the enterprise or between the government and the state-owned capital. In fact, the whole industry is a super monopoly. The Ministry of Railways has attached no importance to making contact with people and media for a long time, so it is an "unpopular department" with some people. Therefore, it is hard for it to avoid falling into the "Tacitus trap."

In the press conference, the spokesman of the Ministry of Railway not only failed to reduce public resentment against the Ministry, but also caused more questions and anger. Then, rumors such as "burying the engine to bury the evidence" and "regarding smooth traffic more important than people's lives" spread like wildfire at the time. The saying of "whether you believe it or not, I do" was satirically named as the "high-speed rail style" by many netizens.

8.2.3.3 The New Media is the Important Platform to Successfully Dissolve the Rumor

The information asymmetry is between the government and the public. The media, being the communication channel between the government and the public, plays an important role in achieving information symmetry between both parties. It can either be the soil for generation and spreading of the rumor or the important platform to refute the rumor. As the media presenting the strongest timeliness, Weibo becomes the cluster of rumors. In the case of the "7.23 rear-end collision of bullet trains," the questions against the rescue work were first proposed on Weibo; and then, as no accurate explanation was given to the public, the questions developed to rumors, which were widely spread. From this point of view, Weibo objectively promoted the spreading of rumors. However, Weibo can also be utilized to publish the true information and eliminate information asymmetry and become the important platform for refuting the rumor. Rumors can make use of Weibo and quickly gather netizens together to blame the government for hiding information, but meanwhile the media can be used to smash the rumor through Weibo by providing accurate and complete details of the investigation.

8.2.3.4 The Public Will Be the Final Propellent for Successful Dissolution of the Rumor by Virtue of Their Unremitting Pursuit of the Truth

The public are vulnerable to the effects of a rumor as they cherish life and master limited knowledge. They may be the communicator of the rumor owing to information asymmetry. However, seen from the whole process from communication, spreading to dissolution of the rumor, the public also challenge the rumor in virtue of their respect for science and pursuit of the truth. When the government and the media constantly provide the information that the public lack, the public will no longer be the communicator of the rumor but support the correct information and become the final propellent for dissolution of the rumor.

CHAPTER 9

New-Media's Public Opinions of the Mass Incident

While undergoing social transformation, China will see increasingly prominent social issues that have been accumulated for a long time, along with the deepening reform of the social management system, great changes of the social structure, profound adjustments to the social pattern of interests, failure of the traditional way of social control and increasingly diversified values. These social conflicts and contradictions have been concentratedly embodied in frequent mass incidents in recent years. According to statistics, "The nationwide mass incidents had increased from over 10,000 in 1994 to over 58,000 in 2009 by 4.8 times, with an annual growth rate of approximately 16.9%."[1]

According to the *2012–2013 Analysis and Prediction of the Social Condition of China* written by Chen Guangjin, the Deputy Director of the Institute of Sociology, Chinese Academy of Social Sciences, the international economy and society was still exposed to unstable and uncertain factors in 2012, when China encountered various issues and challenges in terms of employment, labor relations, income distribution and social management and so on. As indicated in this report, China is now in a period of conflict; and, in recent years, more than tens of thousands, or even over a hundred thousand, mass incidents of social conflicts took place every

[1] Ru Xin, Lu Xueyi, Li Peilin, *The Blue Book of Society—Analysis and Prediction of the Social Condition of China in 2010*, Beijing, Social Sciences Academic Press, 2010.

W. Kuang, *Social Media in China*, Sociology, Media and Journalism in China, https://doi.org/10.1007/978-981-13-0914-4_9

year. The outlook in 2013 was also not optimistic. According to statistics from the All-China Federation of Trade Unions, there were over 120 strikes involving more than 100 people arisen from pay dispute in China from January to August 2012, and more than 270 strikes involving more than 30 people in 19 provinces.

As an important factor affecting social stability, mass incidents have drawn wide attention owing to their frequent occurrence and increasingly fierce confrontation. Many scholars have conducted research on mass incidents from different perspectives in recent years. This chapter, based on previous research, will combine mass incidents that took place in recent years, systematically summarize the definition and major characteristics of the mass incident, particularly the network mass incident, and discuss the process and mechanism of the mass incident.

9.1 The Mass Incident: A Concept with Chinese Characteristics

9.1.1 The Definition of the Concept of the Mass Incident

The "mass incident," also known as the "mass emergency," "mass public security incident," "cluster behavior" or "collective behavior," is a concept with Chinese characteristics. Foreign researchers use different names. The sociological circle in the West regards it as "cluster behavior" and "collective behavior," while Western media are used to calling it "disturbance." Scholars from Taiwan of China refer to it as the "mass event," "crowd activity" and "massive incident" and so on.

Robert Ezra Park, an American sociologist, was the first to give the definition of "collective behavior" (also known as the mass incident) from the perspective of sociology in his book *Introduction to the Science of Sociology*, which described it as "an emotional impulsivity to conduct an individual behavior as promoted and influenced by the collective."[2]

David Popenoe pointed out that the cluster behavior "refers to any behavior conducted in an inorganized, relatively spontaneous and unstable way owing to universal influence and promotion."[3]

[2] R.E. Park. *Introduction to the Science of Sociology*. Chicago: University of Chicago Press, 1921.

[3] David Popenoe. *Sociology*. New York: Prentice Hall Inc, 1995.

Chinese domestic scholars often propose different definitions of the mass incident from different perspectives, which are summarized as follows:

1. Emphasize its influence on and damage to society. According to Kong Lixia, "The mass incident refers to the illegal collective activity where the mass, group or organization sharing the same or similar interests find their interests damaged or dissatisfying, and, as instigated and planned by other people or as irritated by a small detail, finally resort to assembly, demonstration, collective appeal, strike (of students, merchants or workers), siege against Party and government offices, key construction projects or other critical departments, collective block of traffic, collective fight with weapons and even collective beating, smashing, looting, burning or killing and some other ways to seek for the solution to an issue, which result in certain adverse consequences of public security."[4]
2. Emphasize the sudden nature of the incident's initiation. Li Liangdong defined the mass emergency as "illegal pageant, sit-in, demonstration or other forms of large-scale crowd gathering that is sudden or unexpected or has not acquired registration and approval from the competent authority in advance."[5]
3. Emphasize the intermediate factors that initiate the incident. As pointed out by Chen Yuesheng, the mass emergency means "the behavior and activity that suddenly breaks out as incited by certain intermediate social matters, mainly aims to seek for people of common interests, realizes crowd gathering in a spontaneous or organized way and conflicts or contradicts with public order and security."[6]
4. Emphasize the influence on social transformation. In the view of the China Administration Society Research Team, the mass conflict incident taking place during social transformation of China refers to "the mass incident that occurs during China's transition from the planned economy system to the socialist market economy system

[4] Kong Lixia, *Thoughts and Countermeasures of Mass Emergencies*, from *Journal of North Minzu University*, 1999(S1).

[5] Li Liangdong et al., *Stability Is of Overriding Importance*, Page 85, Beijing, Central Party School Press, 1999.

[6] Chen Yuesheng, *Mass Emergencies and Public Sentiments*, Page 12, Tianjin, Tianjin Academy of Social Sciences Press, 2005.

and transformation from traditional agricultural society to modern industrial society, is caused by contradictions among the people or is accumulated or breaks out owing to inappropriate handling of contradictions among the people, involves part of the public, establishes a certain organization, sets the goal, resorts to siege against Party and government offices, sit-in, block of traffic, assembly, gathering a crowd to make disturbances and collective appeal etc., exerts certain influence on the government administration and social order or even launches confrontation of certain intensity in a certain scope."[7]

5. Emphasize the public sentiments in the incident. According to Wang Laihua, the mass emergency means "the incident where a certain number of people reach a consensus within a certain time and space, resort to sit-in, siege, assembly, demonstration and some other ways as influenced or incited by certain intermediate social matters to achieve a certain goal, opposes or confronts the Party and the government authority and incurs the chaos of social order, damages to public or private assets and personal injuries"[8].

The expression of mass incident is more like an official term. The name of the "mass incident" was mentioned in the *Suggestions for Actively Preventing and Properly Dealing with Mass Incidents* forwarded by the General Office of the CPC Central Committee and the General Office of the State Council in 2004, where the mass incident was described as "activities arisen from contradictions among the people where the masses consider their rights and benefits are infringed and express their desire and propose requirements to relevant organizations or units through illegal gathering, siege and some other ways as well as the contact and gathering activities during their preparation."

In 2005, the spokesman of the Organization Department of CCCPC (the Central Committee of the CPC) frankly stated that a few "mass incidents" had arisen as some conflicts could not be solved within the current key period for reform, social transformation and modernization construction of China. At that time, previously used as a derogatory term, the "mass incident" had gradually become a neutral word.

[7] China Administration Society Research Team, *Research on Countermeasures against Mass Emergencies in the Transition Period of China*, p1, Beijing, Academy Press, 2003.

[8] Wang Laihua, *Overview of Public Sentiments Studies—Theories, Methods and Hot Issues*, p12, Tianjin, Tianjin Academy of Social Sciences Press, 2005.

As to these descriptions of the concept of "mass incident," different conclusions have been drawn from different perspectives. However, these definitions actually incorporate the several constituent factors of the mass incident.

1. *Subject*. The mass incident involves a large group of people (no specified number) who pursue the same or similar interests, with or without an organizer.
2. *Reason*. The mass incident generally aims to solve a specific interest issue. Usually, it is directly associated with the interest of a certain group of people, who apply group behaviors to expand their social or political influence, impose pressure on the responsible party to impel the party to solve the specific interest issue. Therefore, the unequal resource allocation constitutes the reason for most mass incidents.
3. *Goal*. The reason determines the goal. As to the mass incident, the group sharing the common direct interest demand or no direct interest demand present their collective strength through group gathering and thus to change their political and economic status and safeguard their interests. Accordingly, the goal of the mass incident lies in correcting and improving improper resource allocation and asking for compensation for the interest loss.
4. *Expression*. Crowd gathering is an important expression form of the mass incident, when a certain number of people, sharing consistent interests, vent their emotions and present their collective strength through various group behaviors, either in a spontaneous or an organized way. Generally, mass incidents in real life mainly adopt political behaviors such as demonstration, sit-in, assembly, block of traffic and beating, smashing and looting. These behaviors are outside the normal political system.
5. *Influence*. The mass incident, regardless of its content and scale, necessarily exerts influence, big or small, on public order and public security in varying degrees and tends to cause conflicts or contradictions, or even social turbulence.

In conclusion, the mass incident is defined as a certain group of people, sharing the same or similar interest demands, gathering in a crowd in a spontaneous or organized way (which exerts influence, big or small, on public order and public security in varying degrees) owing to unequal resource allocation, aiming to correct and improve improper resource allocation, ask for compensation for the interest loss and vent their emotions. Political behaviors outside the normal democratic process are mainly of the form of crowd gathering, including demonstration, sit-in, assembly, block of traffic and beating, smashing and looting.

9.1.2 *The Definition of the Concept of the New-Media Mass Incident*

Along with the constant development of the new-media technology and continuous increase of mobile phone users and netizens, the current mass incidents are all closely linked with the new media. Therefore, in addition to understanding the concept of the "mass incident," it is also necessary to define the "new-media mass incident."

The preliminary research of the "new-media mass incident" is embodied in the research findings about the "mass incident."

Professor Xia Xueluan from the Department of Sociology of Peking University was one of the first to define the network mass incident. He referred to the network mass incident as "network collective behavior" and proposed that "the network collective behavior means that netizens gather in a certain public domain in the network within a certain period in a spontaneous or organized way and have many netizens publish posts for network expression."[9]

Many scholars have since given definitions of the network mass incident, which generally fall into two categories: the first considered the network mass incident as the mass incident combining reality and virtuality; and the second equated the network mass incident with public opinion.

Researchers have reached a consensus on the connotation of the network mass incident—numerous netizens expressing their common appeal in the network. Nevertheless, to some extent, scholars are biased when defining the network mass incident.

As a new form of the mass incident currently, the network mass incident is a product integrating the mass incident and the network. It is irrational to simply regard netizens' appeal as "expressing discontentment," "creating public opinion" and "exerting unfavorable social influence" and so on. As a matter of fact, the network mass incident is a mirror of social dynamics during China's transformation.

[9] Xia Xueluan, *Construction of Cybersociology*, from *Peking University Journal (Philosophy and Social Science Edition)*, 2004(1).

According to domestic and foreign scholars' research and our perspective, we consider the network mass incident to be a group behavior where the new-media group and social group of a certain size, as triggered by a real incident and depending on the new-media platform, concentratedly express their appeal against a certain topic in the new-media space in a spontaneous or organized way, which exerts great influence on the virtual network world and even the real world.

9.1.3 Characteristics of the Mass Incident

9.1.3.1 Collectiveness

Being the essential characteristic of the mass incident, collectiveness suggests the gathering status of people who share the same or similar interests. Generally, these people are holding consistent interest demands and motives. A considerable quantity of mass incidents result from unequal allocation of resources as well as the personal interests of these people, while common interests attract these people and keep them together. Depending on the cause, coverage, crowd mood and influence of the incident, the group may consist of dozens, hundreds, thousands or even tens of thousands of people.

9.1.3.2 Burstiness and Quick Communication

This constitutes an important characteristic of the mass incident. A large number of people may gather together in a very short period of time as suddenly stimulated by an external accident, creating an unexpected scene for which no one is prepared. Furthermore, burstiness is presented in two ways, the burst with a sign and the burst without a sign. As to the burst with a sign, the conflict and the issue have been generated and show a sign of the incident; while for the burst without a sign, the mass incident breaks out suddenly as irritated by certain special conditions. Apparently, the characteristic of burstiness is more evident in the latter one.

The new-media mass incident can be found on-line within two to three hours after the actual incident takes place, is reprinted by several websites after six hours and the replies and discussions on-line reach a peak after twenty-four hours.

Due to the multiple level of trigger factors, different participants, changing content and various forms, the mass incident is often exposed to unexpected changes depending on changes of the causes and the nature and method of the behavior as well as the changes of the controlling measures. Any failure in timely coping with the group conflict may intensify the situation.

9.1.3.3 *Co-existence of Irrationality and Rationality*

Generally, the mass incident is emotional. Emotions exist and play a part in individuals' psychology as well as the masses', and evidently follow the law of "co-frequency resonance." In the mass incident, participants are becoming increasingly irrational owing to the hint, imitation and mutual emotional contagion among the people, until they become fanatical. If irritated by certain social environment, their emotions will be vented in a fierce approach, leading to uncontrollable behavior. Based on the large size of the group, participants of the incident often hold the idea that the law cannot be enforced when everyone is an offender, so they will disregard the constraints of existing social norms and violate laws and social regulations.

The mass incident is an external manifestation of the increasingly intensified profound social contradiction. The subjects of the mass incident—the group of people sharing the same or similar interest and gathering together owing to irrational allocation of social resources—are opposing the competent authority and the responsible department dealing with this incident or another group of people in terms of emotions and interests. This opposition gives rise to the group behavior. The mass incident of general opposition often chooses group appeal or sit-in or similar forms, where participants can control their emotions; but in the mass incident of severe opposition, the subjects of the incident fiercely confront the one maintaining the public security and order, leading to serious consequences such as endangering public order and public safety and causing personal injuries or severe property loss.

9.1.3.4 *Interaction*

The network mass incident often causes a mass incident in real society, or, at least, exerts certain influence on social ideology and culture. For example, it was the mutual effect and the interaction between the network and reality that produced the taxi driver's strike in Chongqing and Sanya.

9.1.3.5 *Cross-Region Property*

Since new media represented by the Internet enables information to communicate rapidly, crossing regions and national borders, a local incident may become a national incident, going beyond the geographical restriction, as it is focused, enlarged and spread by the network.

9.2 The Evolution Mechanism of the Mass Incident

Examining relevant documents on the mass incident known to us, we can see most of the research focuses on the concept, characteristics and causes of the mass incident, but only a few of them mention its internal evolution mechanism. As a discrete random incident, the evolution process of the mass emergency constitutes a complicated system. Only by studying the evolution mechanism and all the factors that influenced the incident, can the early warning and emergency management system that adapts to mass incidents with Chinese characteristics be designed based on the essential characteristics and mechanism of the incident.

Our studies mainly resort to the theory of social conflict and cluster behavior, particularly the value-added theory of Neil Smelser, as the basis, analyze major influential factors of the mass incident and its dynamic and static process of evolution, and thus describe how the influencing factors promote the evolution of the mass incident at every stage.

9.2.1 Theoretical Basis

9.2.1.1 Social Conflict Theory

With the social conflict as the object, the Western social conflict theory is an important trend of social thought in Western sociology and politics. This is a theory of social construction that explains how to cope with and solve social conflicts that arise during social development.

Represented by Lewis Coser[10] and Ralf Dahrendorf,[11] the social conflict theory focuses on studying the causes, forms, constraints and influence of

[10] Lewis Coser, 1913–2003, a sociologist, once served as the President of American Sociological Association, and worked as an executive member of the Association for ten years and later as a director of the Association. He also once took office of the President of East American Sociological Association and the Chairman of the Institute for Social Research.

[11] Ralf G. Dahrendorf, 1929–2009, born in Hamburg, Germany, studied philosophy and classical linguistics in the University of Hamburg, and, after graduation from University of Hamburg, went to London School of Economics to study sociology in 1952 and acquired the PhD in 1956. He had held a teaching post respectively in University of Saarlandes, University of Hamburg, University of Tuebingen and University of Konstanz. From 1967 to 1970, he served as the President of German Sociological Association and started to assume office of the President of London School of Economics since 1974. Ralf Dahrendorf is considered as one of the major representatives of the conflict theory As early as in 1958, he criti-

the social conflict. This theory was proposed upon reflection on and as a contradictory against the structural functionalism theory. While the structural functionalism theory emphasizes social stability and integration and stands as the conservatives of sociology, the social conflict theory stresses the positive role of social conflict in social consolidation and development and stands as the radicals of sociology.

The social conflict theory developed from the structural functionalism theory. In the 1950s and 1960s, the United States was seeing increasingly intensified social conflicts and social instability. This theory was popular in the United States and west Europe in the late 1960s, had made a big sensation in western sociological circle and penetrated into empirical researches of different subdisciplines of sociology. At that time, a large number of works were created based on the framework of the conflict in the field of political sociology, organizational sociology, race relations, social stratification, collective behavior, marriage and family and so on, which had a great impact on contemporary sociology development.

The social conflict theory absorbed the favorable part of the structural functionalism theory, criticized the social equilibrium, stability, harmony and order advocated in the structural functionalism theory, pointed out the common interest disputes as well as common conflicts and contradictions among different classes of society at that time, reasonably explained social issues that bothered people and proposed the methods to solve these issues. In this way, the status of this theory was firmly established in academia.

The dialectical conflict theory created by Ralf Dahrendorf, a German sociologist, also plays a nonnegligible part. According to his central idea, conflicts can never be eliminated in human society, though people can guide and institutionalize the conflict or dispel the intensified conflict form. Power and the authority will necessarily lead to competition, social conflict and social changes, so the power and the authority are considered

cized functionalism and analyzed society in details in terms of the role of change, conflict and other factors in system differentiation as well as violence. He believed that the root cause for modern class conflict lay in the conflict between occupation and no occupation of the means of production, and also the conflict between the sharing and exclusion of the authority. He also put forward the concept of social man. His major works include *Theoretical Discussion of Social Conflict*, *Class and Class Conflict in Industrial Society*, *Leaving Utopia*, *The Social Man*, *Post-class Conflict* and *Life Chances*.

as the key to explain everything related to humans. He proposed an objection against Talcott Parsons's structural functionalism theory that unilaterally emphasized equilibrium and consensus but ignored the conflict.

Ralf Dahrendorf believed that society had two dialectical sides, equilibrium and conflict. Despite the structural stability, society is constantly exposed to changes; despite the system integration, subsystems of society generally contradict each other; despite the synergism of functions, each part of society features both positive and negative functions; and despite the value consensus, a group of social members have to change their own values as suppressed by another group of members. This dialectical view of society steered Ralf Dahrendorf's social conflict theory. Therefore, his social conflict theory was named as the dialectical conflict theory based on this dialectical view of society and the corresponding dialectical analysis.

According to Ralf Dahrendorf, society is always exposed to changes as well as opposition and conflict; the social conflict makes up the fundamental driving force for social changes, while any factor of the society may lead to social conflicts, changes and even disintegration; and social members and organizations formed the society, not for their consensus or interattraction but for the domination and suppression relationship between the two. The domination and suppression, which always exist within society though can be controlled or directed, lay the foundation for the social conflict theory. The most fundamental cause for social conflict lies in the opposition between the economic interests of the two. When the contradictions of conflict groups break out, the confrontation will end, leading to structural changes and redistribution of the authority and interest domination. Dahrendorf also pointed out that it was futile to attempt to suppress and eliminate the conflict once it had been generated.

Lewis Coser, the Western sociologist from the United States, is a major representative of the functional conflict school. Born in a Jewish family in Berlin, Germany, he had been in exile in France from 1933 and immigrated to the United States in 1941. Featuring both the background of the structural functionalism and the standpoint of the conflict theory, Lewis Coser's theory criticized functionalism for overemphasizing social integration and listing any social conflict and aberration as sociopathy, while also opposed Ralf Dahrendorf for overemphasizing the damages of conflict to social stability and integration. Compared with other conflict theorists, Lewis Coser attached greater importance to the process and result of the conflict and paid special attention to analysis of the social conflict. In his opinion, the topic and the social structure of the conflict determine the positive function or the negative function of the conflict. As to the topic of the conflict, provided that the conflict topic does not involve the foundation of both parties, the conflict plays a positive role; and if the core value is involved, the conflict plays a negative role. As to the social structure derived from the conflict, in an open society loosely organized, the non-essential social conflict is positive; and, conversely, in a closed social structure, the conflict will function negatively in the case of no or inadequate tolerance or institutionalization of the conflict. To describe how to vent dissatisfaction and hostility, Lewis Coser put forward the theory of the "social safety valve." The "social safety valve" against social conflict functions the same as the "safety valve" against a boiler, which protects the whole structure from being damaged by continuously discharging the steam. The "social safety valve" mainly has two functions: (1) reducing the social pressure, that is, reducing or relieving the hostility between both parties; (2) giving a social alarm, that is, reporting the public feelings to the ruling class or social administration.

9.2.1.2 Collective Behavior Theory

According to social psychology, man presents both rational and irrational personalities. When individuals become irrational and a group share basically consistent irrational personalities, the group's rationality is much lower than the individual's and the group's spirit of adventure significantly rises; and, in this case, the decision making of the group is severely biased or even goes to extremes. Against this phenomenon, social psychology explores the collective behavior theory.

"Collective behavior" refers to the "unexpected, relatively spontaneous and inorganized behavior that uniformly corresponds to one common irritation in an unstable case."[12] The collective behaviors mainly include "the collective behaviors of primary stage and form such as the rumor, public opinion and propaganda; the behaviors that tend to be adopted by relatively dispersed groups such as fashion, prevalence, panic and fanaticism; the mass incidents that may have a certain organization and goal and take place in relatively more concentrated groups such as gathering and making disturbances, strike, pageant and demonstration; and collective phenomena

[12] David Popenoe. *Sociology*. New York: Prentice Hall Inc, 1995.

in the new electronic and network environment extended from the connotation and denotation of the collective behavior."[13]

Gustave Le Bon,[14] a French scholar, was the earliest to research on collective behavior. Starting from the public, the most fundamental form of collective behavior, he studied on some new characteristics of the public that differ from those of its constituent individuals.

The American sociologist Robert Ezra Park[15] had made a comprehensive introduction to collective behavior in the book *Introduction to the Science of Sociology*, and he believed that "the collective behavior is a product of social interaction."[16]

William McDougall thought that individuals' nature would be aroused by other people's expression of feelings and the primary instinct of individuals that made up the public and their emotional interaction led to the collective behavior of the public.[17]

David Popenoe[18] pointed out "The collective behavior refers to the behavior conducted owing to certain common stimulation and influence in an unstable, inorganized and relatively spontaneous way."[19]

[13] Bimber, B., Flanagin, A.J., & Stohl, C. "Reconceptualizing collective action in the contemporary media environment". *Communication Theory*, 2005, Vol. 15.

[14] Gustave Le Bon, 1841–1931, representative work *The Crowd: A Study of the Popular Mind.*

[15] Robert Ezra Park, 1864–1944, American sociologist, one of the main representatives of the Chicago School. Born in a merchant family in Luzerne County, Pennsylvania, US on February 14, 1864, he attended the University of Michigan and acquired the Bachelor degree of philosophy in 1887. After that, he dedicated himself to the press and was full of enthusiasm about investigations and reports of urban and social issues and the deprived class. From 1898, he took up advanced studies successively in Harvard University and Heidelberg University where he studied under William James, Josiah Royce and Georg Simmel among others. He taught at Harvard as an assistant professor of philosophy in 1904 and 1905 and then assisted Booker T. Washington to work on racial issues. Later, he taught at the Department of Sociology at the University of Chicago from 1914 to 1936. He served as president of the American Sociological Association from 1925. Representative works: *The Immigrant Press and its Control* and *Introduction to the Science of Sociology.*

[16] R.E. Park. *Introduction to the Science of Sociology.* Chicago: University of Chicago Press, 1921.

[17] William McDougall. *The Group Mind.* Michigan: G.P. Putnam's Sons, 1920.

[18] David Popenoe is now serving as the sociology professor and the assistant dean of the School of Society and Behavior Science of the State University of New Jersey in New Brunswick and the sociology professor of the School of Humanities and Science of Rutgers. He has high attainments in studies of social organization and social change, family and social changes etc. and has published numerous works. Representaive works: *Turbulences of the Nest: Changes and Decline of the Family in the Modern Society, Sociology.*

[19] David Popenoe. *Sociology.* New York: Prentice Hall Inc, 1995.

According to David Popenoe, major factors contributing to the occurrence of the collective behavior include the following:

1. *Environment*: People will make common response to the same stimulus in a certain environment, such as the weekend or night when the group is vulnerable to mobilization and influence, a special case where no regulation is provided and the conflict of values and lack of system owing to social changes, and so on;
2. *Relative deprivation*: Relative deprivation means that people fail to acquire what they think they deserve through their effort;
3. *Social control mechanism*: In case of reduction or even collapse of the social control mechanism, people may tend to question the legality of the existing system and try to transform or even overthrow the system for reconstruction through the collective behavior.

Gordon Allport[20] put forward the theory of social facilitation. By a series of experiments on the speed of association, reversible perspective and comparison of psychophysics, the theory proves that the completion of personal tasks will be facilitated by the presence of others, that is to say, an individual will present different characteristics when affected by others of the group compared to when the individual is alone.

The value-added theory of Neil Smelser[21] holds that six conditions need to be provided for generation of the mass incident: environmental condition,

[20] Gordon W. Allport, 1897–1967, American personality psychologist, the father of experimental social psychology, proposed the concept of "social facilitation" and was one of the representatives of humanistic psychologist in the United States. He was selected as the President of the American Psychological Association in 1939 and won the Excellent Scientific Contribution Award released by the American Psychological Association in 1964. His representative works include *Psychology of Rumor, Personality: A Psychological Interpretation, The Nature of Personality* and *Becoming: Basic Considerations for a Psychology of Personality.*

[21] Neil Joseph Smelser, 1930–, went to Oxford University to study as a Rhodes scholar in 1952 and earned his PhD in philosophy at Harvard University. Later, he took up advanced learning in San Francisco Spiritual Analysis Institute. Then he taught at University of California, Berkeley and became a sociology professor there in 1972. He assumed the office of the Deputy Director of the Institute for International Relations twice, respectively from 1969 to 1973 and from 1980 to 1981. He had also served in some sociology institutes and academic societies. His main publications *include Economy and Society (with Talcott Parsons), Social Change in the Industrial Revolution, Theory of Collective Behavior, The Sociology of Economic Life, Collection of Sociology Explanations and Papers, Comparative Methods in the Social Science* and *The Changing Academic Market.*

pressure of social structure, inducing factor, common perception, group emotion and mobilization and failure of the control mechanism.

The social conflict theory and collective behavior theory, particularly the value-added theory, explains the laws of group development and the evolution mechanism, which, from a micro level, concerns the actors' daily life experience, structural resentment and common belief reflected by the inducing factor under the background of social conflict and intensified structural pressure; from a median level, pays attention to how emotional contagion and mobilization further promotes occurrence of the collective behavior; and also, from a macro level, analyzes how the primary and secondary incident lacking control during the interaction finally leads to the network mass incident.

9.2.2 The Basic Process of the New-Media Mass Incident

The basic process of the new-media mass incident is summarized as follows. As affected by numerous stimuli, a certain incident takes place in a special social context. A new media user posts this incident in the network. The post about this incident attracts more attention and recognition of new media users than other posts, so many new media users click to view the post and some reply to express their own opinions, realizing the opinion interaction and emotional contagion with other netizens. Moreover, some new media users advocate applying certain actions, while a few of these suggestions gain much sympathy and response from increasing new media users and finally develop to be the new-media mass incident. At last, the government becomes involved, publishes the information and solves and settles the network mass incident, and everything returns to normal.

On this basis, the new-media mass incident is divided into six stages: incident normality, new-media news, new-media hot incident, new-media mass incident, incident handling and incident settlement (see Fig. 9.1).

Among these stages, the news media news indicates when the new media user posts a certain irritant incident on the network BBS and communicates it to other new media users by personal publishing. The post at this time is just a post of network news.

When the post attracts more attention of new media users, increasing numbers of new media users are clicking and viewing this post and even some new media users reply to express their own opinions. New media users are exposed to emotional contagion, and the common perception and group consciousness are gradually formed. By then, the page views of

Fig. 9.1 Development stages of the new-media mass incident

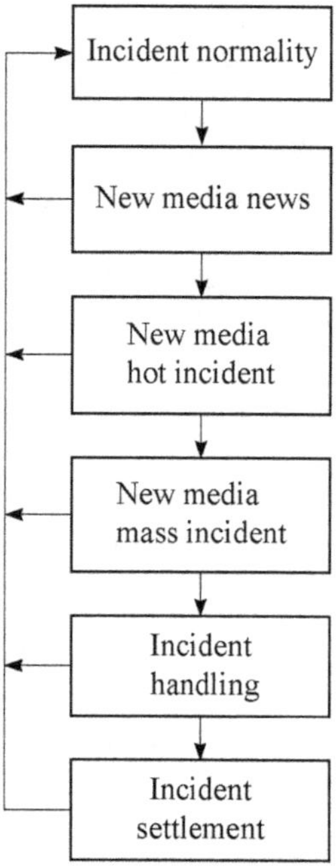

the news post continue to rise, while the post becomes the network hot post and the incident is escalated to network hot incident.

Then, when the emotion of new media users is further intensified, they advocate further action. The suggestion gains much sympathy from increasing new media users. Other new media users respond to it and put it into practices. Upon mobilization, collective behaviors are constantly emerging. Then, this incident becomes the new-media mass incident, and the corresponding post is the network mass-incident post.

9.2.3 Analysis of the Social Context for the Mass Incident

9.2.3.1 Social Transformation and Redistribution of Interests

In recent years, China has made great social, economic, political and cultural progress and people's living standards continue to improve, which has given rise to many profound conflicts and social issues. After having been accumulated to a certain degree, these social conflicts will likely irritate the public, leading to massive explosion of mass incidents in China at the present stage.

It is an evitable outcome of historical development, mainly because China is exposed to social transformation, that is, social changes.

Social transformation in China is embodied in transformation of the economic system, political system, social system and openness. All aspects of society are subject to profound changes brought by the transformation, mainly including: reorganization of the interest structure and class differentiation; loss of traditional authority and transfer of social power; transition of the social system and change of the social development trend; aggravated competitions and conflicts among different social groups, individuals and social forces; belief crisis and diversified values; and anxiety and confusion of social psychology.[22]

Samuel Huntington[23] once pointed out that "Modernity breed stability, while modernization creates unrest."[24] Various profound changes during social transformation finally lead to instability of society, demonstrated by the frequent occurrence of mass incidents.

9.2.3.2 Pressure of the Social Structure

The value-added theory of Neil Smelser and Lewis Coser's constituent factors of conflict are evidently revealed in studies of the changes of the social structure and its social context during social transformation of China. Therefore, as a manifestation of collective behavior, collective action and social conflict, the mass incident is inevitable.

According to Neil Smelser's theory, the following factors are contributing to the frequent occurrence of mass incidents in China nowadays:

1. *Environment.* The rapidly developing new media provides the support platform and the space for the mass incident.

[22] Lin Mobiao, *Basic Features of Social Transformation and Transitional Society*, from *Socialism Studies*, 2004(6).

[23] Samuel P. Huntington, 1927–2008, was a famous international political theorist in contemporary United States. He studied in Yale University, University of Chicago and Harvard University, earned his Ph D in 1951 and stayed on to teach at the school. He had served as an official or consultant in many departments of US government. Huntington had worked as the professor of Albert J. Weatherhead III of Harvard University, the director of Harvard's Center for International and Regional Affairs, the director of John Olin Institute of Strategic Research and a consultant to the state security program of the Carter administration. He was also the spokesman and one of the chief editors of *Foreign Policy* and the author of *The Clash of Civilizations and the Remaking of World Order*.

[24] [US] Samuel Huntington, *Political Order in Changing Societies*, Beijing, Joint Publishing, 1989.

2. *Pressure of the social structure.* As China is exposed to social transformation, emerging social conflicts have bred numerous social risks. Some conflicts may give rise to the vulnerable segmentation of the social structure, which may lead to fracture of the social structure in a severe case.
3. *Inducing factor.* Under the background of tense social structure, the irritant incident tends to stimulate people to vent their dissatisfaction and express their interest demands.
4. *Common perception.* Upon the combined effect of the social structural pressure and irritant incident, the associated people may easily reach certain recognition and sympathy and generate universal perception and common belief.
5. *Group emotion and action mobilization.* Driven by universal perception and common belief, netizens sharing the recognition and the sense of belonging gradually gather together and create the network group. During expansion of the group size, the group, based on emotional contagion, finds collective excitement and responds to the call to action of active figures. In this way, the mobilization is completed.
6. *Failure of the control mechanism.* The constant interaction between and spreading of the primary and secondary incident produce the network mass incident.

In our opinion, pressures of the social structure mainly incorporate the elements discussed in the following subsections.

9.2.3.2.1 Unfairness

Along with the further development of the Reform and Opening Up program and the progress of social transformation, the original social pattern of interests has collapsed, with the different social classes now exposed to new interest differentiation and combination. The possession of social wealth varies vastly among the people, since they own different social resources, political and economic, in addition to the effect of multiple ownerships and distribution methods. The disadvantaged group at the lower level of society, instead of grasping the opportunities brought about by social transformation and sharing the fruits of Reform and Opening Up, suffer too much of the cost of social transformation and reform and have even had their previous earnings reduced. By comparison, the advantaged social group accumulates fabulous social wealth relying on the great quantity of social resources held in their hands. Owing to the unfair social distribution, unfair class development and unfair allocation of resources, the disadvantaged group psychologically feels extremely lost, unfairly treated and relatively deprived and, therefore, holds strong resentment against the government and society. The hatred of officials and rich people is widely spread, social conflict frequently occurs and social risks are constantly accumulated, which constitute the fundamental inducing factor for them to lodge their dissatisfaction to the network, which in turn leads to a network mass incident.

9.2.3.2.2 Government Misconduct

At present, many problems exist in the government's operating mechanism, such as policy making not being open and transparent enough, unclear operating rules of the system, constantly changing policies, insufficient and ineffective international management and lack of effective channels for citizen participation in terms of external communication. Since the negative news may be extended as a result of the increasingly developed network and media and due to the misconduct of local governments, the credibility crisis of these local governments has been intensified, which further endangers the credibility of the whole government.

9.2.3.2.3 The System to Be Improved

Institutions, the normative system governing people's social relations and ways of behavior confirmed by society within a certain historical stage, act as a prerequisite and important support to social stability. The degree of stability of a society mainly depends on the degree of systematization and institutionalization of that society.

Since the Reform and Opening Up program, social transformation in China has accompanied a series of profound and extensive institutional changes, giving rise to complicated social conflicts and contradictions. Affected by modernity, the traditional social system has broken away from social restraint and obstruction and has gradually disintegrated and collapsed. However, facing the great demands of economic, social and political reform, the new means of economic production and economic security is exposed to the shock by the traditional means, and is therefore uncertain and unstable.

In light of the long-term, local and unsystematic institutional transition, the old institutions, norms and values have been denied, while the new ones have either not yet been formed or fail to universally and effectively bind all social members. Hence the issues of "institutional conflict," "institutional deficiency" and "institutional void" have emerged. In this case, social contradiction and social conflict can hardly be regulated and controlled effectively owing to the deficiency or "vacuum" of social norms and authority as well as the lagged and weak social integration and control mechanism. Under these circumstances, the public is prone to behave offensively, which may damage the normal social order, and even a network mass incident may occur.

9.2.3.2.4 Social Psychological Changes

The psychological change constitutes the origin and powerful driving force for individuals to attend mass behaviors. Subjective psychological factors contributing to individual behaviors are mainly manifested by the follows:

First, the public's awareness of safeguarding rights and democratic participation is sharpening. Therefore, when the public's rights and benefits are deprived or damaged, they will actively seek for feasible measures to solve practical issues. Through rapid development of the network and based on its favorable characteristics, the network has become a good platform for the public to safeguard interests and express appeals.

Second, the public are feeling increasing relative deprivation. The sense of relative deprivation means that people feel deprived of their own interests by other groups when comparing themselves to the reference group. The great gap between the poor and the rich in China inevitably brings about relative deprivation. As driven by the sense of relative deprivation, the disadvantaged group will feel discontent and hold a resentment or even hatred and grudge against the group that deprives them of their interests.

The third is the chaos of values. The traditional values, beliefs, morals and social norms have been subject to facture during modernization, so society sees the chaos of people's values, no norms for social behaviors and irresponsible, extreme and vulgar values. Owing to the anonymity of the network, the joining groups are prone to irrational and extreme policies and behaviors.

Fourth, people's law consciousness is weak. Compared to positive changes of people's mind, their cultural quality is lagging far behind. They apply abnormal ways to safeguard their rights, owing to a lack of, or immature, democracy and law consciousness, lack of rational subject consciousness and the universal idea of "the law cannot be enforced when everyone is an offender." As people do not need to worry about being held accountable, more people are encouraged to attend the network mass incident, which affect the frequency and influence of the network mass incident.

9.2.4 Influencing Factors of Evolution of the Mass Incident and Analysis of the Action Mechanism

9.2.4.1 Influencing Factors of Evolution of the Mass Incident

9.2.4.1.1 Irritant Inducing Factors

First of all, an incident tends to trigger the network mass incident if it reflects the typical contradiction and focused conflict, touches vital interests of netizens, gains netizen's experience-based recognition and sympathy and attracts the attention of sufficient netizens. Any occasional incident associated with public interests may result in the breakout and venting of netizens' dissatisfaction and grudges, owing to increasing pressure of the social structure. To express certain common affection needs, many netizens respond actively to the appeal, and gather together, express their demands and mobilize others through the platform of the Internet. In this way, a large-scale network mass incident is generated.

Second, an inducing incident is able to become a network mass incident, when it violates morals and laws and challenges the mainstream values of society but it is legitimate to participate in the incident. This kind of incident will very likely incite netizens' strong but irrational moral outrage for the immorality and unfairness of the incident, and rapidly lead to netizens' resentment and disgust. According to previous experiences, this kind of incident will see rapid expansion of the range of influence and enter the public agenda after reports in the mass communication media, when the corresponding government department has to pay attention to this incident and even apply a solution under the pressure of the superior government and public opinion in the network. For example, in the "poisonous milk scandal" and "oblique building incident," netizens had legally proposed a condemnation and request for accountability investigation against any behavior that violated against laws and morals and challenged social mainstream values.

Finally, when an incident shows a dramatic effect, goes beyond netizens' expectation, attracts wide attention and arouses people's strong interests, it also tends to become a network mass incident. Only by attracting people's attention and arousing their interests can the information successfully trigger people's collective consciousness and joint action and can it make up an inducing factor to the network mass incident. As to the network mass incident, the click rate is considered the indicator to measure how much the information attracts netizens' concern and its influence on netizens. In the network, people have a more visible logic of thinking, simpler and undisguised emotions and more diversified imaginations. Furthermore, the absolute, uncompromising and brief and clear expression of ideas in the network infinitely expands and spreads any tiny feeling, so netizens are vulnerable to hints and are easily moved.

9.2.4.1.2 Psychological Distance and Common Perception

As to the psychological distance, the participant of the incident will first consider his/her psychological distance to this incident before deciding whether to participate in any network behavior (view, reply, share and so on). Provided the incident involves the netizen's vital interests and draws his/her close attention, the netizen shows a shorter psychological distance to this incident and tends to adopt further network behaviors; and, conversely, when the psychological distance to this incident is longer, and the further network behavior will not be triggered.

Common perception refers to a kind of ideological and affective identification among participants of the incident inside a group based on their common attitude, understanding and goal. Generally, common perception is easier to be formed among netizens sharing shorter psychological distance to the same incident. Being the adhesive that binds participants of the collective behavior in a network mass incident, the formation of common perception is of particular significance. Upon the short psychological distance, based on common interests and concerns, common experiences and comparisons as well as common emotions and traditional morals, heterogenous netizens will get rid of their own prejudices, share and follow the same topic and task, form a common perception for a certain subject, intensify group cohesion and further produce the sense of belonging and the sense of identity of the group and stratum. By then, the group presents a powerful common belief, which is constructed for the network mass incident, and which lays the foundation for transformation from individual behaviors to collective behaviors.

9.2.4.1.3 Emotional Contagion

The contagion theory considers the collective behavior as a result of people's emotional contagion. In a group, an individual's emotion is extremely vulnerable to the contagion and hints by the group emotion. The participant of the collective behavior has lost his/her conscious personality, while the unconscious personality dominates. Based on certain social psychology and affected by the hint, people's emotions develop towards a certain direction and tend to be transformed to behaviors. When mobilized or organized in a crowded occasion, people's emotions are vulnerable to contagion, a chained and cyclic course of response. People lack rational analysis and judgment during emotional contagion.

When exposed to high excitement, people enjoy significantly increasing group consciousness and cohesion and very likely believe gossip and rumors, so the rumors spread rapidly among the group and affects group members. This situation will further spur their excitement, and they will show a more evident inclination to adopting actions. Under these circumstances, participants' actions are mainly controlled by their emotions, when they may abandon social morals and norms as well as laws, conduct extreme behaviors and bring about unpredictable consequences.

9.2.4.1.4 Behavior Mobilization

In the network environment, behavior mobilization constitutes a necessary condition for collective behavior. Here we focus on discussing the role of the opinion leaders in network popular feelings, network public opinion, Internet mass hunting and other network collective behaviors. The opinion leaders refers to people who actively join the network of interpersonal communication, often provide opinions, ideas or suggestions to others and exerts influence on others. However, in the network era, the grass-root netizen who is the most active on-line and able to master and analyze information can also be called the "opinion leader." The authority of the opinion leader is constructed based on several factors. Higher authority and higher activeness will result in a higher ability in action mobilization. By frequently publishing information and setting the relevant network subject, an opinion leader consolidates netizens' perception, emotion and attitude formed during the generalized-belief period of structural tension and common perception by means of propaganda, demonstration, exaggeration and hint, calls on netizens to safeguard their own interests or common morals and values and mobilizes netizens to turn their attitude towards an incident to a practical behavior against or response to the incident.

The information initially published by the opinion leaders may be a piece of news, a photo or a dialogue, which, after processing and analysis by opinion leaders, often touches society's most sensitive issues and makes netizens repost the content, reply and even conduct Internet hunting in a big way.

9.2.4.1.5 Interaction Between the Network and Traditional Media and the Emergence of Collective Behaviors

Interaction between the network and traditional media frequently plays an important role in the occurrence of network mass incidents and emergence of collective behaviors. With the rapid development of the network in recent years, the audience relies less on the traditional media. Nevertheless, in view of the development of network mass incident, the incidents that drew wide attention of the public and even aroused the government's concern were mostly published and deeply investigated by the traditional media. The developing process of the incident and the final solution to the issue often depend on the interaction between the traditional media and the network media. By analyzing network mass incidents, we can see that most network mass incidents have gone through the following process: the subject published on line → netizens reposting, replying and following the subject in a massive way → traditional media deepening the subject and setting the media agenda → public agenda → netizens reposting, replying and following the subject again → re-report by traditional media → … → the subject exiting from the public agenda.

The information about the "Sun Zhigang Incident" first came from the "Peach Blossom Castle," a forum of Xici Hutong, where media people from all corners of the country gathered. At the end of March 2003, a postgraduate student studying media in Beijing published a post in the forum, saying that a classmate of his classmate died in Guangzhou for no reason and his family was attempting to find out why. This post was not massively reposted or discussed at that time. However, this incident immediately drew wide attention from the public after having been published by *Southern Metropolis Daily* on April 25, and attracted the public's attention more after Sina and other websites reprinted the news and subsequently became the hot topic in the network. By then, the "Sun Zhigang Incident" developed to be nationwide news from local news reported by the local media and became the focus of the state for some time. Later, news media of different levels and types involved in the report of this incident.

In the network era, the social control mechanism will be constantly weakened. Social control in a traditional sense means that the social institutions or organizations such as the government exert influence on the generation and development of collective behaviors. However, in the network environment, collective behaviors are more vulnerable to the effect of public opinion and communication. Theoretically, the traditional media should fulfill the monitoring duties, select or revise the news information, decide the type and quality of the news delivered and further affect or control the content or direction of public opinions. But, in order to satisfy the audience's demands and fight for the resources of public attention, the traditional media nowadays prefer seeking after hot issues of network public opinion and have weakened or even given up their power of monitoring and control.

In view of the public's decreasing trust in the government's legitimacy and the weakening social control mechanism, more and more people will actively join collective behaviors due to the interaction between the network and traditional media and its influence.

9.2.4.2 Analysis of the Action Mechanism of These Factors

Being exposed to transformation, the Chinese society presents an unequal allocation of resources and tense social structure at a macro level. The relatively disadvantaged masses are inclined to bear resentment against the real environment and hold a hostility and grudge against various advantaged groups, as social conflicts are intensified by social realities such as disappearance of the public discourse space, imperfect mechanism of interest expressing, unequal political status, information deficiency, misconduct of some local governments that damage people's interests and improper social control. The public's disequilibrium and sense of deprivation formed in the real environment produce their externally explicit or internally implicit demands and motives, which constitute the fundamental cause for people to join the network or participate in the network mass incident.

When a piece of network news incorporates the stimuli such as deprivation of common interests, violation against common experiences and injuries of common emotions, it will easily acquire netizens' concern, and by then, netizens will judge their psychological distance to this incident. In case of the short psychological distance, netizens will further follow and participate in communication and discussion of the incident, form belief identity and common perception and share a sense of belonging to the corresponding group and stratum. Conversely, in the case of the long psychological distance to the incident, netizens have no common perception and fail to gather into a group, when this incident will be rapidly covered by the massive information in the network.

As to the specific network behavior, netizens may hope to exert certain influence on an incident, as stimulated by the inducing factor, driven by the psychological demand and called on by common perception. Then, they can show their impact by building the incident to be a hot issue of network public opinions through consistent network behaviors such as clicks, views, replies, reposts, topping or highlighting, and even turn the network news to be a network hot incident.

When these conditions, including social background, structural press, irritant stimuli and common perception and belief, are satisfied, participants' emotional contagion and action mobilization function as the driving force for group construction and collective behaviors of the network mass incident. If the netizens who click, view and follow certain hot issue, find other netizens who share the same interest demand and safeguard the common morals and values and meanwhile accumulate and vent their emotions, and also find any mobilization, response and interaction of group behaviors, they will reply and discuss the post for support or respond to mobilization in other ways, further construct the network group, mobilize group behaviors and promote the network hot incident to become a network mass incident. Conversely, without a corresponding emotional contagion and behavior mobilization, netizens will not further construct the network group or mobilize the collective behavior, while the network hot incident will gradually lower its voice and disappear.

On this basis, the joining in of the traditional media that actively cater for netizens' demand preferences as well as the interaction between the network and the traditional media promote the emergence of and interaction between the primary and secondary incident during collective behaviors of the network mass incident.

The primary incident of the network mass incident indicates the initial incident when the network mass incident first breaks out; and the secondary incident represents the secondary incident derived from the primary incident during the evolution of the network mass incident. Provided the primary incident and secondary incident link closely to and affect each other, the primary and secondary incidents will constantly emerge, constituting collective behaviors. As the original stimulus, the social conflict behind the network mass incident has drawn high attention from netizens as it releases the irritant inducing incident that incorporates various factors attracting netizens. With persistent overheating of the incident, the traditional media join in in a very short time so as to strive for public attention, actively participate in incident spreading, stimulate the audience's emotions and mobilize netizens to express and safeguard their interests; and then, a secondary incident is generated. As supported by the traditional media, netizens will continue to show concern about the incident and respond to action mobilization, leading to the second round of overheating and spreading of the incident in the network; and then the new hot topic of network public opinion will spur the traditional media to participate in and interact with the incident again, promoting the generation of the network hot topic in the next stage and even collective behaviors. Following this circle, primary and secondary incidents constantly emerge and interact with each other, and the network mass incident takes place.

After the network mass incident occurs, the corresponding responsible department will attach great importance to the incident, and the government will investigate and regulate on this incident and publish relevant information, so it facilitates settlement of this incident to a certain extent. Then, the network mass incident gradually lowers its voice and subsides.

9.2.5 *Analysis of the Evolution Mechanism of the Network Mass Incident*

The evolution mechanism of the network mass incident studies the laws of the generation and development of the network mass incident. In our studies, we have reached the theoretical model for the evolution of the mass network incident. The main elements of the evolution mechanism are shown in Fig. 9.2).

In the model shown in Fig. 9.2, the network mass evolves in a dynamic and expanding process, which consists of the following six stages.

The first stage is the normal phase of the incident, when the incident has no attention from netizens. It is still at an embryo stage for breakout of the mass incident.

In the second stage, the accumulated social conflicts and contradictions and the tense social structure give rise to network news of all different sizes, which constitute the background and origin of the network mass incident. Owing to the rapid development of the network and intensified social conflict and structural tension, social conflicts and social risks cannot be effectively regulated and eliminated, while the public, particularly the

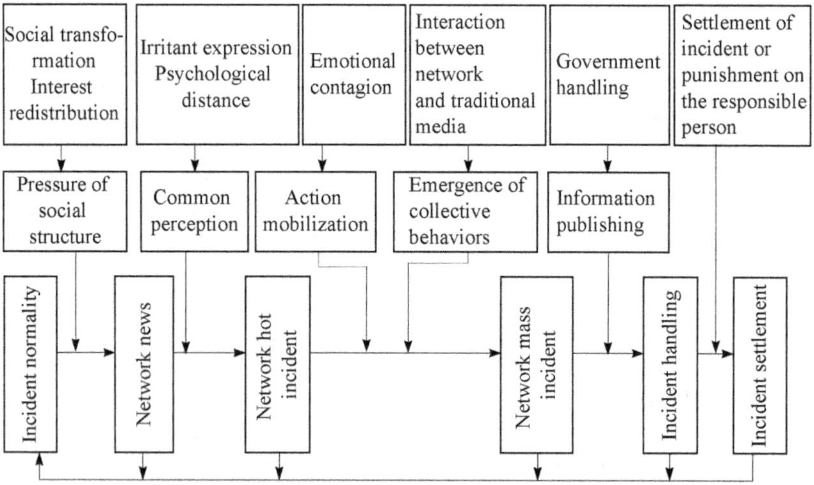

Fig. 9.2 The model for evolution of the network mass incident

disadvantaged group of the public, increasingly feel deprived, hold a dissatisfaction and grudge and have to vent their emotions, relieve their tensions and express their demands through the network due to the imperfect public participation system in the real society as well as their having no way, or only an inhibited way, to express their interest demands. In this way, on-line confiding, on-line help seeking and on-line accusation are often seen in the form of network news, and network news of different sizes are constantly emerging.

In the third stage, based on the network development and the increasing pressure of the social structure, the network news that incorporate irritant stimuli and factors easily attracting netizens' attention and forming the common perception and generalized belief, develop to be network hot incidents. Though thousands of pieces of network news emerge in the network every day, most of which are specific manifestations of accumulated social conflicts and sedimented social risks, not all of them will turn into network hot incidents that then lead to network mass incident. Whether the network news applies irritant expressions and contains stimuli are the key factors to decide whether the incident attracts netizens' interests and attentions. Only when featuring these factors, can it obtain the scarce resources of netizens' attention, further produce common perception and emotional sympathy among netizens and boost formation of the group consciousness and emergence of the network clusters. The click rate of netizens is considered as the direct indicator that reflects how much netizens concern about the incident and how influential the incident is. As the attention rate of the network news increases sharply, the incident develops to be a network hot incident.

In the fourth stage, as affected by netizens' emotions and mobilized by activists, the traditional media and the network closely interact with each other, primary and secondary incidents mutually affect each other, and network collective behaviors are constantly emerging, when the network hot incident transforms to be a network mass incident. In this stage, (1) netizens will gather into a group based on irritant-inducing factors and common beliefs, where they are exposed to mutual emotional hints and contagions and form the depersonalized collective consciousness. As the activists call on netizens to safeguard their interests and uphold justice, netizens may easily go to extremes emotionally; and the internal mobilization is gradually realized. (2) The incident is further spread in a comprehensive way owing to the misconduct of the government, the weakening social control mechanism and joining in of the traditional media that cater for netizens' demand preferences. The interaction and mutual promotion between the network and the traditional media promotes involvement of more and more netizens, mutual effect and wide spreading of primary and secondary incidents as well as constant emergence of cluster behaviors. Therefore, the incident finally develops to be a network mass incident.

In the fifth stage, the network mass incident takes place. The public opinions of the network are spreading, and the influence of the incident is expanding, so the government attaches great importance and makes the information of the incident known to the public. The audience will know about the truth of the incident, which facilitates the solution to this incident.

In this sixth stage, the incident is solved. This mass incident gradually subsides and returns to the normal state.

During the whole evolution of the network mass incident, influencing factors that play a guiding role vary in different development stages. Moreover, these stages are exposed to mutual transformation and intertwining, making up a dynamic evolution process that combines the social context, hot perception elements in the network, emotional contagion of network collective behaviors, action mobilization and constant emergence of primary and secondary incidents based on the interaction between the traditional media and the network.

PART V

Empirical Studies

CHAPTER 10

Empirical Studies on New-Media Public Opinion

The new media, including the Internet and the mobile phone, is one of the greatest inventions in human history. Through stable growth in size, the Internet industry economy has become the important driving force for China's economic development China; the Internet penetrates into various fields and promotes adjustments and upgrading of the economic structure; it also improves the government's ability in administration and public services and promotes development of social undertakings; the Internet and mobile media function as important channels for cultural communication; and the Internet is serving the public and playing an indispensable part in people's life.

We have conducted a large-scale random telephone survey among mobile phone users and a quantitative analysis, and discovered some unexpected new facts and some new findings that have surprised everyone.

We adopted the random telephone survey among mobile phone users. Based on random sampling, the investigation covered the four most representative cities in China: Beijing, Wuhan, Guangzhou and Chengdu. The survey was carried out between June 1 and July 31, 2010. Respondents were all mobile phone users, categorized by gender, age and occupation. The sample size was designed to be 4000 people, 1000 for each condition category in all 4 cities. At the end, 3421 valid samples had been obtained. The closing date for the survey data was July 31, 2010. Analysis results of the survey follow listed below.

W. Kuang, *Social Media in China*, Sociology, Media and Journalism in China, https://doi.org/10.1007/978-981-13-0914-4_10

10.1 The Credibility of the New Media Is Not Less than that of the Traditional Media

10.1.1 The Credibility of the New Media, Represented by the Mobile Media and the Internet, is Similar to that of Newspapers, While the Credibility of TV is the Highest

Though some people believe that the new media has less credibility compared to the serious traditional media, particularly the print media such as newspapers, the credibility of the mobile phone, the network, newspapers, radio and TV is respectively 22.4%, 19.6%, 20.7%, 12.6% and 34.2% according to our investigation.

As shown in the survey, the popular idea of "the credibility of newspapers is the highest" has been overturned, as the mobile media, the Internet and newspapers share the similar credibility. TV is the most credible, since "seeing is believing" and videos are harder to be forged in people's mind.

Our first question was: "Please mark the news information communicated through mobile phones, news in the Internet, newspaper, radio and TV news for their credibility. The full credit is 100."

Many people's prejudice about the low news credibility of the new media has been overturned by our investigation on news credibility.

As a matter of fact, false news is not necessarily associated with media forms, but is determined by the interest drive behind the scene, in other words, whether anyone is making false news to boost the circulation and audience rate, thus to acquire larger commercial gains.

10.1.2 Chinese Netizens Would Rather Believe Weibo

According to the classical communication theory, the news information in Weibo, which is spontaneously uploaded by netizens without information verification and filtration by a "gatekeeper (the journalist and editor)," is less credible than traditional newspapers, radio and TV. However, the survey says: netizens would rather believe Weibo.

Our second question was: "In case of any inconsistency in the report of the same incident between Weibo and the traditional media, you would believe: (1) Weibo; (2) the traditional media (newspapers, radio and TV)."

The survey shows that 63.5% of the respondents chose Weibo, suggesting that Chinese netizens would rather believe Weibo.

This is not a unique instance. The magazine *Well-off* published the data of an investigation on September 4, 2012, showing a similar result to ours.

According to the investigation of *Well-off*, though the network and Weibo was not powerful enough to challenge TV, their credibility (69.7%) had far exceeded that of the two forms of the print media, newspapers and magazine (54%).

This is because media credibility is declining owing to widespread paid news, fake news and vulgar programs and the sacrifice of news authenticity and professional ethics.

Weibo, being relatively independent but depending on the network, was at the fourth place in "the most credible media in respondents' opinion" following the network, and won 27.5% of votes. Radio (19.3%) and magazine (9.1%) were less credible than Weibo, ranking the fifth and sixth. The mobile phone (5.8%) and outdoor advertisement media (2.1%) came last.

Evidently, the credibility of the network and Weibo (69.7%) has far exceeded that of the two forms of the print media, newspapers and magazine (54%)

10.2 The Mobile Media Has Become the New Media of New Media

Using the statistic of the user (audience) scale, the influence of the mobile media far exceeds the coverage of traditional newspapers and radio, and approaches and even surpasses the network media and TV media.

The real and potential audience number is considered to be the important indicator to measure the competitiveness of the media, while the mobile media never worry about user resources. The number of mobile phone users far exceeds the number of netizens and newspaper readers. Compared to the newspaper and magazine with the greatest circulation, the website with the highest click rate and the outdoor media in the station and subway of the largest passenger flow, the mobile media enjoys a larger number of and more extensive audience.

Our idea is also proved by our questionnaire. The third question was: "If you forgot to take your mobile phone when you went out, would you choose to: (1) immediately go back home to get it; (2) go home for it if there is still time; (3) not go home, as no mobile phone is just as well."

As indicated by the investigation, 90.8% of respondents chose to "immediately go back home to get it" and 7.7% chose to "go home for it if there is still time". Only 1.5% of respondents chose to "not go home, as no mobile phone is just as well."

10.3 The New Media Has Become the Mainstream Media

During the 2008 and 2016 US presidential elections, the world truly experienced the influence of the new media throughout the whole process. The new media influenced the US presidential election mainly in four communication ways: the network videos represented by YouTube, the blog websites represented by Twitter, the social networking websites represented by Facebook and personal campaign websites.

Numerous scholars and managers, however, do not consider the new media to be mainstream media. From official and civil, planned and market, in-system and out-system perspectives, there are considerable differences in the debate over the concept of "mainstream media". In 2004, Xinhua News Agency conducted a study called "Research on the Effectiveness and Influence of Public Opinion Guidance," in which the question was whether mainstream media should be assessed based on the following six criteria: First, they bring the propagation function of the party, government and people into full play, stay in the position of authority that common news media can rarely reach, exert special influence and are regarded as the authoritative representative of the will, voice and proposition of the Party, government and the masses by all sectors of the community, both domestically and internationally. Second, they reflect and disseminate the mainstream ideology and mainstream values, which should be the socialist ideology and corresponding values in China, insist on and guide the mainstream of social development and direct the way forward, and have a strong influence. Third, on the basis of high credibility, their reports and comments have received great attention from most people in society, being regarded as the basis of thought and action and having been reproduced, quoted, analyzed and judged by domestic and foreign media. Fourth, their reports focus on the significant dynamics of the political, economic, social and cultural sectors at home and abroad, thereby serving to record the development of progress and preserve it for posterity. Fifth, their basic audience encompasses all levels of society. Sixth, they have large circulation or high audience rating and influence a large, fully representative audience. Collectively, the above criteria have been widely considered a relatively authoritative definition for mainstream media in China.[1]

[1] Xinhua News Agency Research Group on the Effectiveness and Influence of Public Opinion Guidance, *How Mainstream Media Improve the Effectiveness and Influence of Public*

According to the previous definition and debates, however, "mainstream media" was confined to the traditional media, while the new media was excluded. Some people even contrasted the "mainstream media" and the "new media" to the extent that they were virtually in opposition, such as the case in the article by Yang Weiguang titled "Mainstream Media in the Future: New Media."[2]

In our opinion, given the contemporary context of digitalization and networking, the previous definition and debate on the "mainstream media" were based on the traditional media. Such ideas are old and dysfunctional; they are obsolete. Today, the new media is the true embodiment of "mainstream media".

Our idea is also proved by our survey:

Question 4:

Your major ways to acquire news information (choose no more than 2 options):

(1) Mobile phone; (2) the Internet; (3) newspaper; (4) radio; (5) TV

According to the survey, 57.8% of respondents chose the mobile phone, compared to 79.7% of the Internet, 17.8% of newspaper, 8.5% of radio and 36.2% of TV.

Question 5:

The quantity of news media you read every day:

(1) 1; (2) 2; (3) 3 or above.

The result suggests that 47.8% of respondents chose 2, compared 44.7% choosing 1 and 7.5% choosing 3 or above. Evidently, most people will not read more than 2 news media every day.

Question 6:

Please write down the major media where you read news (choose no more than 2 options):

As a result, 27.8% of respondents wrote Sina news, compared to 24.7% of Baidu news, 19.4% of Tencent news, 17.4% of Sina Weibo, 16.3% of NetEase, 15.7% of Sohu net, 15.5% of Phoenix net, 11.8% of Xinhua net, 11.7% of People's Daily on-line, 10.7% of *Reference News*, 10.4% of *Global Times*, 9.7% of *Southern Weekly*, 2.2% of CCTV and 6.7% of other media.

Opinion Guidance 1: Criteria and Evaluation of Mainstream Media, from *Chinese Journalist*, 2004(1).

[2] Yang Weiguang, *Mainstream Media in the Future: New Media*, from *Contemporary TV*, 2009(11).

PART VI

Countermeasures and Prospects

CHAPTER 11

Countermeasures Against New-Media Public Opinion

The response to public opinions refers to a series of management measures against the public opinion crisis incurred by a network incident, including making use of some public opinion monitoring measures, analyzing the development trend of public opinions, strengthening the communication with the network, assuring the authority and consistency of news and information through a face-to-face method and the language style of media, reducing hearsay and false information to the minimum, taking the initiative instead of only making a response, and guiding public opinion in a more accurate, more rapid and better manner.

The primary condition to cope with public opinions is to know the development trend of public opinion and analyze the dynamics of public opinion and perceptions. Comprehensive information and data should be provided by the network public opinion monitoring system.

As the development of network public opinion observes the life-cycle theory, this life-cycle theory constitutes the theoretical basis for responding to new media public opinions (Fig. 11.1).

Like anti-missile interception, as to the management of network public opinions, the earlier response results in a lower cost and better effect.

W. Kuang, *Social Media in China*, Sociology, Media and Journalism in China, https://doi.org/10.1007/978-981-13-0914-4_11

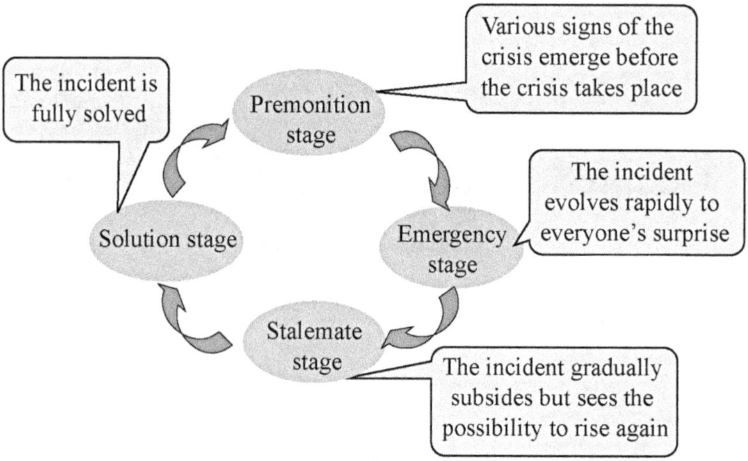

Fig. 11.1 Development of network public opinion observes the life-cycle theory

11.1 Daily Monitoring and Analysis of Public Opinion

11.1.1 Monitoring of Public Opinion

Monitoring of public opinions integrates the technologies of the Internet information gathering and information intelligence processing, satisfies the demands on monitoring of network public opinion and tracking of news topics through automatic extraction, automatic classification and clustering, topic detection and thematic focus of the massive information in the Internet, provides analysis results in forms of briefings, reports and graphs and so on, understands ideological trends of the masses for the customer, correctly guides public opinion and provides the basis for analysis.

There are three necessary conditions for monitoring of public opinions. (1) Only government departments with the enforcement powers can launch the monitoring; (2) The object of monitoring is under strong suspicion for endangering society and the state; (3) The process of monitoring should be rational and legitimate, which shall not infringe personal privacy and normal commercial interests, must safeguard legal rights and benefits of individuals and groups and follow the goal of maintaining national security and stability.

How to correctly cope with any public opinion issue that endangers national and social security, such as rumors and illegal fund-raising? "It will cause more harm to stop the free flow of people's thoughts than to stop that of the rivers." The correct way is, instead of stopping them in an oversimplified and crude way, to discover, s soon as possible, the issue and give an early warning through the public opinion monitoring system, launch the crisis response plan against the crisis immediately, clarify the facts rapidly by means of several public opinion guidance measures such as publishing a post at the official website or mainstream forums and holding a press conference, race against the rumor and tell the public the truth as early as possible. A good public opinion monitoring system shall discover any issue in real time, rapidly prepare the guidance plan and quickly deliver the guiding information to all major websites.

The network public opinion monitoring system features several strengths, such as reduction of the workload of information gathering by man, global coverage, real-time monitoring and assistant analysis of public opinions, which generally consists of three basic modules, the network public opinion gathering system, the network public opinion analysis engine and the public opinion service system.

The public opinion system should make comprehensive use of search engine technology, text processing technology, knowledge management methods, natural language processing and mobile phone SMS platform, and conduct automatic acquisition, extraction, classification, clustering, topic monitoring and thematic focus against the massive information of the Internet, to satisfy users' demands in monitoring of the network public opinion and tracking of hot incidents.

The public opinion system integrates core functions including public opinion monitoring, public opinion gathering, public opinion intelligent analysis, public opinion response, public opinion early warning, public opinion search, assistance to preparation of the public opinion report and automatic SMS alert of the public opinion.

11.1.2 Analysis of Public Opinion

Analysis of public opinions refers to the process of conducting in-depth thinking processing, analysis and studies of public opinion and reaching the corresponding conclusion against a certain issue.

There are mainly two ways to analyze public opinion: content analysis and empirical analysis. Content analysis means to conduct objective and systematic quantitative analysis against the information content, in order to clarify or test the essential facts and trends in the information. It is able to provide a clue to the hidden information implied in the information and predict the development of the incidents. Empirical analysis attempts to get certain conclusions after analyzing a large number of cases and relevant data.

To analyze public opinion, the first thing is to clarify the stage of the incident or topic. An incident may consist of several different stages, including the induction period, incubation period, emergence period, development period, high-tide period, processing period, settlement period and feedback period. Secondly, before analyzing a certain public-opinion hot topic, it is necessary to classify it in a scientific manner. Generally, hot incidents are mainly divided into the sudden natural disaster, the production safety accident, the mass incident, the public health incident, the public power image issue, the judicial incident, the economic and livelihood incident, social thoughts and China-related emergencies.

Concerning the influence of public opinion, association with the public interests and the damage to the image of public departments, the parameter setting and data analysis framework for public opinion analysis should reflect the following conditions: the development overview and course of the incident, main ideas and emotions of the public; whether the public is in the stage of recognition and attitude expression or the stage of action; how influential the public opinion is in leading the public to develop from recognition to social movement and even social unrest; the organizational degree and whether any plan for action; cautious use of political interpretation and analysis of whether any explicit interest demand exists; whether there is any great impact on the existing social system; the possibility to be supported or utilized by anti-China forces; and whether any clear object and goal and which part of the departments and even the system it is directing to. The researchers of public opinion analysis should become the "non-participating observer" instead of the "non-observing participant," being neutral and keen.

11.2 Response Principles

11.2.1 The Rule of the Golden Twenty-Four Hours

The key time to cope with the negative information on the new-media platform is the twenty-four hours after the information is published. If the information is timely coped with within twenty-four hours, the crisis may be defused, and it may not become a public-opinion hot issue; otherwise, it may give rise to a new media incident. In light of this, the publicity and public security departments at all levels should establish a public opinion early warning system against the new media public opinion, track and monitor the new media platform at all times, try to discover any public opinion issue under monitoring or other negative information at the first post and report rapidly to the relevant party and the superior administration.

Publish the news as soon as possible to win the discourse power struggle. Take the initiative. The crisis management is essentially the crisis communication management. Relying on authentic and transparent information, open reports and humanized communication, it will not cause any panic among the public or trouble to the government, on the contrary, it will promote the virtuous interaction between the civil power of the network and the government strength and produce a positive result.

Publish information at the first opportunity. It is an important manifestation of a responsible government to publish the incident information in a timely and accurate manner, which is of great significance for letting the public know the truth, protecting them from the rumor and reassuring the people.

Guide public opinion at the first opportunity. By publishing information at the first opportunity, it will help the government take the initiative in managing the crisis incident, reassure the people and avoid misrepresented reports as well as rumors spreading.

Hold the news dominance at the first opportunity. The crisis will naturally become the focus of public concern and inspire the public's excitement owing to its great damages. If the public opinion is well guided, it will facilitate crisis management; but if it is badly guided, it will endanger the treatment of the crisis. Media is not only the sign of public perceptions, but also the catalyst for public emotions.

In principle, any information about the public opinion on the new media platform should be managed locally. The publicity department at the local place bears the primary responsibility for discovering the public opinion, which, after discovering any local new media public opinion, should launch the response mechanism as soon as possible, contact the relevant units or individuals the public opinion concern, publicize the information on the new-media public opinion, investigate the facts of the incident and collect and organize materials for response to the public opinion. The relevant units and relevant individuals bear the primary responsibility to cope with the public opinion, and should respond rapidly to any information revealed by the new media public opinions.

11.2.2 *The Principle of Information Disclosure*

In the context of the new media, what we should do is to disclose information in a timely way. An information blackout is ineffective and, more importantly, impossible!

It is a principle to disclose information, but, in an exceptional case, some information may not be publicized. As to emergencies, it is necessary to present the facts rapidly and report the causes cautiously. No hiding and no rootless talk.

11.2.2.1 *Relevant Government Departments Should Give Full Play to Home Advantages and Guard against Home Disadvantages*

The home advantages of the government include: the public power, media and information advantage. The "home disadvantages" of the government include: netizens' distrust in the public power, disappointment against judicial justice and lack of confidence in social equity.

The home advantages should be brought into full play when coping with public opinion incidents. The government controls much more comprehensive and professional knowledge than netizens, exerts great influence on news media and, more importantly, carries authority. The publicity department should make full use of the media advantage, with no hiding and no rootless talk, and give full play to the information advantage by providing systematic professional information quickly and utilize the information asymmetry to vigorously guide public opinion. At the same time, the publicity department should be alert to the case where the home advantage is transformed to be the home disadvantage, for example, the loss of the government's credibility.

11.2.2.2 *"Take the Banner" and the Dividing Strategy*

"Take the banner" in network public opinion. In the current context of frequent occurrence of public opinion incidents, it is necessary to hold high the banner of social equity, judicial justice, people orientation and harmonious society, actively investigate and solve any inharmonious or unstable factor of society and safeguard the masses' essential interests. Never leave the banner to opinion leaders on-line for all sorts of concerns and let netizens down.

Make full use of the dividing strategy, that is, dividing the central from the local government, and dividing the government from unscrupulous officials.

Fig. 11.2 Three factors for the response to emergencies

First, guide it rather than blocking it, and assure open and transparent information. The hot emergent incident, particularly the negative incident, necessarily draws wide attention among network public opinion. The network public opinions at this time may encompass all kinds of voices, while the extreme and irrational opinions exist and even sometimes prevail. When coping with the incident, it is suggested to present facts, publish the true information, set up the agenda for the topic and guide public opinions. Blocking the voices or the channels of public opinions, may run counter to the government's desire. Ultimately, only facts constitute the foundation for guiding public opinions.

Second, solve it rather than evading it, and actively bear corresponding responsibilities. In most cases, the breakout of public opinion crisis is incurred when the government avoids accountability for an emergency or responds to it in an inactive way. Accountability is the focus of public opinion about an incident. Hence it is necessary to actively answer the public's doubts when coping with public opinion, not avoidance or rejection.

In general, three factors for the response to emergencies are: facts publishing, official accountability and punishment of illegal people (see Fig. 11.2).

11.2.3 Take the Initiative to Communicate with Media and People

Increasingly government departments and officials have become aware of the necessity to take the initiative to communicate with media and people, and therefore increasing numbers of Chinese government departments and officials open their Weibo accounts. Nevertheless, a few administration and official Weibo accounts regard form over substance and have no regular and real interaction. In Weibo, everyone is equal, and even an official has no greater influence than other people.

The guiding strategy for new-media public opinions can be summarized as: rapidly discovering the new media public opinions, clarifying the responsible subject of the public opinions, actively setting the new media agenda, publishing information at the first time, carefully responding to any question, frankly answering to the public's doubts, giving authoritative comments at the proper time and interacting with public opinions (see Fig. 11.3).

As to emergencies, the government departments should take the initiative to organize and plan for news publicity and win the public through media.

The communication with media is communication with journalists in the end. The journalist, neither your friend nor your enemy, neither your superordinate nor your subordinate, is always your challenger.

Fig. 11.3 Multiple forms of press release

When the emergency occurs, the press spokesman, as the government mouthpiece, should communicate with media as soon as possible, carefully respond to any question and frankly answer the public's doubts.

The crisis management of the press spokesman is embodied in the communication with media. Being the representative of the government, the press spokesman should be the earliest and the first to provide the facts of the incident.

The press spokesman should spare no effort to deliver the key message and should figure out his/her standpoint and the key message before appearing on the scene. That is to say, the press spokesman shall clarify SOCO—the Single, the Over-riding, Communications and Objects.

When responding to media, the specific strategies for communication control in terms of press release mainly include the following:

1. Manage the report: Manage the perspective, requirement, standard and form of the report and provide follow-up reports.
2. Publish the latest news uninterruptedly: Publish the dynamic information of the incident at any time; timely publish the government's countermeasures; mobilize the society to participate actively in countermeasures; and finally publish the results.
3. Give full play to the role of the mainstream media (including the mainstream new media). When the mainstream media accurately and timely provides authentic and authoritative information, the public will not be as passionate as before to collect information through other channels, and rumors and "hearsays" will consequentially disappear. Provided that the government chooses "not to report the information" or "to conceal the truth," it will first affect the information published by mainstream media, when the mainstream media will be placed in a passive position in the public opinion competition. In this way, the effectiveness and influence of the mainstream media in guiding public opinions will be significantly compromised, exerting an adverse effect on social stability.
4. Organize experts to guide public opinions in good time. Relevant government departments should provide authoritative comments in good time, organize a team of professionals to publish comments and guidance and prepare the report focusing on experts' views.

Take the initiative to communicate with media, propose requirements on the reports, control the communication channels of the key message and assure the standard and controllable information.

The five basic principles for the communication with media consist of: honest attitude, open information, consistency, clear information and pre-arranged plan.

The ten golden rules for the communication with journalists: treat every communication with media as an opportunity rather than a threat; be well prepared and understand the arrangement of the journalist; conduct careful investigation and preparation before interview; control the process of interview; be polite, patient and pleased; communicate in a simple and clear way and do not use jargon or conventional verbal exchanges; give a direct and accurate answer; never say "no comment"; never lie, never guess and never speculate; and do not provide personal views.

In case of any emergent disaster, the press spokesman should first express concern and show a caring response to the incident in a humanized way and then give the global view about the actions and the incident. This is because the people are injured and feel panic, anger and confusion about the emergent disaster.

11.2.4 The Fundamental Way to Solve Issues is to Solve the Conflicts in Real Society

The virtual Internet world is actually an incarnation of the real society. The basis to cope with network public opinions should be settling livelihood issues and improving the regular interest expression and game mechanism.

For an instance, house demolition has been the direct cause for many critical incidents. The government and the law enforcement department should play as the judgment during the demolition. Unless for the goal of public interests, the government and the law enforcement department should remain neutral as a judge rather than safeguarding the developer's interests during the demolition. The developer should treat demolition as a commercial activity and evaluate the risks of demolition in advance.

The coolest "nail household (a person or household who refuses to move and bargains for high compensation when the land is requisitioned for a construction project)" may be found in Japan. Since the residents there refused to move, Runway 1 of Tokyo Narita International Airport was completed after a delay of over a decade, Runway 2 has its length shorter than the specified, leading to many dangerous cases during taking off and landing of aircraft, and Runway 3 stays on the drawing board without any sign for the start of construction.

Moreover, airplanes cannot take off or land at night in Narita Airport, pursuant to the agreement with several households inside the airport, thus not to affect these nail households' rest.

These several households have stayed in the airport and fought against the government and the airport for 40 years. Many residents have moved out, while these nail households are still persisting. As the Atsuta family is still living where the planned Runway 3 should be, the construction of the runway has not yet commenced.

The ability in guiding network public opinions is also a kind of governance capacity. If the popular will is ignored in the early stage, it will evolve to be the "popular discussion" in the medium stage and finally develop to be the "popular discontent" in the late stage. Any ignorance or delay of response to the popular at any step will lead to clustering of public opinions. In order to fundamentally solve this situation, it should start by clearing the negative emotions already accumulated.

CHAPTER 12

Future Prospects of New-Media Public Opinion

The application of the Internet started in the United States. In 1969, under the leadership of the US Army, ARPA connected the computers of four famous universities in the southwest of the United States, which was the embryo of the Internet. Since then, the application of the Internet gradually extended from the military to the civilian population and expanded from the United States to the whole world.

In April 1973, Martin Cooper, an engineering technician of the famous Motorola company in the United States, invented the first mobile phone for civil use, and was therefore honored as "the Father of the Modern Mobile Phone." In 1981, the first mobile communication network of the world, Nord Mobile Telephony, was opened successively in Saudi Arabia, Sweden and Norway.[1]

Being the two major typical representatives of the new media, the Internet and the mobile phone were born with the natural properties of media, as people used the Internet and mobile phone to share information. Owing to their own strengths in communication, they had spread widely at a higher rate than any other media form. According to calculation, it took four years for the Internet to develop to reach 50 million users, compared to respectively twenty-eight years and twelve years for

[1] Kuang Wenbo, *Introduction to Network Communication*, Page 196, Beijing, Higher Education Press, 2009.

W. Kuang, *Social Media in China*, Sociology, Media and Journalism in China, https://doi.org/10.1007/978-981-13-0914-4_12

radio and TV.[2] The fixed-line telephone spent 125 years to attain 1 billion users by 2001, while the mobile phone only spent twenty-one years to do so. The global mobile users had grown from 1 billion to 2 billion within three years.[3] Until now, the global Internet users have exceeded 2 billion, and the mobile phone users have exceeded 5 billion.[4]

In addition to reaching a large scale that other media cannot compare, the Internet and mobile phone have also profoundly changed users' lifestyle.

12.1 Prospects of the New Media

12.1.1 The New Media Becomes the Mainstream Media

Based on different discourse systems and standards, the academic world and the industry are both exposed to great controversies on the definition of "mainstream media." Under the official discourse system within the system, media units established at the ministerial level represented by *People's Daily* and Xinhua News Agency are considered as the typical mainstream media. However, based on the market-oriented standards among the people, the mainstream media are defined as the media that embrace a large audience, influence the society with their reports and promote reform of the social system, such as Hunan TV and *Nanfang Metropolis Daily*. Despite various debates on the definition of the mainstream media in the past, they had one thing in common: they all excluded the new media forms including the Internet and mobile media and tended to confine the mainstream media to the traditional media (newspapers, radio and TV).

In our opinion, two aspects should be examined when judging the mainstream media: the number of users and the social influence. On one hand, users of this kind of media are no longer the minority or fringe population of the society; and on the other hand, the media has acquired considerable social influence through the users. If judging "whether the new media have become the mainstream media" from these two aspects,

[2] Wang Shubo, Si Jiuyue, *Challenges and Countermeasures of Information Communication Globalization*, from *Journal of International Communication*, 2000(4).

[3] Kuang Wenbo, *Introduction to Network Communication*, Page 196.

[4] *The International Telecommunication Union: the Number of Global Netizens Has Exceeded 2 Billion*, Tencent Technology, 20110126.

the new media represented by the Internet and the mobile phone have become the mainstream media in the true sense.

In view of the number of users, the new media represented by the Internet and the mobile media have already become the mainstream media based on their strengths in the massive information and even started supplanting the existing traditional media.

The We Media present massive information also mixing the good with the bad, so the new media has suspicions about its credibility. Therefore, the audience credibility also constitutes an important indicator to measure whether a media form falls into the category of mainstream media. In order to accurately answer this question, we have conducted a quantitative research on the credibility of the new media by investigating new media users. According to the investigation on 4000 respondents from 4 cities, Beijing, Wuhan, Guangzhou and Chengdu, people's credibility in the news of the mobile phone, network, newspapers, radio and TV is respectively 22.4%, 19.6%, 20.7%, 12.6% and 34.2%.[5] Many people's traditional idea about the low news credibility of new media has been overturned to a certain extent.

In conclusion, the new media not only reaches and even exceeds the user size of the traditional media in terms of the quantity, but also plays an influential role not second to the traditional media. Hence, no matter whether people admit it or not, the new media has practically become an important part of the mainstream media. As a matter of fact, the "new" and the "old" are only relative concepts. Radio and TV were new media compared to newspapers at one time, but now the Internet and the mobile phone are new media compared to newspapers, radio and TV. There is no doubt that a newer media form will emerge one day. As long as the new media adapts to the social development, it will become the mainstream. It can be seen that the Internet and the mobile media have already become the mainstream of the current age, while their mainstream trend may be even more intensified in the future.

12.1.2 Diversified New Media Platforms and Forms

Looking back on the evolution history, we can see the new media platforms and forms become increasingly diversified. Before the birth of the mass media, people could only know about the news taking place a thousand miles

[5] Kuang Wenbo, *Whether New Media is Mainstream Media?—a Quantitative Research Based on Mobile Media*, from *Journal of International Communication*, 2011(6).

way by arriving at the scene or through long and inefficient verbal communication. After the mass media, newspapers, showed up, people could know about things happening far away by reading the text at home. Later, radio and TV enabled people to acquire information in a richer and more comprehensive way. The emergence of the Internet further overturned people's ways to communicate and receive information, when people have many choices of the content and forms of information, are able to skip any clip they are not interested in and jump to their topic and acquire the first-hand information from another individual on the spot. Since the mobile media is widely spread, people can make use of their "mini-computers"[6] in hands to do everything they can do with the Internet.

The newspaper, radio, TV, Internet and mobile media were all "new media" when they were invented. In a manner of speaking, it is the people's desire to acquire information that has promoted the evolution of media platforms. By now, the "new media" in the latest concept are typically represented by the Internet and the mobile media.

Seen from the evolution of the existing new media platforms, we can conclude part of characteristics of the new-generation media platforms. From the technical perspective, the new media platform in the future will enable people to master information more conveniently and freely. According to Marshall McLuhan's idea of "media is the extension of human," media will help people acquire information that can hardly be acquired with people's physical organs, and this extension is freer from any constraint. In the future, the new media technology will bring information farther away to people in a timelier manner. From the perspective of influence, the new media platforms will further embed themselves in people's daily life and become an integral part of daily life. The new media will be everywhere and will unconsciously exert influence on people's social decision making and lifestyle. No longer being non-essential, new media platforms will become the important tool for people to monitor the surrounding environment and keep pace with social development.

It is an unsolvable controversial topic that whether people are feeling more convenient to apply new media platforms or people's daily life is becoming more constrained by media technologies during the development course of new media technologies, which can only be examined in the future. Despite all these debates, we will never return to the era of

[6] The mobile phone has become the "mini-computer" provided with the communication function.

verbal media. Time will never stop, the "new media" will continue to evolve and the platforms for the new media will be constantly updated.

In the future, the new media will present in diversified platforms, as the hardware, and in diversified applications, as the software. Take the Internet for an example. When the Internet was first applied for civil use, people commonly applied it to acquire more information, under the context of information deficiency.

12.2 Prospects of New-Media Public Opinions

12.2.1 Internationalized New Media Public Opinions

The Internet is technically characterized by hypertext and hyperlink, by which the communication of new-media public opinion may, in theory, be infinitely extended. The boundless scope of communication enables the influence of new-media public opinion to grow out of nothing and develop gradually.

The wide application of technologies makes it possible to extend the technology-based new-media public opinion.

Starting from Tunisia, the Jasmine Revolution had successively broken out in numerous Arab countries since 2010. In this anti-government fight, social media such as Facebook, Twitter and YouTube played a significant role. Based on the great influence of these new-media applications, anti-government sentiments and actions had spread among these countries in an effect similar to dominoes. It was hard to imagine this situation in the past when the media was underdeveloped. Only the issue of space and distance would lead to the collapse of the sentiments and actions. It indirectly proves that the new media are playing an important part in promoting social reforms, while it also demonstrates that the new-media public opinions have been internationalized and the boundaries between countries gradually disappear in the interconnecting Internet.

Scholars from different circles and different countries expressed their different views on the role of new-media applications such as Twitter in the Jasmine Revolution. Some stated that Twitter did not play such an essential role as circulated among the people, and the revolution only followed its previous track of development. In our opinion, the social media were neutral in this incident, and new media was only utilized as an Internet-based technical platform without any bias. People who made use of the new media technology provided the new media with the role to objectively promote development of the incident. The social pressure in real life undoubtedly constituted the major reason for the breakout of the revolution. However, people had no such a platform to spread opinions and information before the emergence of the new media. It was the new media that gathered the people sharing the same behavior tendency together and promoted them to facilitate the generation and development of the revolution through practical efforts. Though the technology only offered the possibility, the possibility was sometimes the key.

The internationalization of new-media public opinion is also revealed by the development of public opinions during a domestic public incident. For an instance, in the "3.14 Incident" of Tibet, some Chinese netizens, in the Internet, challenged the reports on the disturbance written by western media like CNN. They thought that these media had adopted misleading news information and particularly the pictures in the reports and established the website with a domain name of "Anti-CNN" to collect and fight against the misleading reports. In addition to the incident itself, the netizens' actions had caused great discussions on the tendency of media reports at home and abroad. CNN, as spurred by public opinions, also made a response. Realizing this phenomenon, the Chinese government had arranged seventeen foreign media to interview in Tibet on March 25, taken the initiative to publish information related to the incident and prevented the further spreading of misleading information.

With the development of economic globalization and realization of the concept of "the global village," the new media technology will be further spread and the new media applications will be further globalized in the future. At the same time, exposed to increasingly evident internationalization, the new media public opinions will enjoy greater influence as the new media is becoming the mainstream.

12.2.2 Innovative Management Thinking is Demanded for Management of New-Media Public Opinion

The new media feature a large number of users, and the new-media public opinion enjoy increasingly great social influence. Other than its positive influence, the attention shall also be paid to the negative effect of the new media. The corresponding management department should learn to strengthen management over new-media public opinion and assure the new-media public opinion keeps pace with the stable development of society.

Laws constitute the baseline of social justice. Though the new media platform is a virtual space, the real people using the new media should observe the legal system in real life. Against the new media updating with each passing day, the managers shall follow it up and establish and improve the law management mechanism, in order to prevent new-media public opinion from going to the extremes. As the most fundamental and the most important rule, punish any illegal or criminal activity performed on the new media platform.

It is easy to use the new media, but is hard to use it well. "Digitalization" is the first step to guide new-media public opinion. However, the websites the government's Internet programs opened have realized "digitalization" to a certain degree but failed to accomplish "interaction," contributing to their low efficiency.

The new-media public opinion is growing in the social context of the vigorous growth of civil society and redistribution of social power. In this process, the government should take the initiative to adapt to the changes, transform governmental functions correspondingly and gradually change from passive managers to active participants. The new media should become a diversified platform and a quasi-public area, where the voices of common people and voices of the government share the equal status and compete, thus to promote the overall progress of social affairs.

Governments of all countries have to monitor the content of the new media for its negative effect. The illegal or improper contents of new media should be subject to control. The illegal or improper contents highly recognized by governments of all countries include: (1) abetment and agitation; (2) slander, insult, defamation, hostile attack and other immoral expressions as well as false news information; and (3) pornography, which is commonly acknowledged to be the illegal and harmful content that should be controlled in the strictest way.

The legal model for management of new media content varies in different countries owing to their different values, legislative traditions and development levels of new media. Some countries advocate exerting strict control over the new media, adopting necessary measures to safeguard values of the state or the nation, protecting cultural traditions of the state or the nature, creating a pure world on-line and cracking down hard on pornography, violence, bloodiness, terrorism and false information on-line; some countries advocate not intervening in the new media content and regard anarchism and liberalism of the new media first; while some countries set up regulations on the new media content and encourage self-discipline of the industry.

The new media communication features the massive information, detailed and complicated content and diversified forms. The publishing, spreading and treatment of information are characterized by concealment, rapid communication and wide influence. The publishers, communicators and receivers of the information are hard to control. The news communication business of new media involves multiple subjects, including all types of enterprises and news media. Hence the management of the communication content of the new media is extremely complicated.

The new media shows its special laws of industry development and technical characteristics. The feasibility of policies shall be taken into consideration when the administrative policies, laws and regulations on monitoring of new media content are formulated.

Based on the no-threshold communication method of new media communication, anyone from the hundreds of millions of users is able to become the communicator, so it is hard to manage them merely relying on the traditional approval system. In view of the special laws of the new media, it is recommended to manage the new media through the "registration system + investigation and punishment system."

The new media belongs to the world and sees no national boundaries. We can learn from the mature and successful new-media policies and laws at home and abroad. Managers and creators of the new media shall bear the spirit of innovation.

It is an extremely complicated, arduous and long-term task to manage new-media public opinion. It is impossible to solve all issues in harmful information communication in the new media through only one management measure, as one measure only plays a limited role. The monitoring of new media information content shall apply comprehensive management, establish a comprehensive management framework, combine multiple management measures including laws, policies, technologies and ethics and realize mutual cooperation and mutual interaction among these measures. Only in this way can we effectively manage the new media and create the healthy and orderly environment for new media information communication for human society.

References

Works

Guo Qingguang, *A Course in Communication [M]*, 2nd Edition, Beijing: China Renmin University Press, 2011.

Zhang Guoliang, *The Principles of Communication [M]*, 2nd Edition, Shanghai: Fudan University Press, 2009.

Yu Guoming et al., *Annual Report on Public Opinion in China—2012 [M]*, Beijing: People's Daily Press, 2012.

Yu Guoming, *Public Opinion Analysis: A Quantitative Research into the Public in Modern China [M]*, Beijing: Huaxia Publishing House, 2001a.

Xie Xinzhou & Yan Fuchang, *IPTV Technology and Management*, Beijing: Huaxia Publishing House, 2010.

Ding Junjie & Zhang Shuting et al., *Internet Public-Opinions and Bombshell Public Events Index [M]*, Beijing: CPC Central Committee Party School Press, 2010.

Lei Yuejie, *Media Criticism [M]*, Beijing: Peking University Press, 2007.

Chen Lidan, *Studies of Public Opinions—Research on the Orientation of Public Opinions [M]*, Beijing: China Radio Film & TV Press, 1999.

Chen Lidan, *Ten Lectures of News Theories [M]*, Shanghai: Fudan University Press, 2008.

Xiong Chengyu & Jin Jianbin et al., *New Media Research Frontiers [M]*, Beijing: Tsinghua University Press, 2012.

Liu Jianming, *Principles of Social Public Opinions [M]*, Beijing: Huaxia Publishing House, 2002.

Gan Xifen, *Journalism Theory*, Beijing: China Renmin University Press, 1982.

Sha Lianxiang, *Social Psychology*, Beijing: China Renmin University Press, 2002.

W. Kuang, *Social Media in China*, Sociology, Media and Journalism in China, https://doi.org/10.1007/978-981-13-0914-4

Jiang Hong & Xu Jian, *Introduction to New Media [M]*, Shanghai: Shanghai Jiao Tong University Press, 2006.

Gong Chengbo, *Introduction to New Media [M]*, Beijing: China Radio & Television Publishing House, 2007.

Yu Jianrong, *Contentious Politics [M]*, Beijing: People's Publishing House, 2010a.

Hu Yu, *News and Public Opinions [M]*, Beijing: China Radio Film & TV Press, 2001b.

Yu Hong, *Research on the Opinion Leaders of Political BBS: A Case Study on Sino-Japan BBS of Strong Nation Forum [M]*, Beijing: Huazhong University of Science & Technology Press, 2010b.

Wang Tianyi, *Guidance of Network Public Opinions and Construction of Harmonious BBS [M]*, Beijing: People's Publishing House, 2008.

Chen Yuesheng, *Mass Emergencies and Public Sentiments [M]*, Tianjin: Tianjin Academy of Social Sciences Press, 2005.

China Administration Society Research Team, *Research on Countermeasures against Mass Emergencies in the Transition Period of China [M]*, Beijing, Academy Press, 2003.

Wang Laihua, *Overview of Public Sentiments Studies—Theories, Methods and Hot Issues [M]*, Tianjin, Tianjin Academy of Social Sciences Press, 2003.

Kuang Wenbo, *Introduction to New Media [M]*, Beijing: China Renmin University Press, 2012a.

Kuang Wenbo, *Introduction to Network Communication [M]*, 3rd Edition, Beijing: Higher Education Press, 2009a.

Kuang Wenbo, *Introduction to Mobile Media [M]*, 2nd Edition, Beijing, China Renmin University Press, 2012b.

Kuang Wenbo, *Mobile Media: New Revolution of New Media [M]*, Beijing: Huaxia Publishing House, 2010.

Kuang Wenbo, *Analysis of Netizens [M]*, Beijing: Peking University Press, 2003.

Kuang Wenbo, *Media Quality of Public Servants [M]*, Beijing: Xinhua Publishing House, 2012c.

Xie Gengyun, *The Report on Chinese Social Opinion and Crisis Management (2011) [M]*, Beijing: Social Sciences Academic Press, 2011.

Chinese Academy of Social Sciences, *The Blue Book of Society in 2011 [R]*, 2010(12).

Meng Zhiqiang, Peng Jianmei & Liu Youping et al., *Report on Charitable Contributions in China in 2011 [M]*, Beijing: China Society Press, 2012.

Chinese Academy of Governance, *Report on Objective Appraisal of Administration Weibo Accounts in China in 2011 [R]*, 2012.

Ru Xin, Lu Xueyi & Li Peilin, *The Blue Book of Society—Analysis and Prediction of the Social Condition of China in 2010 [M]*, Beijing, Social Sciences Academic Press, 2010.

[UK] Hugo de Burgh, Li Xiguang & Zeng Rong et al., *How to Respond to Western Journalists [M]*, Beijing: Party Building Books Publishing House, 2012.
[US] Walter Lippmann, *Public Opinion [M]*, Shanghai: Shanghai Renmin Press, 2006.
[US] Walter Lippmann, *Public Opinion [M]*, Beijing: Huaxia Publishing House, 1989.
[UK] Andrew Chadwick, *Internet Politics [M]*, Beijing: Huaxia Publishing House, 2010.
[US] Everett M. Rogers, *Diffusion of Innovations [M]*, Beijing: Central Compilation & Translation Press, 2002.
[US] Cass R. Sunstein, *Republic.com. [M]*, Shanghai: Shanghai Renmin Press, 2003.
[US] John Fiske et al., *Key Concepts in Communication and Cultural Studies [M]*, Beijing: Xinhua Publishing House, 2004.
[US] Gordon Allport et al., *Rumor Psychology*, Shenyang, Liaoning Education Publishing House, 2003.
[US] Samuel Huntington, *Political Order in Changing Societies [M]*, Beijing, Joint Publishing, 1989.
[GE] Hans-Joachim Neubauer, *Fama [M]*, Beijing, CITIC Press, 2004.
[FR] Francoise Reumaux, *The Black Widow—the Meaning and Spreading of the Rumor [M]*, Beijing, The Commercial Press, 1999.
[FR] Jean-Noël Kapferer et al., *Rumors [M]*, Shanghai, Shanghai People's Publishing House, 1991.
Martin Fishbein & Icek Ajzen, *Predicting and changing behavior: the reasoned action approach [M]*. New York: Psychology Press, 2010.
David Popenoe, *Sociology [M]*. New York: Prentice Hall Inc, 1995.

Articles

Kuang Wenbo, *Analysis of the Concept of "New Media" [J]*, *Journal of International Communication*, 2008(6).
Kuang Wenbo, *'Butterfly Effect' in New Media Communication and Its Countermeasures [J]*, *Journal of International Communication*, 2009b(8).
Kuang Wenbo, *Cool Thinking of the Weibo Popularization [J]*, *News and Writing*, 2012d(2).
Xia Xueluan, *Construction of Cybersociology [J]*, from *Peking University Journal (Philosophy and Social Science Edition)*, 2004(1).
Han Yunrong & Gao Shunjie, *Exploration on the Model of Public Opinion Communication in Weibo [J]*, *Modern Communication* (the Journal of the Communication University of China), 2012(7).

Dai Lina, *A Study of the Method of Identifying Microblogging Public Opinion Leaders and the Management Strategy [J]*, *Shanghai Journalism Review*, 2012(9).

Yu Hong, *The Primary Exploration of the Model to Select Public Opinion Leaders in On-line Forums [J]*, *Journalism & Communication*, 2008(2).

Chen Ran, *Identification and Selection of Public Opinion Leaders in On-line Forums—An Emperical Research on Kaidi Forum [J]*, *Contemporary Communication*, 2010(2).

Wang Yu, Zeng Jianping, Zhou Baohua & Wu Chengrong, *The Cluster Analysis-Based Way to Find Opinion Leaders in On-line Forums [J]*, *Computer Engineering*, 2011(5).

Li Yuanyuan, *Analysis of the Formation Mechanism and Characteristics of Weibo Public Opinions [J]*, *The Press*, 2010(6).

Zhang Xian, *Weibo and Public Domain*, *Literature and Art Studies [J]*, 2010(12).

Li Yiping & Zhao Ling, *On the Loss of Public Spirit in the Public Area of Weibo [J]*, *Southeast Communication*, 2011(6).

Liu Yanbo, *A Brief Analysis of the Relation Between Weibo and Public Domain—with Weibo "Cracking Down on the Abduction of Women and Children" as an Instance [J]*, *News Information*, 2011(3).

Huang Yan, *Media Characteristics of Weibo and Response by Traditional Media [J]*, *Southeast Communication*, 2011(1).

Zou Ying, *Web 3.0—the New Era of Internet [J]*, *Computer & Telecommunication*, 2009(12).

Song Hua, *The Trend for Questioning Administration in the Public Domain of Weibo [J]*, *Contemporary Views of Social Sciences*, 2011(3).

Ren Mengshan & Zhu Zhenming, *Discussion on the Political Communication Role of Social Media in "Twitter Revolution" in Iran [J]*, *Journal of International Communication*, 2009(9).

Zheng Yan, *The Freedom and Boundaries of Netizens—Reflections on the Free Speech in Public Domain of Weibo [J]*, *Social Sciences Studies*, 2012(1).

Xue Ke & Chen Xi, *A Study of the Communication Model of Influence of "Opinion Leaders" in BBS—'Yin Shui Si Yuan BBS' of Shanghai Jiao Tong University as an Example" [J]*, *Journalistic University*, 2010(4).

Index[1]

[1] Note: Page numbers followed by 'n' refer to notes.

W. Kuang, *Social Media in China*, Sociology, Media and Journalism in China, https://doi.org/10.1007/978-981-13-0914-4

CPSIA information can be obtained
at www.ICGtesting.com
Printed in the USA
LVHW081504181118
597555LV00012B/741/P

9 789811 309137